Consumer Reports

GUIDE TO BABY PRODUCTS

Consumer Reports

GUIDE TO BABY PRODUCTS

**SANDY JONES
AND THE EDITORS OF
CONSUMER REPORTS**

CONSUMER REPORTS SPECIAL PUBLICATIONS

YONKERS, NEW YORK

A Special Publication from Consumer Reports

Director, Special Publications Andrea Scott
Project Manager Linda Coyner
Project Editor Maggie Keresey
Medical Editor Marvin M. Lipman, M.D.
Designer Susi Oberhelman
Page Composition Eric Wayne Norlander
Illustrations Armen Kojoyian (products), Tatjana Krizmanic (tips)
Special Publications Staff Robert Markovich, Michael Quincy, Pauline Piekarz, Joyce Childs

Consumer Reports

Editorial Director Jacqueline Leo
Editor Julia Kagan
Executive Editor/Director Editorial Operations Eileen Denver
Design Director George Arthur
Managing Art Director Tim LaPalme
Director, Publishing Operations Maggie Brenner
Retail Sales and Marketing Will Michalopoulos
Manufacturing & Distribution Steven Schiavone

Technical Director R. David Pittle
Senior Director, Technical Operations Jeffrey A. Asher
Director, Technical Policy & Public Service Edward Groth III
Testing Director, Recreation and Home Improvement Geoffrey Martin

Consumers Union

President Rhoda H. Karpatkin
Executive Vice President Joel Gurin

Baby-care tips © Meadowbrook Press. Reprinted from "Practical Parenting Tips" by Vicki Lansky with permission of the publisher, Meadowbrook Press, Minnetonka, MN, USA.

First printing, May 1999
Copyright © 1999 by Consumers Union of United States, Inc., Yonkers, New York 10703.
Published by Consumers Union of United States, Inc., Yonkers, New York 10703.
All rights reserved, including the right of reproduction in whole or in part in any form.

ISSN: 1091-0557
ISBN: 0-89043-918-4

Manufactured in the United States of America.

GUIDE TO BABY PRODUCTS

INTRO   **Welcome to baby world** **13**

CHAPTER 1   **Buying basics** **17**
Baby products sources • Be baby-ready • Baby shower help • Shopping savvy • The big baby industry • Money-savers

CHAPTER 2   **Furnishing your baby's room** **35**
Planning the nursery • Choosing a crib • Shopping savvy: mattresses • Crib alternatives • Bedding needs

CHAPTER 3   **Traveling in the car** **59**
Car-seat options • Car seat buying plan • Seat installation • Air bags and children • Car seats on airplanes

SPECIAL SECTION   **Ratings of car seats and travel systems** **75**

CHAPTER 4   **The latest baby wheels** **89**
The many stroller choices • Double and triple seaters • Sports strollers • Bicycle trailers

CHAPTER 5 **Baby-carrying convenience 111**
Shopping savvy for all carrier types • Slings • Strap-on soft carriers • Framed back carriers

CHAPTER 6 **Sitting pretty 121**
Baby seats • High chairs • Booster seats for chairs • Hook-on chairs • Automatic baby swings • Traditional playpens • Travel play yards

CHAPTER 7 **Bathing and diapering 145**
Bathing your baby • Diapering • Diaper rash • Changing tables • Diaper pails • Diaper bags • Toilet training

SPECIAL SECTION **Ratings of diapers and training pants 166**

CHAPTER 8 **Dressing your baby 173**
Practical baby clothes • Shopping savvy • Clothes for toddlers • Footwear

CHAPTER 9 **Feeding time 183**
Breastfeeding • Nursing bras • Choosing a breast pump • Bottle feeding • Juices and sweetened beverages • Using bottled water • Facts on pacifiers • Introducing solid food

Chapter 10 **Playtime gear 215**
Baby toys • Playtime options • Walkers • Stationary entertainers • Jumpers

Chapter 11 **Keeping baby safe 237**
Baby-proofing your house • Baby monitors • Gates

Chapter 12 **Product recalls 259**

Resource guide 287

Index 295

ACKNOWLEDGMENTS

Sandy Jones would like to express her appreciation for the invaluable assistance of Barbara E. Franklin and Dr. James L. Freeman toward the completion of this book, and to acknowledge the insightful guidance of Andrea Scott, Director of Special Publications for CONSUMER REPORTS.

PREFACE

Guide to Baby Products is published by CONSUMER REPORTS, the monthly magazine best known for test reports, product Ratings, and buying guidance. We are also a comprehensive source of unbiased advice about services, personal finance, health and nutrition, and other consumer concerns. Since 1936, our mission has been to test products, inform the public, and protect consumers. Our income is derived solely from the sale of CONSUMER REPORTS magazine and our other publications and services, and from nonrestrictive, noncommercial contributions, grants, and fees. We buy all the products we test, just as you do. We accept no ads from companies, nor do we let any company use our reports or Ratings for commercial purposes.

PRODUCTS AND SERVICES FROM CONSUMER REPORTS

CONSUMER REPORTS. Published monthly, CONSUMER REPORTS magazine provides impartial information on brand-name products, services, health, and personal finance. When you subscribe, you get the annual Buying Guide as well. To subscribe (12 issues, $26), write P.O. Box 53029, Boulder, Colo. 80322-3029.

CONSUMER REPORTS ONLINE. The CONSUMER REPORTS web site can be found at *www.ConsumerReports.org*. Free areas of the site give general buying guidance, a comprehensive list of product recalls, manufacturers' phone numbers, and other useful information. Members-only sections provide searchable Ratings of electronics, appliances, cars, and more, along with the current issue of CONSUMER REPORTS and participation in message boards. Membership is $2.95 per month or $24 per year ($19 for subscribers of CONSUMER REPORTS magazine).

CONSUMER REPORTS BY REQUEST. Specially edited reports are available by fax or mail. Call 800 789-3715 for an index of what's available. The index costs $1.

ZILLIONS. Our bimonthly magazine for kids ages 8 and up, featuring toy tests, games, and "money smarts." To subscribe (6 issues, $16), write us at P.O. Box 54861, Boulder, Colo. 80322-4861.

CONSUMER REPORTS ON HEALTH. Our monthly newsletter devoted to your health and well-being covers fitness, nutrition, medication, and more. To subscribe (12 issues, $24), write us at P.O. Box 56356, Boulder, Colo. 80322-6356.

CONSUMER REPORTS TRAVEL LETTER. Our monthly newsletter with money-saving travel information and the best travel deals. To subscribe (12 issues, $39), write us at P.O. Box 53629, Boulder, Colo. 80322-3629.

NEW CAR PRICE SERVICE. Our comprehensive reports compare sticker price to dealer's invoice for a car or light truck and for factory-installed options. Call 800 651-4636.

USED CAR PRICE SERVICE. Find market value and reliability summary for most 1983–1997 used cars and light trucks. Call 800 422-1079.

AUTO INSURANCE PRICE SERVICE. Compare the cost of insurance for the coverage you need; find the best price. Now available in Ariz., Calif., Colo., Conn., Fla., Ga., Idaho, Ill., La., Mich., Miss., Mo., Nev., N.C., N.J., N.Y., Ohio, Pa., Tenn., Texas, Utah, Va., Wash., and Wis. Call 800 944-4104.

CONSUMER REPORTS TELEVISION. Produces a nationally syndicated consumer news service, Consumer Reports TV News.

OTHER MEDIA. Information from CONSUMER REPORTS is available on radio around the country and in columns appearing in more than 500 newspapers.

Consumer Reports

GUIDE TO BABY PRODUCTS

Introduction

WELCOME TO BABY WORLD

**Congratulations—you're expecting!
Now expect to make a multitude of buying decisions
to get ready for your baby.**

There are few events in life that are more exciting than having your first child. Strike that: There are none. Expectant moms can be found in baby stores all over the country, cooing over infant clothes, imagining their babies snuggled in a beautiful crib on the softest of teddy-bear-decked sheets. Baby product choices are heartfelt and personal. Parents who want what they think of as the best for their child will often spare no expense to get it. And that's why the baby business is booming.

As you decide on your own selections, consider our "Guide to Baby Products" your personal shopping "consultant." This easy-to-read handbook covers a wide range of baby products, consolidating the latest information on quality, safety, and cost into one basic source to assist you in making smart, informed buying decisions.

Our research and testing will help you navigate the sea of complex and sophisticated baby merchandise, such as multifeatured strollers, car seats, cribs, and high chairs, pointing you to the best products—and away from the-less-than-the-best. The extensive listings in the back of the book give you direct access to manufacturers, web sites, and catalog sources. In addition, we've detailed vital product safety procedures and included current recall information. And throughout the book, you'll find hundreds of practical

product tips to help you feed, diaper, dress, and care for your baby. In short, the guide helps you make the right choices for the new addition to your family and get the most value for your money.

The big-bucks baby marketplace

According to the Juvenile Product Manufacturer's Association (JPMA), the trade organization of product manufacturers, retail sales of juvenile products (excluding disposable diapers and toys) reached an all-time high of $4.42 billion in 1997 (the most recent figure available when this book was written). The Toy Manufacturers of America (TMA) reports that baby-toy sales were $564 million in 1997.

First-time parents are the biggest spenders—of course, veterans already have many essentials. A survey published in 1997 by the American Baby Group revealed that first-time parents averaged $7,250 for clothing, furni-

ture, accessories, day care, and medication the first year alone.

Nursery expenses, such as furniture, averaged $600. Baby clothes and other essentials, including baby-care items such as diapers, wipes, and shampoo, added another $600. Nonessential baby toys and books amounted to $800.

A 1996 U.S. Department of Agriculture survey found that baby expenses averaged between $5,600 and $11,600 for the first two years. Annual food costs were $810; clothing $370.

You can see that it's easy to get carried away when shopping for baby supplies. And your first shopping trips may be overwhelming. But rest assured that a newborn doesn't need much besides a place to sleep, simple clothes to stay warm, and diapers to stay dry. So our very first piece of advice is to begin with the essentials. You can then decide which extras you really want.

Baby product ABCs

Some pieces of baby equipment are so useful they must be termed necessities: a crib, a car seat (required by law in all states and by hospitals before they'll allow you to take baby home in your car), basic clothing, diapers, some type of diaper bag, and, for most parents, a stroller.

Soft carriers, backpacks, breast pumps, changing tables, and bottle warmers help make caring for your baby easier—but you can do just fine without them. Such items as crib mobiles, baby swings, door-hung jumpers, and most baby toys have a brief lifespan, so understand that they're fun extras.

Finally, some products are downright risky to your baby's safety. Conventional wheeled walkers can plunge down staircases. Older model portable play yards may have rivets and dropsides that create safety hazards. Bath seats have figured in over 45 deaths; and pressure-mounted "safety" gates can gradually work their way off the wall, leaving staircases or hazardous areas exposed.

How can you know for sure what to buy for your baby? "Guide to Baby Products" can serve as your principal reference. But since baby goods are always evolving (and manufacturers are frequently bought out or taken over), the exact product descriptions, model numbers, and prices may change.

So we recommend that you also keep up with parenting magazines and product-advice publications such as CONSUMER REPORTS. Talk to experienced parents and childbirth educators. Surf every baby-product web site you can find, and scout stores to see merchandise for yourself.

Do remember that because products are constantly redesigned, anything you buy now may be outmoded in two to three years. And you may not use a purchase again unless you plan on another child. So your primary buying goals right now are safety, reliability, convenience—and top quality for your investment.

Chapter

1

BUYING BASICS

The booming baby business wants your dollars. Product facts and a buying plan help you avoid overspending.

Never has there been such a variety of baby goods and services—and so many people eager to sell expectant parents products they may or may not need. From pricey boutiques to giant discount chains, web sites to catalogs, and telemarketers to corporations that crowd your mailbox with brochures and coupons, the baby-product industry hopes to make the sale.

This chapter will streamline your selection process, alert you to shopping pitfalls, and help keep your baby budget in balance.

BABY PRODUCT SOURCES

The easiest place to start your search for good baby products is the classified section of your local telephone directory under "Furniture—Children's," or "Accessories—Children's." You can also conduct a web search for nearby baby product sources in your zip code, using the business directories offered by search engines such as Excite or Yahoo!

Large discount chains that carry general merchandise, such as Wal-Mart, Kmart, Target, Sam's Club, Cosco, Shopko, Bradlees, and Service Merchandise, also carry baby items.

Sears, JC Penney, Spiegel, and Montgomery Ward have a limited selection of cribs, clothing, car seats, and baby accessories, but not at rock-

Contents

Product sources, page 17

Be baby-ready, page 18

Baby shower help, page 22

Shopping savvy, page 24

The baby industry, page 27

Money-savers, page 31

BE BABY-READY
Basics to have before baby arrives

Item	
Car seat Pages 59 to 88	An infant or convertible safety seat must securely fasten in a rear-facing position in your car's back seat. Car seat/stroller combinations are also available. **Special advice:** *Never* buy used. The seat may be defective, damaged, or a recalled model. The sharp angle of some standard models may cause breathing difficulties for preemies: Get a recommendation from your physician.
Stroller Pages 89 to 110	Avoid any model that exceeds one-fourth your own body weight. Take a "test drive" to check brakes, ease of handling and lifting. Try out folding mechanisms. **Special advice:** Don't buy used. Brakes or folding mechanisms may be worn, or the model could be a recall. Newer models may be easier to handle.
Crib Pages 39 to 54	A sticker indicates a certified manufacturer. Test bars to see that they can't be moved or rotated and dropsides for ease of handling. **Special advice:** Don't buy used. Components and hardware could be worn and weakened. New designs and construction can be safer.
Mattress Pages 50 to 54	Choose from foam or innerspring, getting the firmest one you can find. Mattresses are standard-size to fit cribs exactly. Gaps between mattress and crib are a suffocation hazard. **Special advice:** A store return policy is more important than a manufacturer's warranty, which may cover only minor flaws.
Crib bumpers Page 57	A tie-on bumper keeps baby's arms and legs from getting captured in the crib bars. **Special advice:** Bumpers must fit snugly and tie or snap into place. Ties should be no longer than seven inches.
Bedding Pages 57 to 58	Stock up with four to five crib sheets, four or more lightweight cotton blankets (receiving blankets), three waterproof mattress protectors. **Special advice:** Sheets should be soft and elasticized all around so they don't loosen and entrap baby. Layered sleepwear is a better option than covering baby with blankets. Look for quilted, stay-put mattress pads.
Diapers Pages 149 to 157	*Cloth:* Buy four to six dozen, plus four small snap-on, wet-proof outer pants, and two to three sets of diaper pins. *Disposables:* Get at least 100 newborn size, 100 in size 1, plus one or two dozen cloth diapers as backups and milksops. **Special advice:** Don't overbuy small-size diapers. Your baby may grow fast.
Diaper pail Pages 159 to 161	*Cloth diapers:* Choose a bucket-style pail with locking lid. *Disposables:* Get a Diaper Genie or comparable pail with several boxes of refills, or use a garbage can with easy-to-seal liners. **Special advice:** A diaper pail used for soaking must have a locking lid; a tot can drown in the soaking water.
Diaper bag Pages 161 to 163	Look for heavy-duty, moisture-resistant material, such as vinyl-backed luggage fabric; well-reinforced seams; secure handles. **Special advice:** The most durable models come from mail-order catalogs. Consider size and carrying comfort. You can also adapt other bags.
Diaper-changing table Pages 157 to 159	Look for a stable, sturdy model. If it's light, make sure it has a wide stance. All-wood is least likely to tip. You may also use the crib with one side dropped down. **Special advice:** Fold-down adapters for the top of a nursery chest may tip the whole chest if baby's weight is placed on the outer edge.
Feeding supplies Pages 183 to 214	*For breastfeeding:* Buy two or three nursing bras; a box of washable or disposable breast pads for leaks. Lansinoh nipple cream is available from the La Leche League. *For bottle feeding:* Get a set of eight to 12 bottles, nipples and rings, plus a dishwasher basket. Have a month's worth of the formula suggested by your baby's pediatrician. **Special advice:** Consult the La Leche League web site for breast-feeding reference books (see Resource Guide). If you're bottle feeding, boil bottles and nipples at least five minutes before first use to remove any chemical residues. Stay with major formula brands. Non-formula soy milk and off-brand formulas can cause serious malnourishment problems.

Item	

Pacifier
Pages 204 to 206

Buy several, equipped with a small nipple, preferably silicone. Some babies who are breastfeeding may not take to a pacifier. **Special advice:** Boil pacifiers five minutes before first use to remove any chemical residues.

Clothing
Pages 173 to 182

You'll need six to eight nightgowns or one-piece suits, the same number of T-shirts, a small baby cap. **Special advice:** Used clothing is a great buy. Check garage sales, resale shops, classifieds. Avoid elastic bands, metal zippers, scratchy seams, and tiny decorations (a choking hazard).

Bathing/grooming
Pages 145 to 149

Have two to four soft towels; a package of baby washcloths; fragrance-free cleansing bars, like Basis, Dove, or Neutrogena; a pair of blunt-tipped scissors or a baby-sized fingernail clipper. **Special advice:** Any soap can irritate a newborn's skin, so stay with plain warm water for the first few months. Avoid lotions, creams, and powders—their chemicals and fragrances can irritate or cause allergic reactions. It's easiest to trim nails while baby is sleeping.

Medicine chest stocks
Page 156

Ask your baby's doctor to recommend a pain and fever-reducing formula, like Infant's Tylenol. Choose a glass rectal or digital underarm thermometer. A nasal aspirator is a bulbed device for suctioning baby's nose if it becomes congested. **Special advice:** Talk to your doctor for further medication recommendations.

Night-lights
Page 39

Install a dimmer switch in your bedroom and the nursery. Or use a lamp in each room with a low-watt bulb. **Special advice:** Use plug-in night-lights in baby-safe, out-of-reach outlets only.

Optional equipment
Pages 36 to 37 and 115

You may want a rocker or glider for late-night nursing or a nursing support pillow. A soft carrier can make it easier to get around. **Special advice:** Soft carriers are useful for only a few months.

bottom prices. The large department stores in most towns and malls usually carry upscale baby clothing and linens, but not furniture, car seats, or other big-ticket items. You can also go to the baby-supply sources below.

Discount chains

Huge stores such as Toys 'R' Us, Babies 'R' Us, Baby Superstore, and Baby Depot (usually located inside a Burlington Coat Factory) offer a wide selection of baby products in a variety of price ranges. A decade ago, no one could have predicted that these stores would succeed with a focus on the diaper set, but they've tapped into a giant market.

The big baby chains promote products to parents primarily through advertisements (in local newspapers and national and regional parents' publications), floor circulars, and coupons. Most also offer computerized gift registries (discussed on page 22). Close-out sales and "baby week" promotions using "loss leaders"—deeply discounted car seats or other big-ticket items—are a common enticement to come inside and shop. Just don't let a sales associate talk you into a higher-priced model once you're there.

Specialty shops and baby boutiques

Every state has a number of independently owned baby stores and chains, such as Small Fry World in Texas; Baby 2 Teen in Virginia; USA Baby in New York, New Jersey, and other states; Baby Town in Iowa and Illinois; and Kid's Warehouse in California.

Increasingly, these small stores target upscale parents seeking what they see as the best for their young. Merchandise includes high-end safety seats, cribs, and a huge supply of convenient or fashionable accessories, including baby-proofing products, baby-food grinders, and stylish diaper bags. But you'll pay higher prices than you would for identical items at a discount chain (if you can find them at a chain).

When the giant discounters and baby and children's megastores slashed baby product prices, they also cut out one essential ingredient—the human touch. But baby specialty stores offer it in abundance. Knowledgeable salespeople will listen to your queries, answer them thoughtfully, and offer personalized buying advice. They'll bend over backward to be sure you're satisfied, going out with you to your car to try out a safety seat, taking back a broken stroller, or doing all they can to help you when products fail. You'll discover that managers and salespeople (often grandmotherly figures) have

Show off

"Stall" visitors who come to see the baby so that the older child can be the center of attention for a few minutes. Show pictures of the child as well as of the baby. Then let the child help you show off the baby.

their own product biases and will tell you in detail why they prefer one car seat or stroller over another. Their opinions aren't always based on solid facts, but they will patiently talk to you about your product needs.

The majority of these stores carry familiar domestic brands of strollers, cribs, and accessories; but many are changing their focus to products from the European marketplace, high-end bedding and baby clothing, and toys or other baby accessories not found in the mass retailers.

Browse all you like. When it comes to a hand-painted crib priced at nearly $1,000, Ralph Lauren and Christian Dior outfits, silver rattles, or brilliantly artsy crib sheets and comforters priced in the hundreds, looking is what's fun.

Keep in mind that newborns and toddlers couldn't care less about wearing designer duds or sleeping on the latest trend in fabric patterns. Babies just want to be held, rocked, soothed, and fed. All the rest is, well, window dressing.

By the way, although specialty shops and boutiques often take special orders, we don't recommend ordering cribs, furniture, or other critical baby items from them. The store may promise delivery in weeks, but it's not uncommon for orders to drag on for months. Once the product arrives, you may have problems returning it should it have flaws. If the item is not immediately available, we suggest you don't buy it. You don't want your baby to arrive and not have a place to sleep!

Web stores and catalog shopping

Web sites specializing in baby goods are the newest trend in the baby market. One example is iVillage's iBaby, which carries over 20,000 products from more than 200 baby brands. The site has been configured as a virtual department store with a customer service department, a store directory, a gift finder, a baby registry, and a clearance center. It also offers consumer information, such as recent product recalls, product ratings, and shopping lists to aid new parents. Most products are shipped within days, and the site has a liberal return policy. (See the Resource Guide for web site information.)

Virtual web stores offer a wider selection of safety seats, high chairs, and strollers than most local stores can. But unless you've actually seen the product—with the same model number—in a store, your web-store purchase may not be exactly what you've pictured. You'll then have to pay to ship it back. And when you comparison shop, don't forget to include shipping and handling charges, which may add $5 to $10 or more to the purchase price.

If you're just starting out on the web, most local libraries now have computer access, and librarians will help their patrons with web surfing. Using a search engine such as Excite or Yahoo!, try entering keywords such as "baby products + links" or just "baby + links," and you'll be led to listings of sites to pursue, although you can't use the library computer to order. (For a list of representative baby product web sites, see page 290.)

Catalogs are an easy and convenient way to shop for baby needs from home. (You may especially appreciate them later, when caught up in caring for your baby!) We suggest ordering one or two items initially to be sure of the quality, and to be sure that everything matches up with catalog photos and descriptions. Also, double-check sizing measurements, which can sometimes vary, and read the order form to confirm return policies. (See page 291 for a list of baby product catalogs.)

Baby fairs

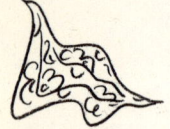

Special

Ask your older child to take care of something special for you while you're in the hospital— perhaps a scarf or piece of jewelry.

Baby expos, happening in many cities across the country, give manufacturers, retail stores, and local nonprofit agencies a chance to show their wares to a select audience—you and hundreds of other expectant and new parents. They also give you a great opportunity to schmooze with other parents about their strollers, high chairs, or diapering preferences, or to ask experts your burning questions.

The best day to attend is the last one. Bring some cash, and prepare for old-fashioned haggling. If you find a stroller or high chair that's already on your shopping list and you're sure about the actual retail price, ask the sales reps how much they'll take for the unit. You have the advantage. A rep doesn't want the hassle of packing up the product and paying to ship it back to headquarters. If you're lucky and first in line, you may be able to carry away your desired product for half price or less.

Baby Faire Consumer Expo puts on baby fairs in large cities, such as Atlanta, Boston, and Chicago. (See the Resource Guide, page 292.)

BABY SHOWER HELP

Is a friend or relative giving you a baby shower? Guests may need coaching about what you want and need.

How product registries work

Baby specialty shops and retail chains all over America, including Babies 'R' Us, Target Stores, JC Penney, and Sears, have hit on baby-gift registries to capitalize on gift-givers and shower-attendees. The service registries aim to prevent duplicate or unwanted gifts.

Once you fill out the store registry form, you receive a walkie-talkie-sized wand for scanning the zebra-striped UPC product codes of the items you like. Don't get overzealous. A 20-page printout listing your 150 wishes for baby gifts may be more confusing than helpful.

Smaller specialty shops may save your registry information in a three-ring notebook. The big chains use computer systems to store your name, your partner's name, your address, your baby's anticipated birth date, and your gift choices—all in a giant nationwide database. The information is accessed when your name or other pieces of information are entered by a gift-shopper. Your list is then printed on command from the terminal in the nursery goods department.

Once retailers have captured your personal information, they're ready to set their promotional and marketing wheels turning. That might be a plus if you get money-saving offers but could be a downer if you're deluged with promotional telephone calls and junk mail when your private data is sold to other companies.

The automated systems, such as those at Sears, JC Penney, and Target stores, aren't fail-safe. Screens may be virtually illegible from the glare of store lights; computers and list printers may refuse to cooperate. Plus, when we questioned baby shower shoppers walking around with huge lists print-

Gifts What you don't want

SHOWER GIFT NO-THANK-YOUS

You won't want to buy these yourself either!
- Scratchy or constricting baby clothes.
- Delicate or hand-washable clothing—impractical for a newborn.
- Uncomfortable, elasticized, baby headbands.
- Bottles shaped like animals or footballs, with nooks and crannies that can harbor bacteria.
- Any toy small enough to fit through the center of a toilet paper roll—a choking hazard.
- Stuffed quilts, pillows, and large stuffed toys—they could suffocate a baby.
- Potentially dangerous items like a conventional walker, baby bath seats, and some play yards.
- Fabric diaper stackers—instead of helping, they just get in the way.

ed out by the store's computer, the reviews were mixed. Some said they were happy to know exactly what the guest of honor wanted. Others were totally confused by 14 or so stapled pages of product names, not always identified by product category.

Another option that may be less intrusive into your life is to create your own baby wish-list of both big and smaller items and distribute the list to friends. Perhaps one of the friends, or your baby's grandmother-to-be, would be willing to provide a telephone number and be the "checkpoint" for what's already been purchased. The list also helps givers who want to pool their resources toward one or two big-ticket items.

SHOPPING SAVVY Baby basics

Baby products are so cute, they're tough to resist, even when you're not bubbling with anticipation. But extras and impulse buys can put a big dent in your budget. So plan all purchases in advance—and stick with your list.

Choose carefully, buy gradually

Before shopping, consider how you will use each product. For example, if your car has a tiny back seat, a small-sized, rear-facing infant car seat may work better for you than a "convertible" model. The stroller you choose depends on whether you plan to take baby on long walks in the country or just for quick shopping jaunts. Your baby's high chair will need to fit the space you've got in your kitchen.

Because baby products are constantly redesigned—and because babies outgrow them so quickly—they're not long-term investments. Hold that thought as you eye costly baby suites, expensive wall hangings, or elaborate quilt and bedding sets. (The latter usually end up folded away in the closet anyway.) A baby swing is useful for four to five months, tops. Baby mobiles, soft strap-on carriers, walkers, and jumpers will serve for only a brief window of time.

Don't feel pressured to buy everything immediately. In fact, it makes sense to postpone buying those items you won't use right away. For example, you can decide later about purchasing a high chair, a changing table, a front carrier, baby toys, or a sports stroller like your neighbor's. Once you bring your baby home, you may discover you don't really need as much as magazines and well-meaning friends and relatives suggest.

Put quality ahead of fashion

Clever, licensed characters help sell baby products. The top 10 licensed properties are Winnie the Pooh; Disney characters such as Mickey Mouse; Looney Tunes; Sesame Street; Teddy Bear Bear; 101 Dalmatians; Paddington Bear; Crayola; Barney; and Bananas in Pajamas.

But baby sheets, clothing, feeding accessories, and toys featuring these familiar faces come at a price. You're likely to pay between 10 and 15 percent more for these items than for very similar or identical goods from the same company without the well-known characters.

The same goes for brands like Carter's, a firm associated with upscale baby clothing that licenses its name for safety seats, strollers, and stroller/car seat combos manufactured by Kolcraft. Fisher-Price, of toy fame, now shares its name with NoJo, a bedding manufacturer, as well as Stork Craft, a crib-maker. NoJo also manufactures bedding under the Baby

Gifts What to ask for
A PRACTICAL SHOWER GIFT LIST

Here's a most-wanted list of shower presents, based on a poll of experienced parents.

- **A case of size-1 disposable diapers.** You can also include a package of fabric diapers. Even when parents plan to use disposables, soft fabric diapers come in handy as burping cloths and milksops.
- **Practical baby clothes.** They should be one or two sizes larger than newborn—especially plain T-shirts, onesies, elasticized-hem nightgowns, and caps.
- **Large receiving blankets.** These soft cotton blankets are always "layerable" and washable.
- **Gift certificates.** That way, Mom and Dad can buy what they want and need, instead of having to exchange duplicate or unusable gifts.
- **A unisex diaper bag.** Please, no bunnies or teddy bears! Diaper bags are for dads, too. A sturdy bag or diaper backpack in neutral navy or black with lots of easy-access storage space is just the ticket. (See pages 161 to 163 for diaper bag suggestions.)
- **A baby bathtub.** Ideally, it's equipped with baby towels, washcloths, shampoo, gentle cleansing bar, and, of course, a rubber ducky. (See page 146 for bathtub ideas.)
- **A baby sling or soft front carrier.** Make sure it's washable and easy to put on and take off. (Carriers are discussed on pages 111 to 120.)
- **A post-birth beauty makeover.** Pampering for Mom.

Guess name. Yet, product-by-product, you can get goods of equal quality at a considerable savings by shopping the original, less-illustrious manufacturers' product lines, rather than the "named" line.

Guard against impulse buys

Beware of being "sold." Expectant parents, especially first-timers, may be unfamiliar with products and think they need everything. Even though in-store helpers may appear totally impartial in their guidance, remember that their job is to sell as much as they can.

Plan your shopping trips. You may innocently set out to browse in the crib section and end up buying a top-of-the-line mattress ($150), a set of cute bibs ($10), and a musical mobile ($30). Then, in the rosy glow of it all, you throw a $300 quilt, pillow, and sheet ensemble into the cart because it's printed with clever Noah's ark animals all over it and is so adorable you just can't resist. Only later do you realize you've charged nearly $500 and

List — Baby supplies

WHAT OTHER PARENTS OWN

Source: American Baby Group Survey of 1,500 expectant and new mothers, The American Baby Group and Bruno and Ridgeway Research Associates, 1997.

haven't even looked at strollers, baby clothes, high chairs, or the other essentials you really wanted.

Then there are music buttons, now attached to exercisers, walkers, night lights, and lots of baby toys. The music may sound okay, even appealing, in the store. But unless you enjoy tinny, computer-chip music like that hidden in birthday cards and are eager to hear, say, "Twinkle, Twinkle, Little Star" a thousand times before the battery wears out, our suggestion is to pass on musical products.

Make a list before you shop, and stick with it. Spend time in baby stores—but make it clear that you're "just browsing, thank you." When you feel a well-intentioned impulse to get your baby whatever strikes your fancy, curb it with the thought that those tempting extras may not be worth the money in the long run.

Confirm return policies

Always find out the seller's return policy before you buy anything. Sometimes manufacturers offer extravagant "lifetime" or "10-year" warranties on mattresses, strollers, and other baby products that you will use for only a few years.

Warranties like that are often simply sales gimmicks to bump you up to the next price level. The companies offering the warranties often don't really back them up, but will send you back to the retailer from whom you bought the product.

If you do end up returning a product to the manufacturer, you'll most likely have to pay shipping. And you may get a replacement with the same generic problem as the original one you purchased. Read the fine print in any warranty, but also determine in advance the store's overall return policy. Does it guarantee satisfaction with the product? Or does it limit your right to return a product to days, months, or a year? These facts are more important than a warranty against "defects in workmanship," or other vaguely worded promise.

THE BIG BABY INDUSTRY

Feel like the stores are flooded with baby products of every description? You're right. Over 200 companies manufacture these items, creating a constant flow of merchandise. And despite all the bears, bunnies, and fuzzy fabrics, the baby business is very competitive.

Familiar

To help the family dog or cat adjust to the new baby, bring home one of the baby's diapers or blankets the day before the baby is brought home, and give it to the pet to play with and sniff. The baby's odor will then be a familiar one.

Who makes what

A handful of larger companies whose names you'll see over and over in this book and in the stores—Century, Cosco, Evenflo, Fisher-Price, Graco, and Kolcraft—make, import, or put their names on most of the baby gear sold in this country, including car seats, high chairs, strollers, playpens, and numerous other baby accessories. Some of these companies also sell cribs, although most cribs come from baby furniture specialists, including Child Craft, Simmons, and Stork Craft.

Small and medium-sized companies produce limited numbers of products (usually each with their own specialties), such as baby bottles, fabric baby carriers, toys, sports strollers, and baby bedding.

Foreign companies also sell their products in the U.S. You'll find two kinds of imported goods. On one end are makers of poorly constructed imports sold at cut-rate prices. At the top, you'll find importers of very costly items usually carried by exclusive baby boutiques—strollers from Japanese manufacturers such as Aprica; strollers and high chairs from the Italian firms Peg Perego and Chicco; and lush Italian cribs imported by such companies as Bellini, Pali, and Ragazzi.

Baby skin care products (shampoos, powders, and soaps) are made by giant manufacturers of drugs or other sundries, including Johnson & Johnson and Mennen. The multibillion-dollar disposable-diaper industry is dominated by two companies—Procter & Gamble, maker of both Pampers and familiar household products, and Kimberly-Clark, which manufactures Huggies and other paper goods.

Baby formulas come from huge pharmaceutical concerns, including Ross Laboratories, a division of Abbott Laboratories; Mead Johnson Nutritional Group, a division of Bristol-Myers Squibb; and, more recently, the multinational Nestlé, marketing under the name Carnation. The baby food industry is headed by Gerber, with smaller shares going to food makers Beech-Nut and Heinz.

As companies change, products change

The highly competitive baby product industry, like many others, is constantly in flux, with buyouts, takeovers, and sellouts common.

For example, Century, a manufacturer of car seats and baby accessories, is now owned by another baby-product company, Graco, which has been purchased by Newell-Rubbermaid, maker of familiar household products.

Cosco, a general baby-products manufacturer, is now owned by Dorel, a Canadian firm. Gerry, a maker of backpacks and car seats, has been acquired by Evenflo, which produces a huge variety of baby products. Evenflo, in turn, is now owned by Kohlberg, Kravis & Roberts, a private investment firm. Fisher-Price, well-known for its toys, has been bought by toy giant Mattel. Playskool, a baby product manufacturer, is now owned by the other toy giant, Hasbro.

All this change has made it hard to keep up with who makes what. That means it's doubly important to supplement our research with your own.

How competition affects product quality

On the plus side, keen competition produces increasingly sophisticated designs and problem-solving products—and helps keep prices down. In general, baby goods just keep getting better.

Protective car seats for babies and preschoolers continue to improve year after year. New angled baby bottles appear to make feeding easier. Knee-press hardware, allowing crib sides to lower silently and effortlessly, can be a genuine improvement over awkward foot pedals and squeaky metal rods used in the past. Stationary baby entertainers are a welcome alternative to wheeled walkers that injured hundreds of thousands of babies, usually when they fell down staircases.

Competition leads manufacturers to try to outdo each other. Typically, when an innovative baby-product manufacturer invents a wonderful new product and it sells well, others race to their drawing boards to create something similar. Often the new design improves on the original. Sometimes the clone is cheaper, too.

Sometimes, design one-upmanship leads to overpriced products glutted with features that detract rather than enhance. Take strollers, for instance. Manufacturers have long competed to pack on the most accessories, but every extra also piled on weight and bulk. Snack trays were attached to the front, then snap-on toys added to the trays, then huge storage bins appeared underneath. Wheels kept getting larger, and fold-down canopies got longer and longer. Then stroller-makers introduced the concept of securing car seats on adapted strollers. Result: Relatively efficient strollers morphed into heavyweight awkward contraptions.

But then the competitive spirit kicked in again. Japanese and Italian importers entered the marketplace with remarkably intricate strollers carrying the same features of our behemoths—at half the weight. They were costly, but upscale parents were willing to invest a hundred dollars or more for convenient, better-engineered models.

The competition-driven evolution goes on. Canadians have entered the crib marketplace with well-finished, stylish models. An Italian firm created a multiple-height high chair so smooth to operate it edged out less-expensive four-legged designs. Another Italian firm cloned that adjustable wonder, and now sells it for less.

The downside of competition

More rarely, the rush to the marketplace leads to serious product flaws. Easy-to-handle portable play yards, made with tubular frames and lightweight fabrics, appeared to be a wonderful new baby invention. They could be quickly put up and folded down, stored in a durable carrying case, and thrown into a car trunk or a plane's overhead luggage bin.

However, an unanticipated flaw in the folding mechanism resulted in some models with sides that didn't snap into a rigid, open position but rather folded into a V-shaped indentation. Over a dozen babies died when their necks were entrapped. At present millions of models have been recalled because of that and other problems, such as protruding rivets. (For a list of current product recalls, consult page 259.)

How the industry targets you

Along with constant innovation and a "captive" buying group, manufacturers have another tool—direct contact with parents.

Prepare yourself. Once discovered to be expecting, you're fair game for those marketing a myriad of products and services. For instance, disposable diaper makers invest millions of dollars each year to purchase the names, addresses, and telephone numbers of expectant and new parents.

The big-time marketers are so efficient, they'll discover your good news almost as soon as you do. Their secret? Reporting systems in obstetricians' offices. Then you get "demographed." Perhaps you're a DEWK—dual-employed with kids. To marketers, this means you've got bucks to spend on your baby.

Once in the loop, you'll find your mailbox filling with coupons, catalogs, and samples, plus the company-sponsored brochures and baby magazines that are basically product-peddling tools. You may also receive dinnertime

Save

Get unisex clothing in boys' departments; it's usually more rugged and often costs less than items in girls' departments.

telephone calls from "market research firms" wanting to probe your family profile and acquire personal data so you can be flooded with even more mail and calls.

Some of the material you'll receive is helpful, and the coupons can be handy. A number of parents even call the toll-free customer service numbers and announce themselves to formula, baby food, and diaper makers to get the perks. Others just post a trash can near the front door and toss everything but coupons.

MONEY-SAVERS

This list can help you save money as you shop—and you'll find a lot more economical ideas throughout the book.

Buying basics. You can start with a car seat, stroller, crib, diapers, and basic baby clothes. Then wait to see what others give you. The stores will still be open after your baby comes, and by then you'll know better what you need.

In the meantime, get friends and relatives to lend you outgrown clothing in promise for a similar exchange later if needed, and check garage sales and thrift stores for clothing and toy bargains. There's no need for tons of expensive clothes. Just dress baby for comfort—layers in the winter, T-shirt and diapers in the summer.

Canny shopping. Comparison shop for every big-ticket item before you buy. Once you know what models and brands you want, you may be able to save $50 or more by checking out stores, catalogs, and web sites. But always determine all return policies. Why get stuck with an unsatisfactory product?

Resist the urge to buy everything in newborn sizes. Babies don't stay tiny very long, and some are large even at birth. Get T-shirts, gowns, and footed sleepers in a larger size, and let baby grow into them.

Before shopping for a car seat, check with your insurance company. Some companies offer their customers car seats at nearly wholesale prices. You may also get a deal at Midas Muffler shops or through hospital loaner programs—fine as long as the seat is new. And check sales and coupons from big discount chains such as Toys 'R' Us. You will find racks of promotional magazines in the front of the store.

Feeding economy. Breastfeed your baby, if possible. You'll save between $1,200 and $3,600 over feeding with formula—and breast milk also has health benefits (see pages 183 to 184). Invest in good breastfeeding manuals or hire a lactation consultant to help you succeed.

If you bottle feed, buy formula in bulk from baby megastores or discount stores, rather than from the grocery store. Ask your baby's pediatrician for coupons and samples. Join grocery-store and drugstore baby clubs for more coupons and discounts.

Call the toll-free customer service lines for all of the formula and disposable diaper companies and sign up for their new-mother programs. Most likely, you'll get coupons and free samples, and you may get put in the loop for other special offers, too.

If you want to prepare your own baby food, use organically grown produce. Freeze the pureed food in ice cube trays and then store the cubes in plastic bags. Buy one or two flexible molded-plastic bibs, rather than a number of the terrycloth type, then wipe them clean after every meal.

Diaper tactics. Launder your own cloth diapers. (They make great

List Getting ready
14 THINGS TO DO BEFORE BABY ARRIVES

1. Study the car seat section (page 59), then track down a rear-facing seat, infant or convertible. Using the manufacturer's instructions and your car's manual, install the safety seat securely in the center of your car's backseat (or wherever your car's manufacturer recommends) so it won't budge.

2. Select and interview a pediatrician for your baby. Make notes on the hours allotted for answering telephone queries. Also ask for recommended formula brands so you'll know what to buy if baby is bottle feeding.

3. Post emergency telephone numbers, including your baby's doctor-to-be, and numbers and contacts for family members next to the kitchen telephone.

4. Check on smoke alarms and install new batteries, if needed. Also, install a carbon monoxide alarm. Put large street address numbers at the entrance to your driveway for the fire department to see, and plan to put a sticker on the nursery window to indicate your baby's room.

5. Turn the thermostat on your water heater down to 120 degrees F to reduce the risk of burning baby's sensitive skin.

6. Get a water filter installed under the kitchen sink, especially if you're using well water.

7. Get your baby's room redecorated right away. You'll want to allow time for the chemical fumes from new paint, wallpaper, drapes, and carpeting to subside before baby comes

burping pads, too). Your initial investment of $150 to $200 will last for years in contrast to up to $80 per month for disposables.

If you use disposables, try to buy them from discount stores when they're on sale, or when you've got coupons. Try out alternative brands, such as Luv's, which are less expensive than Pampers and Huggies.

Use a damp washcloth rather than baby wipes, which are full of chemicals that don't belong on baby's skin. Store a couple of damp washcloths in plastic bags for your diaper bag. Or soak soft paper towels in water.

Instead of buying a baby bathtub, bathe baby in the kitchen sink with a folded bath towel lining the bottom. Or take the baby in the tub with you. (Use lukewarm water, and get somebody to help you lift him in and out.)

Pass up baby powder (talcum powder can cause pneumonia if inhaled in large quantities by your baby), lotions, and other baby "cosmetics." Your baby's skin doesn't need them.

home. (The best wall paint is the fungicide-free, water-based latex variety.)

8. Air out new furniture and anything made of plastic or particleboard in baby's room to lessen their fumes.

9. Make sure all new baby clothes and bedding have been laundered in a fragrance-free detergent to remove sizing and chemicals. Don't use fabric softener liquid or sheets. The fragrance can irritate baby's sensitive nose and throat.

10. Remove any plug-in room deodorizers in the house. They can irritate, too.

11. Arrange for family members or part-time helpers such as high school or college students to help out with laundry and household responsibilities for a month or two after baby arrives.

12. To give yourself a dishwashing break and keep the kitchen sink from piling up with dirty dishes, stock up on throw-away plates and cups.

13. Freeze extra meals or stock the freezer with easy-to-prepare frozen entrees from the grocery store. Check local takeout sources.

14. Pack a bag for baby's homecoming day: You'll want two or three small nightgowns, preferably elasticized-hem styles; a lightweight cotton receiving blanket for warm weather; or a fleece or thermal blanket plus a small baby cap for cold weather. If you're bottle feeding, include several small pacifiers with silicone nipples. The hospital may provide disposable diapers, but if you plan to use fabric diapers, have four or five plus a waterproof diaper cover.

Nursery know-how. Save 10 to 15 percent on bedding, strollers, clothing, and other items by passing up well-known cartoon and fantasy characters or fashion labels. (The companies pass the licensing expense on to consumers.)

Purchase sheets, bedding, and simple baby clothing at discount chains such as Wal-Mart and Kmart. Department stores and mall baby stores charge twice as much as chains do for footed sleepers and other baby garments.

Instead of a changing table, use a soft changing pad on the floor for diapering.

Buy a sturdy, new crib, but pass up the matching chest, changing table, and armoire ($1,000 to $5,000). Get open shelves or a sturdy three-drawer chest ($75 to $150) instead. Fasten either one to the wall with an L-bracket so your baby can't pull it over on top of himself.

Find freebies. Call your health department about free immunizations. Sign up for every baby registry you can find. You'll automatically be put on lists for coupons and money-saving offers. Subscribing to parenting magazines will have the same result. If you don't mind wading through junk mail, you may be able to find good savings opportunities.

Be a bargainer. Sometimes smaller furniture stores are so eager to make a sale, they'll discount cribs and mattresses, if you negotiate with them. The best time to bargain is very late afternoon, when the store will soon be adding up its sales for the day.

Baby fairs held in most big cities are a great place for deep discounts. Once you've chosen the brands and models you want, offer to buy the model off the showroom floor on the last day. You may be able to get a big discount if you're willing to carry the model away.

Shop outlet stores for clothing and furniture, and look for clothing sales during season changes.

Chapter

FURNISHING YOUR BABY'S ROOM

You can create a cozy, safe, convenient nursery—
without breaking the piggy bank.

Planning a nest for your baby is part of the fun of getting ready for your child's birth. Enjoy creating a cozy and inviting room. Some parents select a single, coordinating theme, such as Winnie the Pooh, Disney characters, or animal motifs, then hunt down wall coverings, sheets, blankets, and other decorating items that echo the image throughout the room. But many are shifting away from well-known characters to simpler approaches, blending colors and patterns to make baby's room visually attractive without being too cutesy or repetitious.

However, like most parents, you'll also consider other issues besides appearance. A 1997 survey conducted by the American Baby Group showed that while furniture brand name and company reputation were important, quality and safety were the key concerns.

PLANNING THE NURSERY

Because putting together a safe, attractive nursery can be a big job, it's easiest to take it in steps.

Divide up the space

Babies' rooms naturally divide into zones: a sleeping area where the crib will be; your "nursery nest" for holding baby while you feed him; a diaper-

Contents

The nursery, page 35

Choosing a crib, page 39

Buying a mattress, page 50

Crib alternatives, page 54

Bedding needs, page 57

changing center, and a place for storing diapers, clothing, bedding, and other baby supplies. Begin by measuring the room so you know exactly how much space you have for each area. Don't forget to size up windows, too, to have dimensions for curtains or shades.

Crib location. The center of the room is a safe crib spot, protecting your baby from reaching out to pull anything down from walls, furniture, or windows. The simplest starting point for choosing a crib is to select the type of finish. You'll find a wide variety of wood finishes in baby stores—sleek Scandinavian naturals, dark Victorians, country-cottage whites, or cherries and other tones. You can then select other coordinating furniture, if you want—new or used. (How to choose a crib is discussed in detail, beginning on page 39.)

Nursing nest. Ideally, this will center around a rocker or other comfortable chair with side arms and an ottoman, or even a daybed with high endboards that allows you to snooze while baby nurses during the night.

Baby Safe

A secure nursery

Since you will be leaving your baby for long periods of time in the nursery, you'll want to be very careful about safety.

• Position furniture so you have a clear path when you enter the room at night. Keep the floor uncluttered by toys or other objects.

• Keep wall hangings with ribbons or streamers out of reach of the crib. Blind cords can strangle babies in cribs. Use a cord shortener, and be sure to place the crib well away from the window. Clip crib bumper ties so they are no longer than seven inches.

• Regularly check crib bars and hardware. Immediately stop using a crib with broken or missing parts.

• Purchase window locks or guards from a hardware or home supply store and install them following manufacturer's instructions. Or have locking shutters made that will close off the bottom part of the windows. Position chairs or other furniture away from windows to prevent your tot from crawling up and falling out.

• Start working on your fire escape plans. If the room's on the second floor, purchase a rolled-up ladder with "stand-offs" (so it's easier to descend) and store it high enough so that there's no chance of injury to your child.

• When your tot graduates to a toddler bed, install a screen door for the room. It will allow you to see and hear your child, and will let air circulate in the room, but will keep him securely inside if he awakens before you do.

Add a side table to hold a reading lamp, a drinking glass—and a bottle warmer, if you're bottle feeding. A clock radio with a tape or CD player will let you listen to soft music and keep tabs on the time. If you're breastfeeding, a nursing pillow will keep your arms from getting tired.

Changing station. If your bathroom is large enough, put your diaper-changing center there. If not, you'll want to create one in your baby's room. Baby should have a secure place on which to lie, such as the crib with one side lowered, a diaper-changing table, or a chest with a changing pad well fastened on top. You'll want a surface with a safety belt and high sides to prevent baby rolling off. And don't forget a child-resistant garbage can or diaper pail. (Diaper-changing tables are discussed on page 157.)

Storage. Closet-organizing systems will allow you to maximize the space for storing folded baby clothes, small things on hangers, and toys. (Some parents even build a changing station right into the closet.) Shelves or a chest having at least three drawers can be used for diapers, supplies, and baby clothes. Open bookcases will do the job, too. All storage units should be fastened to the wall so they won't fall over on a climbing tot. (Tip-resistant furniture with safety brackets designed specifically for children's rooms can be ordered from Mommy's Helper. See the Resource Guide.)

Stackable plastic bins, available in bold primary colors or pastels, are another storage plan. Be wary of chests with lids or self-locking latches. A free-falling lid can hurt a child's fingers or entrap his neck, and a latch may lock a tot inside. Open shelves cause less clutter and confusion when your child starts searching for toys.

If limited space requires that your baby's room double as a guest room or home office, you might consider having a set of floor-to-ceiling cabinets, such as kitchen cabinets in wood finished to go with the crib. Recessed lighting and a changing counter with an unbreakable mirror in the back will fascinate baby. Don't forget an enclosed but vented cabinet to hide the diaper pail. If you need it, you can build a desk area into the system, but be sure to include a locking door to keep a tot out of your office supplies, computer, and all wiring and electrical outlets.

Select your colors

Wall and trim colors form the background of the nursery. Spark your decorating imagination by clipping appealing pictures of rooms and scenes (even if they're not nurseries) from magazines. You'll see how colors combine and patterns and fabrics go together before you commit yourself. Store your clippings along with the schematics of the room's measurements in a large, inexpensive photo album with self-sticking pages.

For more ideas, collect samples of paint shades from hardware and home supply stores. Investigate wallpaper patterns or simple borders that you can paste around the room near the ceiling and even around the windows. You can then coordinate the borders with other fabrics, colors, and patterns in the room.

If you're painting the nursery, look for fungicide-free, washable, scrubbable latex for easy cleanup when your tot leaves handprints or crayon marks on the walls. If your house was built before the 1980s, the current paint and trim may contain lead. Sanding and stripping the walls may release lead dust into the air, so you may want to consult a professional about doing the job for you.

Add decorative touches

Unless you paint it yourself, a big mural for the nursery's wall can be too expensive. Instead, experiment with textures using sponges, rags, or other painting techniques. You can find how-to's in crafts books in the library. While you're there, browse in the children's picturebook section—their artwork offers wonderful color ideas. You may even buy a few children's books and have the drawings mounted and framed, then hang them at a level visible from the crib but high enough to be out of a toddler's reach. Arts and crafts stores and the crafts section of most Wal-Mart stores also carry stencils that let you add a personal touch to walls.

You might also like enlargements of family pictures, posters of babies, or farmyard and wild animals, even a big, unbreakable mirror.

The fabrics you choose for curtains and valances, crib dust ruffles, and wall hangings also add texture and shading. Your options include pristine white laces, pastel ginghams, playful jungle or farmyard themes, or rich solids such as burgundies and greens. Don't forget that stuffed animals and bright toys will add their colors to the palette.

Thick, light-blocking window shades or wooden shutters with no finger-pinching potential may help keep your tot from crowing like a rooster at dawn. Shade or blind cord loops are a strangulation hazard, so cut them in half and roll them out of reach.

For safety's sake, resist the urge to buy costly pillows and quilts. Even though decorative nursery ensembles appeal to the eye, your baby is much safer without them. A recent study conducted by the U.S. Consumer Product Safety Commission (CPSC) found a correlation between soft bedding—pillows, quilts, and sheepskins—and baby suffocation deaths. (See the Sudden Infant Death Syndrome—SIDS—discussion on page 53.)

Have a baby-friendly ceiling—and a safe floor

Babies spend a lot of time on their backs looking around. You can make bare ceilings more engaging with colorful fabric kites suspended out of reach, or billowing fabric draped through rings on the ceiling. Most babies are fascinated by contrasts of light and dark, even something as simple as the pattern created by leaves fluttering outside the nursery window. Vinyl prism stickers, available in nature stores, break up light into colorful beams and "project" the colors onto the wall. Or stick glow-in-the-dark stars and a moon on the ceiling for an appealing nighttime pattern.

Although useful and decorative, night-lights attract crawling babies and sometimes can be fire hazards. Use a lamp with a low-watt bulb and a fire-resistant shade, or one with a three-way brightness control that dims the light when you touch the base. Tape the lamp cord out of baby's reach. Install a dimmer switch on the nursery's switch plate (and in your bedroom as well) so you can adjust the lighting at night as you check on your sleeping baby.

For the floor, you might consider replacing dust-collecting carpets with smooth, washable floor surfaces such as nonskid, mar-proof vinyl. Easy-to-clean, low-pile carpets or area rugs can help to soften the look of the room, but make sure your choices are washable or at least stain resistant. All small rugs should have nonskid backings to keep you or your growing tot from slipping or tripping. You may want to adhere them to the floor with rubber backing or double-faced adhesive.

You needn't feel pressured to have a perfect nursery before you bring baby home. As with most decorating, you can add touches gradually—or even wait until your baby graduates from the crib to create a toddler's environment. And you may discover in the day-to-day caring for your baby that room decor isn't that important after all.

CHOOSING A CRIB

Your baby has lots of sleeping options: a full-sized crib, from basic to luxurious; a crib that later converts into other furniture, such as a loveseat; a

Colorful

Put a colorful poster, kite, or piece of wallpaper on the ceiling above the dressing table.

portable crib; a bassinet; a cradle; or a bedside sleeper.

Most parents choose a full-sized crib. The selection can be overwhelming—picture a huge showroom filled with models offered by a giant discount chain. But a crib is basically a simple device. It's a box with coil-spring mattress supports and legs with wheels. The sides and sometimes the endboards are made of bars or slats so you can see inside—and baby can see you. Except for special promotions, the mattresses and fancy bedding you'll see on display are sold separately.

Your main concerns in selecting a crib are sturdiness and safe, quality construction.

Where to buy a crib

Full-sized cribs are the most widely used of all baby products. In fact, more American families own a crib than any other piece of baby apparatus. Cribs are sold in some furniture stores, in local baby specialty stores, and in nearly all discount and megastores specializing in children's products.

The easiest place to start looking for a crib is in the business advertising listings of your local telephone directory, under headings such as "Furniture–Children's." Stores such as Toys 'R' Us, Babies 'R' Us, Baby Superstore, and Baby Depot carry a wide range of cribs in a variety of wood finishes. Sears, JC Penney, and Montgomery Ward offer brand-name crib models as well as lower-end models.

The big discount chains display a mind-boggling selection of mostly lower- and mid-priced models. Prices begin at around $60 for a lightweight model painted white, and go up toward $250 for dark wood stains and natural finishes. Models from the biggest crib manufacturers, Simmons and Child Craft, will stand alongside less familiar brands such as Angel Line, Baby's Dream, Bassett, Cosco, Delta Enterprise (Baby Luv), Evenflo, Generation 2 Worldwide (Childesigns, Next Generation brands), La Chambre de Bebe (Forever Mine), Million Dollar Baby, Okla Homer Smith, Stork Craft, and Tracers. Some of these companies produce only cribs and baby furniture; others offer cribs as part of their multiproduct baby lines.

Local specialty stores and boutiques targeting upscale parents focus on well-finished domestic models, such as the Child Craft Legacy line, and heavyweight imported cribs, such as Italian Ragazzi and Pali models, with prices soaring to $500 and $700 or more per crib. Bellini stores also offer their own brand.

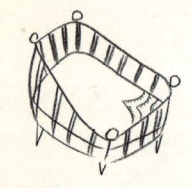

Quick change

Make up your baby's crib sheets and pads in layers so all you need to do is pull off a top sheet and pad to "change" sheets.

Check both price and quality

Federal regulations govern crib safety. So your crib selection will mostly depend on your own furniture preferences and how much you wish to spend. You can create a showpiece nursery suite for thousands of dollars. Or you can simply buy a well-constructed crib—the option most parents take. ("Assessing a crib," pages 43 to 47, has the pointers.)

Crib pricing is inconsistent within both the crib and the retail industries. When carefully inspected, two cribs in the same price range may show noticeable quality differences. And two seemingly identical crib models from the same manufacturer may also have subtle differences—one may be perfect while the other may display rough spots, bubbles, and other flaws in finishing and workmanship.

Crib prices range from about $60 for a no-frills white model to $700 or more for a heavyweight, imported crib that looks more like a furniture masterwork than a baby bed. There are unmistakable differences between the lowest- and highest-priced cribs on the market, but those in the middle range are very similar from one model to another.

Cribs priced under $100 are likely to have simple, squared posts on all four corners and thin end panels. You will probably find surface defects, such as rough edges and textures, or portions with uneven paint. Look under the display mattress and you may spot flimsier hardware and springs than on higher-priced models.

Typically, the lowest-priced cribs are painted white, allowing crib manufacturers to cover over mixed wood grains, unsightly knots and flaws, and variations in wood tones. (More transparent finishes demand better wood matches.) However, a white crib is not necessarily a poorer choice. In fact, some painted models are made from denser hardwoods than more costly, stained models.

As with other big-ticket baby items, price and quality don't always match up. If you know what to look for, you can find a crib that's a great value for $200 to $300 or even less. It will have furniture styling without being a showpiece, and you'll be pleased with the finish, the hardware, and its low-key decorative touches.

Most cribs are constructed of wood. Manufacturers use at least a dozen different kinds of wood, from porous and easily dented pine to stronger and more durable hardwoods, such as ash, beech, oak, hard maple, or imported varieties. As a rule, the harder the wood, the more dense it is, and the heavier it makes the crib. More rarely, cribs may also be constructed of other materials—steel, brass, or molded plastic.

Wood colors are probably the first thing you'll notice when you begin crib shopping. Expect a wide palette of shades and finishes: stark whites; washed whites that show the wood's grain; natural wood colors, such as blonds; and gradations of deeper wood stains, from lighter maples and cherries to dark, reddish mahoganies.

Often, heftier cribs have heftier price tags, too. Solid wood endboards, carved trimming, and other embellishments, as well as rich stains and glosses, are usually found on more expensive models. Some may even mimic heirloom pieces—heavyweight, Victorian-style sleigh beds and old-fashioned four-posters with canopies. For example, a Ragazzi Country Cottage Sleigh Bed in cherry with curved, solid wood endboards, one side stabilizer bar, and a single dropside with a lift-and-knee-press mechanism costs $600 at an upscale baby boutique in Midlothian, Virginia.

But in the mid-priced range, you can also find a Stork Craft crib in a sleigh style in dark wood. It features dual stabilizing bars underneath, a sin-

Choose your crib based on style and sturdy construction. All cribs must meet government safety standards, making safety issues less of a worry. Try the dropsides—they should be easy to operate. Request delivery and in-home assembly so you can inspect the fully assembled crib for flaws.

42 ■ Guide to Baby Products

gle dropside using metal rods, swivel casters, and well-glued teething rails. The cost was $229 at a large discount baby warehouse in Denver, Colorado.

The $600 Ragazzi, as beautiful as it is, appears so heavy, it will increase the darkness factor in a nursery, making the room seem smaller. The Stork Craft crib, on the other hand, achieves the same sleigh effect with subtle curving, but the ends have bars instead of dark, solid wood. In fact, if your baby's room were long and narrow so that a crib had to fit with one end toward the door and the other toward the window, you might like the Stork Craft even better than the Ragazzi. You'd be able to easily look in on baby, and baby would be able to see out the window.

Assessing a crib

By federal law, cribs have to meet certain safety standards: They are required to have firmly locking dropsides, with a backup to prevent accidental lowering; a lock-release mechanism beyond a child's capability; and bars no more than 2⅜ inches apart (the width of a soda can). Interior dimensions have been standardized so that all crib mattresses fit snugly (gaps are a suffocation hazard). Mattress supports must be low enough in their highest position so that a child cannot easily climb out. Plastic bags, which some parents use to protect crib mattresses, must now carry suffocation-hazard warnings.

Grow

Trace your child's silhouette from a shadow every year or so.

When shopping, you'll want to evaluate a prospective crib for durability and construction. Keep these features in mind when looking for a well-made crib.

Sturdiness indicates construction quality. A certification sticker, located somewhere on the crib frame, shows that the manufacturer has passed testing for product durability. Tests evaluate overall construction, side rails, latching mechanisms, and teething rails. Remember, the sticker does not certify the crib model—just the maker. (See Product Recalls for crib certification details.)

A simple in-store test that you can conduct yourself for solid crib construction is a sound shaking. If you hear metal knocking on metal, or the crib frame seems loose rather than solid, the construction may be faulty. Or the looseness could simply be a sign of sloppy assembly by the retailer. If so, you will notice that the screws on the endboards aren't tight. A single dropside makes a crib sturdier.

One or more stabilizer bars—metal rods fastened to both endboards underneath the crib—help to steady the frame, definitely an advantage over cribs whose design includes no additional stabilization.

A poor finish may warn of other flaws. A little roughness in the finish isn't a problem as long as there is no splintering or peeling paint. But if those problems are coupled with other glaring flaws, then consider the model defective and avoid it.

Check drawer durability. Typically, cribs with drawers underneath are priced higher than cribs without them. Drawers are not usually attached to the crib frame but are freestanding and roll out from under the crib on casters. Pull any freestanding drawer all the way out from under the crib to inspect it. You may find that it's poorly constructed, with a thin, cardboard-like floor that could bow and give way when loaded with linens or clothing. Look for a floor made of a hardboard, such as Masonite, that will hold up over time.

Faulty railings are a safety hazard. Crib sides are constructed by fitting bars (sometimes called spindles or slats) into drilled holes in the top and bottom rails, then securing each bar with glue and one or two metal pins. The small holes made by the brads are usually filled and covered with a finish so they're invisible.

How well bars and rails fit and stay together makes the difference between sturdy sides and those more likely to separate—and this can be a matter of life and death. Between 1985 and 1996, the CPSC reported receiving information about 138 incidents in which one or more crib bars disengaged from sides, or were loose, missing, or broken. These incidents involved cribs manufactured by at least 26 different companies. Twelve of these incidents resulted in the death of a child, and five in injuries. Injuries and deaths occurred when a baby slipped through the gap between broken or defective bars and caught its head, causing strangulation.

Examine the connection where bars fit into railings. Try rotating each bar to see if it's well secured. Also look for spots of dried glue spilled on the railings. Loose bars and glue spots are signs of poor workmanship.

Top railings on most cribs have a teething rail, a glued-on plastic shield that runs the length of the crib rail and serves to keep babies from gnawing on the wood. (Oddly, there's nothing to prevent babies from chewing on endboards.) Test teething rails to see that they're tightly secured and can't be lifted from the rails. The plastic should extend from one end of the rail to the other and shouldn't have sharp edges that could cut a baby's fingers. And be sure there are no posts or protrusions that could capture baby's clothing.

Mattress supports should be stable. The support holds up the mattress, allowing it to be raised or lowered, depending on the size of the child. The standard support consists of a metal frame with coiled springs attached.

Springs have definite drawbacks. First, babies need a firm, flat surface on which to sleep, not the mushy postural support that some adults prefer. And because the springs are unshielded, they press unevenly on the underside of the mattress, increasing its rate of wear. They can also punch holes in the mattress covering. In addition, springs gather dust and contribute to the trampoline-like surface that encourages babies to use the mattress as a springboard, increasing the chance of a fall inside the crib.

A few manufacturers have begun to offer hardboard mattress supports as an alternative to springs, with a single board positioned on ledges around the crib frame. But if the board isn't thick enough, it could bow over time, and both board and mattress could fall, causing injury. If you decide to purchase a crib with a mattress support board, make sure that there is sturdy backup hardware to hold the board in place. The best attachment for mattress supports are metal components that bolt both to the support and the endboards.

All full-sized cribs offer two or three mattress support positions—from the highest for infants to the lowest for toddlers able to pull up to a standing position. Manufacturers use a huge variety of metal assemblies to allow parents to raise or lower the supports. To prevent a baby from falling out, most safety experts recommend the mattress be lowered as far as possible as soon as a baby is able to sit or pull up.

Wheels need locks. Wheels can be standard rollers or round, multi-directional, ball-shaped casters made of plastic or metal. Casters make the crib easier to push around. Lockable wheels will keep your tot from "walking" the crib across the room when he shakes it, and will help keep other children from rolling the crib when your back's turned.

Dropsides must be accident-proof. Cribs usually have one or two sides that can be lowered, called single or double dropsides. One dropside is actually preferable to two because the nonlowering side helps create a more stable frame.

Raising a crib's side is simple. Just pull it until you feel the click that signals it's locked. Lowering a side is a whole different story. In fact, it's one of

Sound sleep

Position the baby in a corner of the crib or bassinet, head touching the bumper or soft padding to provide a feeling of security. This also allows you to move the baby from corner to corner if the sheet gets wet or soiled.

the most exasperating parts of trying out cribs. You can jerk, rattle, kick, and push, but most crib sides balk and refuse to cooperate.

By law, today's cribs require lock-releasing actions that only an adult can perform, to prevent toddlers or brothers and sisters from accidentally lowering a side. Typically, lowering a crib's side requires a double motion—a lift of the bars, followed by a second action, which depends on the lowering mechanism, varying with different cribs. Here are the three standard ways:

Metal rods. With this mechanism, the crib's dropside slides up and down metal rods located at both ends of the crib. (Sometimes the rods are called "J-rods" or "canes" in the crib industry because of their curved ends.) Lower-priced crib rails simply have a drilled hole to accommodate the rod; others may have a nylon sleeve glued inside the hole for reinforcement. Neither method appears to reduce the squealing caused by the rods when the sides move up or down.

You'll find the release in the center of the crib, directly in back of the side you're going to lower. With your foot, you must push in either a U-shaped metal tab called a kickbar, a toe-trip release, or a treadle, while pulling up slightly on the crib rail. Some cribs may require you to use two hands when pulling up so both sides are even and won't jam. And with experience, you'll learn to quickly move your foot from under the crib to protect your shins from getting hit by the side as it lowers.

Metal-rod systems make a crib more prone to rattling than other options. If the crib is subjected to a lot of shaking from a jumping toddler, the screws fastening the rods into the endboards can work loose from the wood—ruining their holes in the process.

Trigger releases. Instead of metal rods, some cribs have knobs, or triggers, on the upper left and right sides of the crib, that have to be tugged simultaneously to release the locks. The triggers require a lot of pressure, and are purposely spaced far enough apart so that only an adult can make them work. The advantage of trigger systems over metal rods is that they operate silently and are less likely to jam—but they're a tough pull, and you have to use two hands. Rarely, the springs operating the pins may jam. These models are easier to assemble than those using metal-rod systems.

Knee release. The most recent development in side-release systems involves two easy steps—raise the side slightly, then press lightly into the lower part of the bars with one knee. There are two types of knee-release mechanisms: those that are mounted on the surface of the crib, and those that are hidden from view, sometimes called "Euro-style" releases. Either one allows you to lower the sides effortlessly and silently with only one hand. And again, cribs with knee-release systems are simpler to assemble than cribs with metal rods.

But use caution. Knee-release mechanisms are still being perfected, and some versions are prone to failure. Poorly constructed plastic components can warp and bend. The sides of some expensive European-style cribs found in baby specialty stores can drop without the bottom rail being pressed in, falling when only moderate pressure is placed on the middle of the rail. Thus, a toddler may accidentally lower the rail from the inside and fall out. And the endboards of some cribs have recessed tracks that could endanger small fingers when the side is raised. Before you buy a crib with a knee-release system, test lowering the sides repeatedly to make certain that hardware is sturdy and fail-safe, and that there are no capture holes.

SHOPPING SAVVY Cribs

The baby product manufacturing season revolves around the Juvenile Products Show held sometime in September or October in Dallas, Texas. Thus, retailers will often put their floor models on sale during late August through early November to get rid of old designs and clear space for new ones. Floor models may have nicks and scrapes but still be in usable condition. To make certain that the model hasn't undergone a safety warning or recall, contact the CPSC. (See the Resource Guide for contact information and Product Recalls for recent recalls.)

Inspect a floor sample carefully to make certain all parts are in working order. Dropsides should slide up and down easily, and all the hardware should be there, including everything needed for the mattress support. Screws should be tight and still flush against the endboards, with no loosening from wear. The manufacturer's instructions must be included with the crib, or you risk reassembling the crib incorrectly at home, causing serious safety dangers.

Don't buy a used crib. Avoid buying a secondhand crib. First, stringent federal monitoring and frequent recalls combine to produce cribs that are safer than those sold only a few years earlier. Certainly, new designs may still have flaws, but over the long haul, construction techniques and

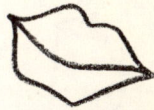

Needy

Kiss the child's palm and close fingers into a fist, explaining that if there's a need for a kiss, there's one in there, ready and waiting.

safety measures continue to improve year after year.

Second, you may not be able to spot the flaws in a used crib. Dropsides, bars, and hardware are a crib's most vulnerable parts. Siblings tend to perch or jump on crib rails. Some toddlers rattle cribs like a freight train, weakening components and hardware. If a mechanical rocking device has been fastened onto the side of a crib to vibrate it, the joints could have loosened. Every time a crib is disassembled, the screws become looser.

Wood shrinks and expands with humidity and heat, weakening the glue that holds bars and rails together. And storing a crib in an attic, basement, or garage under extreme temperatures or humidity accelerates the process. More rarely, a crib may have been refinished with lead-based paint, which could poison a child who gnaws on endboards or peels chips off the rails. Buying a new model reassures you that you're getting a sturdy crib, not one that's weakened or damaged.

Bypass baby furniture suites. In most stores where cribs are sold, you'll also find chests, armoires, and dressing tables designed to coordinate in style with certain crib models. When priced together, a matching furniture set can cost anywhere from $1,000 to over $7,000.

If saving money is a priority, a matching furniture ensemble could be classified as a luxury. From a practical standpoint, your baby honestly won't notice where you put him down to sleep. A baby's central program is to be in your arms—carried around if possible—and fed as soon as hunger pangs strike. That's it.

Pieces made expressly for use in a nursery do have a few positive qualities to recommend them. Usually, drawers have stops in the back to keep them from being pulled all the way out and dumped—something tots like to do. Some pieces will have rounded edges and recessed drawer pulls so baby won't be hurt as badly if he falls into them. However, a roller-track system that glides drawers open and closed may be great for you but potentially bad for baby fingers.

In nearly every case, nursery furniture designed to match cribs is overpriced for the quality offered. Looking closely, you'll find that every chest in one manufacturer's line will be virtually the same basic unit, except each one will have a wood overlay finished to match a specific crib. Drawer fronts will be glued on. The back of what looks like a well-made piece may only be cardboard attached with staples.

So consider some other options. Postpone big-time furniture buying for a

Hush!

Apply petroleum jelly or spray nonstick vegetable oil to the side rails of the crib to keep them from squeaking when they're raised or lowered. Or rub them with waxed paper.

few years. By then your child will be old enough to help you pick out sturdy items designed to last through high school. Most likely you'll select twin beds, a chest, a desk, and a bedside table.

In the meantime, if you need a place to store baby's stuff, try shopping in regular furniture stores, especially during seasonal sales. Or you may be able to uncover a real bargain in a thrift or antiques store—a top-quality, recycled piece of furniture sold for hundreds of dollars less than poorly constructed nursery furniture. For safety's sake, you can always install drawer stops yourself and change the drawer pulls if they have sharp edges or stick out too far. And always bolt all nursery units to the wall with angle braces or L brackets. Unbolted furniture can topple over if your baby (like most) climbs on drawers or shelves.

Skip convertible cribs. A convertible model will morph into a loveseat, swing, toddler bed, or double bed when no longer used as a crib. Some models also have a tall, narrow chest fastened on one end that can stand alone later.

Convertibles aren't as practical as they first appear—unless you won't need the crib for another baby; your child's room will accommodate a loveseat along with other furniture; or you can easily fit a double bed into your child's room. And like a nursery suite, a convertible commits you to a particular furniture style you may not want forever.

In addition, baby cribs and mattresses are too deep and firm to make comfortable loveseats, even with lots of comfy pillows. And there are bound to be exposed screw holes where the crib's sides used to fasten.

Cribs with attached chests can be dangerous. Instead of dropsides, most have gated siderails with crossbars halfway up the side. Babies routinely use these bars to get a foothold for climbing out—sometimes falling over the side in the process. Toddlers have also been injured when they climbed up onto the attached chest only to plummet to the floor from a much higher place than if they had simply fallen from the crib.

Ask for store assembly. Once you've chosen a crib, you must get it home and set it up. Most stores sell cribs sealed in the carton. For maximum safety, it's important to carefully follow the instructions enclosed inside the carton.

Although screws and hardware are provided, you will probably need a Phillips screwdriver and a wrench. Expect the task to take two people and at least an hour.

Assembling a crib that uses metal rods for the dropside mechanism is the most challenging of all. Depending on the manufacturer's words, you'll be dealing with "bumper springs," "conical springs," "post brackets," "gate shoes," "dropside rods," and a "toe-trip release." Then once you've assembled the crib, it may not fit through the nursery doorway.

Rather than coping with the hassle, see if the store offers free assembly or if they will assemble the crib for an additional fee. Besides saving tempers and fingers, store-assembly allows you to inspect the finished crib on the spot—and to reject it if you find hardware problems or flaws in the crib's finishing and frame.

SHOPPING SAVVY Mattresses

Although cribs are displayed with mattresses inside, the mattress is actually a separate purchase. And it's also a "blind buy." That means that although two mattresses may feel identical in firmness and appear the same on the outside, there can be real differences in internal quality that affect how well a mattress will hold up over time. (By "over time," we mean two years for each baby. The total amount of use ultimately depends on the number of children you plan to have.)

A number of companies—some reputable, some not—make mattresses. The most well-known and reliable mattress manufacturers include Century/Gerber, Child Craft, Colgate, Cosco, Evenflo, Kolcraft, Sealy, and Simmons.

Mattress prices range from $30 for a bottom-line foam model to several hundred dollars for an innerspring with hundreds of coils, heavy internal hardware, and padding. Baby stores make a big profit on their mattresses, so sales assistants are anxious to sell you the most expensive mattress in the store to accompany your new crib.

Once in a while, stores will throw in a promotional mattress as a "giveaway." But this offer simply may be an inducement to get you to trade up to a more expensive crib, so weigh the total cost to see if you're getting a good deal or not. And do evaluate baby's mattress for adequate firmness (so your baby is protected from suffocation), covering thickness, and quality materials.

At the bottom end of the mattress chain are flimsy foam models with thin vinyl covering and vinyl edging. Next come firmer foam mattresses with thicker vinyl coverings, small metal air vents added on the side, and fabric edging. With each step up, the foam gets more dense, the covering thicker, and the product claims more alluring. (Foam density translates into weight, so the denser the foam, the heavier the mattress.) At the top end of the foam lines are mattresses so firm that they feel like bricks, accompanied by claims that the mattress is triple-laminated and has antibacterial qualities.

Innerspring mattress prices start at the middle of the foam range and quickly rise. The least expensive, like foam mattresses, have thin vinyl coverings and edgings and mushy surfaces. As prices go up, more springs ("coils") are added, starting at around 80 coils and going up to 500 or more.

Springs may be "covered" or "independent" (so they operate separately). Then manufacturers add internal hardware, such as edge rods to support the outer rim of the mattress. Coverings are now thick, puncture-resistant triple-laminates and germ-killing hospital-grade surfaces.

Be skeptical of claims. Don't be seduced by scientific-looking mattress displays with cutout cross-sections that allow you to peer inside. Basically, all you'll see is a mass of shining springs and the multiple layers of padding and other structural features.

Warranties aren't all that significant, either. It does seem that a mattress with a lifetime warranty is somehow superior to those with only five- or 10-year warranties, or none at all. But if you read the fine print, you'll see that the warranties cover only such things as stitching, not, say, a toddler's jumping damage. If you challenge the manufacturer on a true defect in materials and workmanship, you're likely to be referred back to the store. So a store's return policy is more important than a mattress-maker's promises.

The mattress may have a label claiming it's "nonallergenic" (translation: made completely of man-made materials). Or the claim may be that surfaces (ticking) are "stain resistant," "nonabsorbent," or have "antistatic features"—none of which is remarkable because all crib mattresses are moisture resistant, and static is not an issue.

Sometimes mattress labels appear to be purposefully ambiguous. A manufacturer will state that a mattress cover is "three-layer reinforced nylon," which sounds a lot like a triple-laminate cover, but it's not.

Antibacterial claims, as appealing as they sound, simply mean that a few drops of a chemical were added to the vat when the vinyl was in a liquid form. But, in fact, no chemical can prevent the active reproduction of bacteria on a damp mattress surface.

Putting a waterproof-pad cover over the mattress is a better solution for keeping bacteria down. You may also clean the mattress every now and again by wiping it with a damp cloth or sponge and a mild cleaner, such as

Sleep tight

Give night feedings in dim light so the baby will realize that they're different from daytime feedings. And put your baby in the crib only at night; naps during the day can be in a carriage or playpen.

heavily diluted dishwashing detergent or diluted hand soap solution. Just wipe up all the soap residue with clear water, then dry the surface with a towel or paper towels.

Foam vs. innersprings. Foam mattresses have practical qualities to recommend them. Dense foam is very firm and lightweight, which makes changing baby's sheets much easier. Foam is also less springy and therefore less apt to encourage your tot to jump. Some parents worry about foam "outgassing"—giving off toxic fumes—but Sudden Infant Death Syndrome studies have shown that the problem is minimal.

Foam mattresses are available in different firmness levels, depending on density. Labels don't indicate firmness, but you can judge foam density by the comparative weights of different foam models and by giving the mattress a squeeze test—press your palms into both sides at once.

A high-density foam mattress should keep its shape as well as an innerspring mattress, although cheaper, low-density foam may soften with use. A high-density foam model typically weighs seven or eight pounds, making it easier to handle than an innerspring weighing a hefty 20 to 25 pounds.

Innerspring mattresses are not only much heavier than foam but less pliable, which can make sheet-changing more difficult. Coil count and firmness don't always match up—a model with 150 coils can be firmer than another with 600 coils. Put the sample mattress on the floor and lie on it.

Innerspring quality doesn't just mean the number of coils but also the thickness of the steel, the number of layers of padding and their quality, and whether border rods have been added at the top and bottom of the mattress to give extra edge support. Generally, the thicker the rod, the better the edge will hold its shape.

Mattress measurements. Most mattresses are six inches thick. If you opt for a four- or five-inch-thick mattress, the sheets you buy may not fit tautly, which can create a suffocation or entrapment hazard.

If you're using an older crib, measure it carefully before you shop for a mattress. The mattress should fit snugly in the crib. If you can fit two fingers between the mattress and any side of the crib, the mattress is too small for the crib, and a child's body or head can get trapped in the gap between mattress and crib, a potentially fatal danger.

California law requires that baby mattresses be fireproof, so most major manufacturers will meet that requirement—but check the label.

Judging quality. Because a soft mattress is a suffocation hazard, select the firmest mattress you can find, foam or innerspring. Look for double- or triple-laminated ticking, fabric binding along the seams, and plenty of vent holes.

Look closely at the binding. Quality mattresses will use cloth binding rather than vinyl, and the stitching will be even, with no loose threads. Pinch the ticking to see how thick it is, and use the pinch test to compare one mattress to another. Vents on the side or end of the mattress (small, metal-lined holes or a pocket at each end) help the mattress "breathe," which may keep seams from splitting when a tot starts jumping. (A jumping, active child is the ultimate consumer mattress test—and the results won't be in for a year and a half or more.)

Keep puffy and "non-breathing" materials away from baby's face. Quilts,

Baby Safe
SUDDEN INFANT DEATH SYNDROME

A seemingly healthy baby is put to bed but is later found dead. In the United States, Sudden Infant Death Syndrome (SIDS), sometimes called crib death, strikes nearly 5,000 babies every year. Typically, SIDS happens to babies under six months of age, peaking at 2½ months. Boys are slightly more prone to SIDS, and deaths are two-thirds more likely during winter months. The true cause of SIDS is not completely understood, but recent research suggests that some SIDS babies may have had unusual heart rhythms or signaling abnormalities in their brains. But other factors probably play a part in SIDS deaths.

Stomach sleeping doubles the likelihood of SIDS—back sleeping is much safer. Fortunately, by the time your baby is able to turn from his back to his belly, the risk of SIDS has largely passed. Bedding that can bunch up around a baby's face and head could be fatal: The list includes overly soft mattresses in bassinets and other baby beds, crib quilts and comforters, lambskins, pillows, soft toys, futons, waterbeds, beanbag chairs, and sofa cushions.

Overheating may also be a contributor. Keep the temperature in baby's room between 68 and 70 degrees F. Use layers under a blanket sleeper on cold nights instead of puffy blankets on top, and put baby in lightweight pajamas during warm weather.

Ban smoking around your baby. Exposure to cigarette smoke doubles the risk of dying from SIDS. Adult bedding and bed-sharing when parents use alcohol or sedating drugs can also be dangerous.

Breastfeeding appears to offer a baby some protection from SIDS.

pillows, lambskins, or any other loose, bulky items all can cause a baby to suffocate or become entrapped. Plastic can also cause suffocation.

CRIB ALTERNATIVES

If you choose any of these alternatives to a standard crib, be aware of the hazards—and take precautions.

Bringing baby into your bed

Some parents choose to let baby share their bed. But doing so has some dangers. Babies fall overboard. Or, they get their heads captured between the mattress and either headboards or side tables. Sometimes babies suffocate on pillows and soft bedding—particularly waterbed mattresses. And rarely, babies die when parents roll over on them in the night.

If you bring baby into bed with you occasionally, keep soft covers and pillows away from baby's face, and keep baby on his back. Never sleep with a baby if you've been drinking or are on medication that affects your awareness of your child.

Portable and bedside sleepers

Portable cribs. Sometimes called "grandma cribs," these are small, rectangular wooden or metal baby beds that mimic full-sized cribs but are compact enough to roll through doorways. Some portable cribs have legs that lower, so the bed portion sits close to the floor, similar to a playpen.

Portable cribs are somewhat safer than unstable bassinets (discussed on page 55) and fold compactly for traveling. Some models, however, may have a hinged side that folds down from the center of the bars, instead of a dropside. A toddler can climb up on the crossrails of this hinged construction and fall from the crib.

Bedside sleepers. So small they could be called "cribettes," the sleepers are designed for newborns and nursing infants. They allow baby to sleep in his own protected, small area adjoining your bed. The sleeper fits flush against the side of your bed, at the same height as your mattress, with an open side next to your bed allowing easy access to baby. The other three sides of the sleeper are enclosed by bars or a high, padded rim. The bridge between your mattress and the sleeper is usually a length of fabric that you secure between your mattress and springs.

However, sleepers pose a specific danger: If a sleeper isn't completely joined with your bed, or isn't the identical height of your bed, a gap or ridge could be formed that might capture your baby's head or neck.

Your baby will outgrow a bedside sleeper in about two months and a portable crib as soon as she is able to pull up on all fours—usually between five and six months.

What's available

Delta's Luv Cradle "N" Table (Model 5100, $100, birth to 18 months) is a small wooden bassinet for newborns that converts into a changing table with side bars, a safety belt, and three shelves.

Cosco's Portable Crib (Model 10-T58, $80, for babies up to 35 inches or 50 pounds) is made with a one-inch tubular steel frame. It has a two-position wooden mattress platform and casters, and folds to less than eight inches thick for storage.

Arm's Reach Concepts' Bedside Co-Sleeper ($160 to $200, from newborn to 35 inches tall or less than 30 pounds) is a low, portable play yard with one side that lowers to allow access to your baby from your bed. A strap attaches the sleeper to the side of the adult bed. As with other bedside sleepers, it must fit with the adult bed and leave no gaps.

Bassinets and cradles

Like portable cribs and sleepers, cradles and bassinets are small sleeping beds that offer a nest for a newborn near a parent's bed. They present an alternative to putting your newborn into a large crib but are meant to be used only in the first few months of a baby's life. You'll have your baby close by for multiple nighttime feedings and diaper changes. And small babies also seem more at home in a confined space than in a large, airy crib. But once your baby begins to thrash around and seems uncomfortable (or when he nears the upper weight limit recommended by the manufacturer), then it's time to move him to a crib.

Bassinets. These small, wheeled baby beds are made of wicker or woven wooden splints. Most come with a rigid hood attached on one end. They take up little space and can be rolled easily from one room to another. But they have several disadvantages: The large hood may get in the way when you pick up or lay down your baby. Some models have relatively rough, sharp edges on the inside that could cut an infant. Models with soft sides may present entrapment hazards. And they don't offer the stability of portable cribs.

Lullaby

Tape-record the sound of a running dishwasher, a running shower, or water filling the tub, and play it back to lull a child to sleep.

The most troublesome defect is the soft, thin mattress. Since January 1994, over 30 babies have died in this country while lying facedown in bassinets. The cause of these deaths is not clear, but one possibility is that the mushy mattresses covered the babies' faces, causing asphyxiation.

Some bassinets, designed to fold, have hinges on their legs that lock into an open position. Sometimes hinges have accidentally folded, collapsing the bassinet to the floor and entrapping babies in a position that caused them to suffocate. Other babies have suffocated when their heads became trapped between the soft mattress and the hard sides of the bassinet, even when the bassinet was in an upright position. Nonfatal bassinet accidents usually happen when siblings try to lift babies from bassinets and accidentally drop them or cause the bassinet to topple over.

If there are older siblings in the house, you may want to consider a safer bed for your baby, such as a crib. Should you decide to purchase a bassinet, we recommend that you always place baby faceup for sleeping (unless your baby has a medical condition requiring facedown sleeping). Never add more mattress padding, cover the mattress with a plastic bag, or use pillows of any size. Do not even buy a bassinet unless the mattress pad is extra firm and fits snugly against all sides.

Cradles. Although they have a romantic, old-fashioned look about them, we suggest that you resist buying a cradle. Their side-to-side motion

Baby Safe

TAKE CARE WITH BASSINETS AND CRADLES

The most frequent injuries involve children falling either when the bottom of the bassinet or cradle breaks, or when the whole thing tips over or collapses. Suffocation has also been reported in products not structurally sound, or when pillows or folded quilts were placed under the baby.

• Look for a bassinet or cradle with a sturdy bottom and a wide, stable base. Follow the manufacturer's guidelines on the appropriate weight and size of babies who can safely use the bed.

• Check to make sure that spaces between cradle bars are no wider than the crib standard of 2⅜ inches.

• If legs fold for storage, make sure that effective locks are provided to ensure that legs do not accidentally fold while in use.

• Mattresses and padding should be firm and smooth and fit snugly. Never use pillows.

can roll a tiny baby until the child is helplessly pressed against the side (even the baby's weight can cause the cradle to shift to one side). Cradle frames suspended on hooks have a gentler motion—but still roll from side to side.

Babies do love rhythmic motion, but experts advise that the most effective rocking direction is a head-to-toe motion, similar to what they experience when held on a parent's shoulder in a rocking chair.

In addition, cradles may not be as safe for babies as they appear. When rocking pushes babies into the side bars, some get their arms trapped between the bars and can't breathe. Babies should never be left unattended in freely rocking cradles, and locking pins should be bolted into place so cradles cannot tilt to an angle greater than five degrees.

BEDDING NEEDS

Once you have the crib, you'll need more equipment to turn it into a safe, comfortable bed.

Crib bumpers protect arms and legs. Bumpers are pads that tie onto crib rails around all sides to keep baby's arms and legs safely inside. If you buy them, make sure they fit around the entire crib, tie or snap into place, and have straps or ties for at least six locations on the top edge and an equal number at the bottom edge.

To prevent your baby from chewing on the straps or becoming entangled in them, trim ties or straps as short as possible, not to exceed seven inches per individual tie or strap. Use bumpers only until baby can pull up to a standing position. Once on her feet, baby might use bumpers to climb out of the crib.

As of this writing, no safety standard for this product is yet in effect. But voluntary industry efforts are under way to set standards, such as length of tie tapes and type of stitching.

Mattress pads absorb moisture. Quilted pads, usually made out of cotton or synthetic fiber, cover the mattress securely and help to keep urine and spit-ups away from the mattress ticking. You'll want several.

Some moisture-proof pads are latex backed, others have a center of vinyl with flocked facing. They protect crib sheets—and may be put underneath baby when you're changing him. You'll find a variety of sizes, from one large sheet you can cut up to suit your needs to smaller versions that are handy for newborns. Buy four or five.

Sheets should fit snugly. Most crib sheets come with fitted corners or are elasticized all the way around—a plus, since babies can get wrapped up and entrapped when sheets don't stay firmly wrapped around the mattress. Sheets come in woven cottons and cotton blends, in plain colors or brighter patterns. Knitted sheets, although they cost a little more, fit the mattress better and don't show wrinkles as much. You may also like the flannel sheets sold by mail-order companies such as Lands' End (toddler-bed and crib-bed sheets are the same size).

Look for softness and thickness. You shouldn't be able to see your fingers through the weave. The elastic should be dense and form a tight curvature to ensure that the sheets won't work loose of the mattress with baby's motions. Avoid sheets with a strong chemical scent from fabric-treatment processes. Plan to launder the sheets twice to get out all sizing and chemical residues before your baby sleeps on them. Your baby won't spend much time in bed when she's awake, so don't feel compelled to purchase costly designer sheets or patterns.

Blankets are secondary to layering. It's better to dress baby warmly in layers than to try to cover him up with heavy blankets. A lightweight blanket will be all you need.

Receiving blankets come in handy for layering on baby and also for sopping up spit-ups, protecting baby's car seat from heat in the summer, or covering both baby and seat when it's cold or drafty. Get a half-dozen large blankets in 100 percent cotton.

Baby proppers pose dangers. The latest information on the relationship between baby positioning and SIDS has led to a multitude of new products designed to prop babies on their sides or backs. Proppers—also called wedges—are usually firm bolsters, some made in a triangular shape. But these proppers can be just as dangerous as pillows (if not more so) should a baby's neck become captured over the edge of the propper, blocking airways. Simply laying your baby on his back should be sufficient.

Bed warmers can harm baby's skin. A baby's skin is extremely sensitive to heat, and your child can be burned by temperatures that would seem comfortable to an adult. Don't be tempted to use an electric blanket, a heating pad, or a warm water bottle to heat your baby's crib.

Chapter  3

TRAVELING IN THE CAR

A car seat can save your baby's life. But the model you choose must fit your car correctly and be securely installed.

The toll from car crashes is heavy on babies and children. Crashes are estimated to kill some 600 U.S. youngsters under age five every year. Another 60,000 to 70,000 are seriously injured. Most accidents happen within 25 miles of home at speeds of less than 40 mph.

A study by the National Highway Traffic Safety Administration (NHTSA), the federal agency that oversees car seat regulations, found that in 1997, 54 percent of kids under age five killed in crashes hadn't been fastened into car seats or safety belts—despite laws in every state requiring babies and young children to be properly secured in child car seats when riding in a vehicle. And many children ride in car seats that are installed incorrectly.

Some parents mistakenly believe they can hold a baby in their arms during a car crash. But the forces of a crash are dramatic: In a 30-mph crash, a 15-pound baby is hurled through space with a force of almost 300 pounds, striking solid objects or other passengers in the process. If the parent holding the baby is sitting in the front seat and wearing a seat belt, the baby will be pounded into the dashboard by the force of the adult's body. Furthermore, a deploying air bag could prove fatal to the baby.

Car seats—also called child safety seats or car restraints—are hard, molded seats designed to protect babies and young children during crashes. The

Contents

Car-seat options, page 60

Shopping savvy, page 61

Buying plan, page 66

Seat installation, page 67

Air bags, page 70

Car seats on planes, page 71

Traveling in the Car ■ **59**

seat shell is covered with quilted fabric or thick upholstery, usually removable for washing. Adjustable straps, called a harness, secure the baby in the seat. An adult seat belt threads through slots in the seat's shell and is tightly buckled so the restraint is firmly lashed down. (Don't confuse car seats with lightweight seats for in-house use with baby—see pages 121 to 124.)

Car seats must be installed in the back seat to surround a child with a buffer zone of protective space and to distance them from the front seat's hostile dashboard, windshield, and air bags. Babies weighing less than 20 pounds need to ride in a rear-facing position so the safety seat's shell will better support their heads and spines. Since a baby's head is much heavier than the rest of its body, babies are vulnerable to whiplash.

Starting with your baby's first ride home from the hospital, don't put your key into the ignition until you're certain your baby is buckled correctly into a rear-facing safety seat, properly secured to the automobile's back seat.

CAR-SEAT OPTIONS

Car seats are grouped by the child's age and weight and the direction the seat faces inside the car—rearward for babies, forward for toddlers. You'll find infant seats, convertible seats which can convert from rear-facing to front-facing, and booster seats designed for older children. (See "Seat choices" on page 63.)

Seats can also be described by how they secure a child. "Five-point" harness systems have five straps: two for the shoulders, two for the waist, and one between baby's legs (crotch strap). Smaller infant seats have "three-point" harnesses—two shoulder straps and one crotch strap. Most seats have simple straps, and a few also have a front shield.

Booster seats (not to be confused with high chair substitutes, page 65) are designed to raise preschoolers so they can see out. They also guide adult belts comfortably across a child's body. Some have removable five-point harnesses for lighter-weight riders.

Chrysler, Ford, GM, Toyota, and Volvo offer a built-in child car seat as an option in some vehicles. Usually, these are toddler seat/boosters for children older than one year and weighing more than 20 pounds. The seat is tailor-made for the car, and no installation is needed—but you must make sure that it's comfortable for your child. CONSUMER REPORTS has not crash-tested these seats, but because they're tightly secured and the child sits farther back than in a separate car seat, we believe they'd perform very well.

SHOPPING SAVVY Car seats

More than three million children's car seats are sold or given out by hospital loaner and commercial discount programs each year, and car seat sales are between $250 and $300 million annually. But in order to protect your child, the seat must meet certain criteria.

Check the basic requirements. You want the right seat for your baby's weight—and for your car's back seat. If a safety seat is too large for your car, it won't fit properly, which could compromise your baby's safety. The harness must contact the baby's whole body well. And it has to be fed into the correct shoulder slots for your baby's height. The harness should adjust easily to accommodate your baby as she grows.

When correctly installed, a rear-facing seat should not tip more than a 45-degree angle and should be so firmly belted down that it barely moves.

Cost doesn't guarantee quality. A more expensive seat won't necessarily protect your baby better. All seats have to pass rigid, federally monitored crash tests and specifications.

That said, there are differences in the crash performance of various mod-

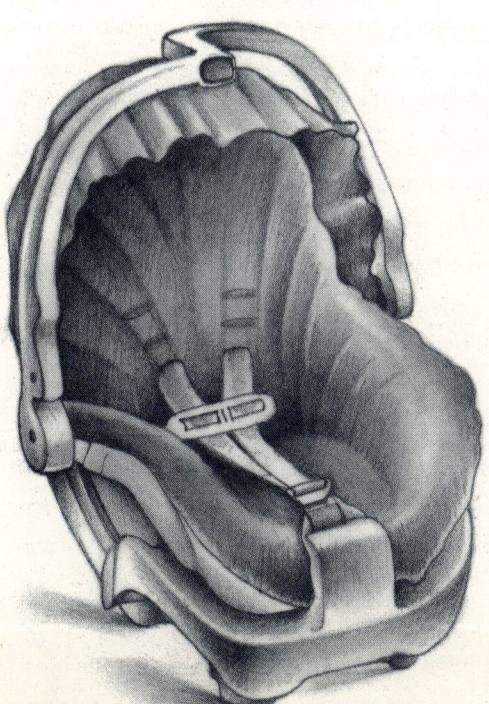

Infant seat

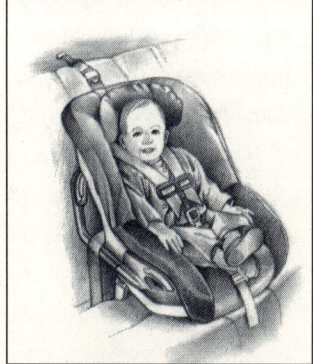

Convertible seat

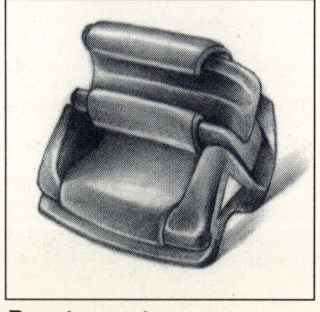

Booster seat

The three basic seat choices, according to the size of your child. **Infant seats** face rear and are often part of a car seat-stroller system. **Convertible seats** switch from rear-facing for infants to forward-facing for toddlers. They often have a tether strap for additional stability and safety. **Booster seats** are for kids who've outgrown car seats but are not yet big enough for adult safety belts.

Traveling in the Car ■ **61**

els, and noticeable variations in shell thickness and rigidity between some low-priced convertibles and those in mid- and high-price ranges. (For a more detailed discussion of federal standards, see page 72.) But usually when you examine differently priced models from the same manufacturer, you'll find nearly identical shell construction.

A seat to fit your needs. Before shopping, establish the kind of model that will work best for you.

If you will be shifting baby from one car to another, consider a lighter weight, rear-facing infant seat with an attaching base, plus another base for your second car.

Should you want to use a tether once your toddler can face forward, look for a convertible seat rather than an infant seat or seat/stroller combination.

A car seat/stroller combination might be handy if baby will go wherever you do. But if your car's trunk is small, you may want to purchase the seat and stroller separately. Strollers that can accommodate a car seat are fairly large. Since everything not tied down should go in the trunk when baby's on board, you'll want enough trunk room left over for groceries and parcels.

Will you be having a heavy or tall baby? It's hard to tell in advance, but if you know your baby is going to be a boy, and you and your partner are both tall, chances are your baby will outgrow an infant-only seat months before his body is mature enough to sit facing forward. A rear-facing convertible seat with a heavier weight limit in the infant position might be a good solution.

If you have a small or low-birthweight baby, your hospital or your baby's pediatrician may recommend a special car seat, such as one without a shield (shields fit small babies poorly), or a car-bed that lets a baby completely recline. Before leaving the hospital, your baby may be observed in a car seat to see if the semireclined position adds to or causes possible breathing problems.

Children with special health problems or medical conditions may need other restraint systems. Talk to your pediatrician, or contact the toll-free number for the National Easter Seal Society (see the Resource Guide) and ask about the KARS (Kids Are Riding Safe) programs.

Beware of used seats. While it's great to buy baby clothes, soft carriers, and sturdy toys at yard sales and thrift or consignment stores, buying a used car seat isn't a good idea. Stringent federal monitoring and the fierce competition between manufacturers have improved car seats every year. Plus, unless you know the history of the seat, you won't know if it's been in a crash or not. Although there may be visible changes in the seat's color where the shell has been stressed or marks on the belts that resemble melting, caused by severe stretching, most fractures and frame stress points won't be visible.

Critical instructions from the seat's manufacturer may be lost. The seat won't be registered in your name, so you won't be in the loop for future recalls. And, unless you've consulted NHTSA's web site to print out an up-to-date car seat recall list (see page 288), you won't know if you're taking home a safe seat or a dangerous lemon.

Buy a new safety seat from a trustworthy store with a generous return policy that allows recourse for installation or performance problems.

Seat choices

Infant seats. These are created to hold babies, from newborns to those between 9 and 12 months, in a semireclined position, facing the rear of the car (toward the trunk). They are secured by the car's adult safety belts, which thread through special slots in the safety seat, and are safest when anchored in the center of the car's back seat. The car seat's handle rotates from an upright position like a basket handle for carrying to laying behind the seat for transport.

Slots in the seat's base are designed to attach to the frame of a shopping cart. Some mid- and high-priced models offer a base attachment (like a docking station), so the seat may be detached while the secured base stays behind. Stroller/infant seat combinations are available (see our Ratings, page 86), as are car seat/bed combinations that ride lengthwise on the car's seat and fold into an upright position.

Infant seats are lighter and less expensive than larger models (they range from $30 to $70), and appear to fit a baby's shape better. A bed model is useful for infants with medical conditions that create breathing problems when the baby is in a sharply reclined seat.

Most infant-only seats have no waist belts. The seat with baby inside is heavy and cumbersome to carry. Baby may exceed the seat's size and weight limits before his neck and back are strong enough to allow him to face forward and then require a convertible seat. Although infant seats may be advertised for home use as rockers and seats, their weight can pose a crushing or suffocation danger if the seat falls. So never place one, with baby inside, on a raised surface, even for a moment.

Thirsty

Use the lightweight plastic bottles that bicyclers use as spill-proof containers for kids.

Convertible seats. These heavier, convertible seats are usually more expensive—$50 to $210. They have a reclining mechanism so they can ride facing rearward for a baby, or forward for a toddler or young child. Weight specifications vary by model. Weight limits for rear-facing models range from 5 to 10 pounds for newborns, with top limits of 20, 22, or 30 pounds; and forward-facing, up to 40 pounds.

Some models have five-point harness systems. Others have U-shaped and T-shaped shields that lower over the baby's head and fasten with a buckle between the legs, or T-shaped shields that resemble upside-down bicycle seats, with the buckling assembly embedded in the narrow end.

Most now also offer a tethering option (see page 65).

When reclined, however, they take up a lot of room in cars with small

Baby Safe
CAR SEAT PRECAUTIONS

• Adjust the harness. When your baby or toddler is in the safety seat, all harness straps should fit snugly across the "strong" parts of the body—shoulders and thighs—not the soft belly. And the harness should lie flat when buckled. The plastic or metal clips that may hold shoulder straps together should be level with your baby's armpits.

• Avoid padding. Do not add padding or blankets under the straps, and watch out for bulky clothing, too. All could interfere with the fit of safety-seat straps. If your baby slides down in the seat, you can wedge a rolled cloth diaper between the crotch and the seat buckle.

• Stash all hard objects. Any loose items in the back seat, such as toys, trays, or packages, will become projectiles during a crash. Stow groceries and parcels in the trunk, and use only small, soft toys as playthings.

• Check the seat every time. Each time you buckle your child in, check the following: Harness straps fit snugly, allowing maximum two fingers' room between the straps and your child's chest. Shoulder straps are fastened into rear slots of the seat no more than one-half inch below the baby's shoulders. Adult belts are tightly and correctly installed through safety-seat channels.

• Using a car seat as a baby seat in the house can be dangerous. A car seat's weight makes it vulnerable to falling off high surfaces and to tipping over if baby squirms or someone (including a pet) bumps the seat. Babies have been injured as they plunge to the floor with the seat or are trapped underneath a seat that tips. If you leave baby in the car seat for a few minutes, be vigilant.

back seats. Some models, particularly those with front shields, don't fit babies up to two months old very well—seat angles can be too flat, harness slots too high, and the distance between the crotch and seat back too wide.

Boosters. Booster seats and high-back boosters are designed for kids who've outgrown convertible seats but are still too small for adult safety-belt systems. More conventional boosters have a rigid base and/or shield that positions adult belts across the thighs and away from the child's neck. High-back boosters resemble convertible seats but are taller. Some only serve as vehicle belt positioners, others have a five-point-harness system that can be removed when a child exceeds 40 pounds.

Boosters raise a child so she can see out and offer better protection than no belts or poorly positioned adult belts. But they won't work if the center of the back seat lacks both adult waist and shoulder belts, and some are difficult to install and adjust. Seats with a high back may block a driver's rear view in smaller cars, and some are difficult to install and adjust. They are not approved for use on airlines. Prices range from $25 to $150.

Tethering for safety

Tethering a convertible seat designed for children heavy enough to ride in the forward-facing position adds an extra margin of safety. A tether is an adjustable strap: One end loops over a metal clip or bar installed on the back side of the car seat; the other hooks to an anchor screwed into the metal frame of the rear window shelf.

Even in a properly fastened safety seat, a child may be injured in a head-on crash if the car seat vaults forward, causing his head to collide with the back of the front seat. Crash tests commissioned by CONSUMER REPORTS showed that tethers improved the protective ability of seats, turning otherwise fair seats into excellent performers. Tethered seats reduced forward head movement of crash-test dummies by about one-fourth, or eight inches. (See the special car seat report, page 75.)

Increasingly, forward-facing safety seats for children weighing 20 to 40 pounds include a tether as standard equipment. Even models lacking a tether have built-in insets or holes cut for tethering hardware. Some car seat manufacturers, including Evenflo and Century, recommend that a tether be installed to stabilize newer convertibles when standard installation doesn't work well. (A well-installed seat can't be pushed more than one inch front to back, or one to two inches side to side.)

Diversion

Before embarking on a long car trip, wrap a variety of small personalized gifts for your child. Have him or her open the gifts at predetermined times.

If you decide you want to add tethering to your child's front-facing seat, first check with the car seat manufacturer to make sure your model can be tethered. (Their numbers are listed in the Resource Guide.) Tethering kits—strap, hardware, and directions—are available from baby stores or directly from your car seat's manufacturer for about $15. However, assemblies aren't interchangeable, so you must get the right brand to start with.

Ask your car seat manufacturer who is authorized to install the tethering anchor. The corner mechanic may not be up to the job. Most recent domestic car models have the anchor hole predrilled to conform to Canadian car seat standards, but screw sizes aren't uniform among car models. Vehicle manufacturers usually offer the tethering bolt and anchor installation for free or at a small price. If you run into blank stares, tell the dealer you want your car equipped with a "Canadian tether." If you're still having problems, check your car's owner's manual for the original service number.

Seats for special-needs babies

Your hospital or baby's pediatrician may recommend a special car seat for small or low-birthweight babies, such as one without a shield (shields fit smaller babies poorly), or a car bed, which lets a baby completely recline. Before leaving the hospital, your baby may be observed in a car seat to see if the semireclined position adds to or causes possible breathing problems.

Children with special health problems or medical conditions may need alternative restraint systems. Talk to your pediatrician. (See the Resource Guide for further information.)

CAR SEAT BUYING PLAN

Check your car owner's manual. Car makers often include extensive information on what fits in their vehicles.

Contact your auto maker. Ask if the auto maker offers a free how-to brochure or video. (Either may take weeks to get, so request them early.) And, if you want a tether, find out how to get it installed.

Check out the back safety belts. You may have to pull the whole seat bottom forward to retrieve buried belts and then test buckles to see that they really work. Check if side and middle belts are the same. Are waist and shoulder belts all one piece or two separate units? Do you have a center arm rest? It's dangerous in a crash and blocks seat installation.

Shop sooner, not later. You need time to find the model that delivers the rock-solid installation critical for safety. Give yourself lead time, too, in case you decide to buy a different car, or need to adapt the seats you've got, either by installing a different set of safety belts or adding a metal clip to make adult belts cinch tightly.

Use the car seat store's resources. Stop at the customer service desk to quiz the manager. Is a particular salesperson knowledgeable about safety seats and how to install them? What's the store's return policy for safety seats? Can you arrange to take seats out to the parking lot to try them in your car before deciding? Are there extra copies of the instruction booklets for the seats if there's none on the display sample?

Don't be manipulated. Salespeople may be misinformed or naïve about products displayed, especially in big warehouse stores, so question any pronouncement. Worse, some baby stores may advertise a deep discount on a popular safety seat model, only to do a bait and switch maneuver, trying to convince you to purchase a pricier model. If a seat's price is almost too good to be true, it could be a showroom sample with missing directions or a torn cover. Or the model might have been issued a federal safety advisory.

Take 'em down and try 'em out. Write down manufacturers' names, the names of models and model numbers, and prices. (A single car seat, such as Century SmartFit, a rear-facing infant seat, may have a variety of differently numbered models, some with bases, some without, and each with different seat cover patterns.) Take seats down from the shelf for a thorough inspection. Scan installation instructions for product warnings and to acquaint yourself with parts and installation. Put similar-looking models side by side to compare features, weights, and prices. Try out handles and buckles. Recline the convertibles and measure how much space they'll need.

Check add-ons. Extras pump up the price: thicker upholstery or padding; fashion imprints like Osh Kosh B'Gosh or Carter's; licensed cartoon or fantasy characters; handlebar cushions; small storage shelves; elasticized side pockets; more sophisticated reclining mechanisms; front shields instead of simple straps; adjustable head pillows; side cushioning on seat wings.

SEAT INSTALLATION

Surveys show that as many as 80 percent of all car seats may be installed incorrectly. The most common mistakes are a wrong size seat for a child's weight; loose shoulder and waist straps; and loose car belts; or car seat belts threaded through the wrong slots.

Stimulation

Tape greeting cards, pictures from magazines, even a swatch of a baby's wallpaper to the back of the front seat, so the back car seat rider will have something interesting to look at.

Sometimes, the problem is with car seats and belts. Vehicle back seats are designed for adult comfort, not for children's safety, and some are too shallow or sharply angled to accommodate a child seat. Or, safety belts and buckles may not anchor a seat firmly enough.

Fastening down children's safety seats will eventually be a simple process. In fact, you won't have to grapple with adult seat belts at all. Regulations issued by the National Highway Traffic Safety Administration (NHTSA) in March 1999 require that all new cars and domestic trucks provide a uniform anchoring system for child safety seats. The new regulations are expected to be gradually phased in over a three-year period beginning September 1, 2000.

New vehicles will have two small metal rods resembling U-shaped drawer pulls installed in the crease in the center of the back seat. And children's car seats will all have straps on both sides that hook into the rods. The car seat's straps will be hooked into the anchors, then tightened.

All forward-facing toddler seats will be required to have adjustable tether straps that will fit into an anchor installed in the upper, rear window shelf of the newly equipped cars. However, until you purchase a new car with the built-in anchoring system, you'll still have to cope with car seat and safety belt compatibility problems. Allow a half hour or more for installing—and a helper wouldn't hurt.

• Consult the car owner's manual. It should have information and graphics on how your car's belts should be used to fasten down the seat. If you get stumped, contact your local car dealer or consult your owner's manual for the regional service office to see what information and help is available.

• Read the car seat instructions. You should find a leaflet or brochure stuffed into a slot or pocket in the back of the restraint. Coordinate car seat instructions with those for your automobile.

• Read the messages on the car seat. Look for installation warnings on the inside, both sides, and the back bottom of the seat.

• Place the seat in the back of the car. The seat should be positioned so your baby (under 20 pounds) looks toward the car's back window. The center is the best seat placement unless there's an arm rest or the seat dips down too deeply to support the restraint. Then you must install the seat next to a window. The car seat manufacturer may recommend that you stuff a tightly rolled towel or receiving blanket in the auto seat's crease so the car seat won't pitch too far forward. Many infant seats have a level indicator on the side, such as a small bead encased in plastic, to show when the seat is angled correctly.

• Feed the adult belts through the seat. Be careful not to mix up rear- and forward-facing installation instructions for a convertible seat.

• Press down hard on the seat. A rear-facing model may require standing up inside the back seat compartment while pushing down into the seat. Dig your knee into a forward-facing toddler seat. Your object should be to embed the seat as deeply as possible into the car's upholstery.

• Tighten the adult belts. Apply as much belt tension as you can while the seat is pressed down. If properly installed, the seat won't budge more than one inch either way when pulled forward or backward or more than one to two inches when you tug on either side.

Where to get installation help

It's vital that the seat be installed correctly. If you can't do it, ask for assistance from these sources.

• The store where you bought the seat. Sometimes (but not always), stores selling car seats will have at least one staff member who's knowledgeable about installation and is willing to offer hands-on help.

• The dealer for your model car. Usually at least one employee at a car dealership knows car seat installation. (Since others may only pretend to know, save yourself time and trouble—start with the manager and work your way down.)

Pit stop

Change your baby in the open trunk of the car (with a blanket inside) or on the tailgate of a station wagon, instead of crouching uncomfortably in the backseat.

• Safety Belt Safe USA Safe Ride Help Line (listed in the Resource Guide). You'll need the car seat's manufacturer, model name or number, and the date the seat was made. You leave a message and help line personnel will get back to you with suggestions.

• Local police department or state patrol headquarters. In many states, officers have installation inspection training and will make sure the seat is correctly installed.

• The National Safe Kids Campaign. As part of the "Safe Kids Buckle Up" child-safety program, over 250 coalitions nationwide offer local car seat checkup events to ensure that seats are properly installed. Call for events in your area, or check out their web site (in the Resource Guide).

• The American Academy of Pediatrics. This organization periodically issues safety seat recommendations ("The Family Shopping Guide to Car Seats: Safety and Product Information"). You can find the most recent version listed on their web site or order by mail. See the Resource Guide.

• NHTSA offers helpful information about car seats on their web site. (See the Resource Guide.)

Solving installation problems

Here are some common installation problems and their solutions.

Continuous loop belts. An automobile belt system consisting of waist and shoulder belts made of one continuous strap plus a sliding metal tongue (the part that clicks into the buckle) may not lock, except in a sudden stop or crash. This seat-belt system requires a heavy-duty, metal locking clip to hold a seat firmly. (Don't confuse this with the harness clip that holds your baby's shoulder straps together.) You can find the clip attached in the back of the safety seat.

Long, rigid buckle-stalks. Some adult safety belts have buckles attached to long stalks too inflexible to feed through safety-seat channels. You may need to have different belts installed.

Buckles too far forward. In some car models, the seat belt buckle doesn't emerge from the seat's crease but is fastened to the upholstery a few inches forward of the crease. A child car seat in such an installation can pitch too far forward or backward in a crash. This problem is hard to fix, short of getting a new belt installed.

Shallow rear seat. Some seats are simply too shallow to correctly support a safety seat; others are too sharply angled, or are contoured to fit adult bodies. There's no ready solution other than trading your vehicle in for a more family-friendly model.

Lack of stability. Sometimes car seat manufacturers will suggest a tethering kit to correct stability problems (see the tethering discussion on page 65). Just be sure the tether stops any side-to-side motion, too.

AIR BAGS AND CHILDREN

Air bags are designed to generally deploy only during a front-end crash, not during side or rear collisions or when a vehicle turns over. In a crash, sensors trigger an explosive charge, forcing a nontoxic gas into the bags and instantly inflating them into a shield.

The air bag protects a full-sized adult from crashing into the dashboard or windshield. Air vents then allow the bag to partially deflate. Once an air bag deploys, it must be replaced. Passengers are always cautioned to wear safety belts, even when they're sitting in front of an air bag, since being out of position in a crash can be deadly.

Air bags can be fatal for children sitting in the front seat. Babies sitting in the front seat in their rear-facing car seats are the most at risk. An air bag can turn a minor, 10-mile-per-hour fender-bender into a 140- to 210-mile-per-hour head impact for the baby. A toddler in a forward-facing convertible seat or booster seat is also endangered, as are toddlers and children sitting in the front, buckled in or not.

The air bag for the front passenger seat is usually found just above the glove compartment. Vehicles with a passenger-side air bag carry a warning label alerting you to not place a child in a car seat in that seat.

Do you want on/off switches? In January 1998, NHTSA issued the ruling that allows repair shops and dealers to install "on-off" switches for air bags in passenger cars and light trucks. An individual letter of authorization from NHTSA is required to install this option.

You must meet certain criteria to have the switch installed, such as owning a car with no rear seat or one too small to accommodate a rear-facing child restraint; or having a child with a medical condition that needs constant monitoring in the front seat.

For most families, having the switch installed is an unnecessary expense. For maximum safety, all children should ride safely secured in the back seat anyway, whether there are front air bags or not. An air bag could still save lives by protecting older children, teens, parents, or other adult family members in the front seat. Plus, you may forget to turn it back on.

If you do decide to have the switch installed in a vehicle you own or lease, first obtain a copy of NHTSA's brochure "Air Bag and On-off Switches: Information for an Informed Decision" and the accompanying form, "Request for Air Bag On-off Switch." You'll find a copy at new car dealers, state motor vehicle departments, and AAA clubs, or you can order one directly from NHTSA. (See the Resource Guide.) You'll be required to certify on the request form that you have read the brochure and that you or other riders in your vehicle meet the risk definitions. NHTSA will then send you an authorization letter to take to your dealer or repair shop.

CAR SEATS ON AIRPLANES

Because babies have been wrenched from their parent's arms in plane crashes, more and more parents now purchase separate tickets for their babies and toddlers and use safety seats when flying. Studies have shown

Handy

Tie toys to a child's car seat with short strings so that you won't have to pick them up constantly.

that in a crash landing, a 30-pound child thrusts outward with a force equivalent to a 480-pound object. Even though U.S. Federal Aviation Administration (FAA) regulations require that adults wear safety belts and that everything else in the plane, including luggage, be secured during a flight, babies don't have to be. The FAA is drafting a proposal for a regulation that requires children under two to be restrained, but it may take several years to be enacted.

Which seats are safe?

During the mid-1980s, the NHTSA and the FAA used similar approaches in determining which child restraints would be approved for vehicles and for airplanes. The standard was called Federal Motor Vehicle Safety Standard (FMVSS) No. 213. Seats that meet this standard are allowed to be used on planes. (See "Look for the sticker," page 73.) Other seats are not deemed safe.

According to a study by the FAA's Civil Aeromedical Institute, children under 40 pounds are better protected by children's safety seats than by boosters, vests, or harnesses. (Just as in automobiles, babies under one year old should ride facing rearward in a safety seat; older babies should face forward.) Children weighing over 40 pounds would fare better with regular aircraft safety belts than with booster seats.

Booster seats (tall car seats resembling convertible seats) and vest- and harness-type child restraint systems have been found to be unsafe as a plane takes off, lands, and taxis. Belt-positioning booster seats also do not offer adequate protection during crash simulations. Airplanes lack an adult shoulder harness to hold them in place, and without that harness, these seats can fail. Boosters and vest- and harness-type restraints are banned from planes.

Besides lacking automobile belt systems, airline seats don't act like auto seats during a crash. They tend to fold forward, either by themselves or when they're struck from behind.

Booster seats with front shields were found to put too much pressure on a child's abdominal area, particularly combined with the sandwiching effect of an airline seat in a crash.

Children's separate safety vests and harnesses (not attached to a safety seat) didn't protect well because of the way they fastened to the adult safety belt. They allowed a child's body to vault forward too much. There was also a danger that a child could slip under the belt and get hurt.

Babies could be endangered if put inside the same belt as a parent, either thrown into the seat in front or crushed by the forward-bending motion of the parent's body.

For more information about flying with a safety seat, the Federal Aviation Agency has a toll-free Consumer Hotline—see the Resource Guide.

Look for the sticker

Most car seats manufactured after January 1, 1981, are federally approved for use in airplanes. Airlines call an acceptable car seat a CRS (child restraint system).

If the car seat is approved, you'll find a label that states "This restraint is certified for use in motor vehicles and in aircraft," along with the letters FMVSS, standing for Federal Motor Vehicle Safety Standard. The sticker should be somewhere on the seat's shell. (Should the seat not be usable on a plane, the label will probably say so.)

If the seat does not have this approval sticker, airline personnel may not allow you to take it on the plane, and you will have to check it as luggage. Even if the seat has the sticker, call the airline, just to be sure.

Making flight plans

Although most airlines let babies under age two fly for free, you won't be guaranteed a seat for your baby unless you pay for a ticket—especially since many flights are overbooked. You can inquire whether a plane is full when you make your reservations, but the status might change before takeoff.

On a fully-booked flight without a child's ticket, you may have to check your child's seat at the gate or stow it on the plane. Or, if there's a single seat somewhere, your flight attendant may allow you to switch rows so you and your baby have two seats together. But without a ticket, you can't count on a space.

These tips can give you and your baby a safer, smoother flight:

Check with the airlines. When making your reservations, ask the airline about their least busy days and times. By flying off-peak days and hours, you're more likely to snag an adjoining empty seat.

In many cases, airlines will allow you to put a child under two with a CRS in the empty seat for free. But confirm the airline policy regarding empty seats.

Feedback

Take a picture of your child playing with or wearing a gift received from a relative or friend, and send it as a thank-you note to the gift giver.

Ask the airline if they offer a discounted fare for a child traveling in a CRS. (Many airlines do.) If you elect to purchase a regular plane ticket (discounted or full fare) for your child, you'll be guaranteed a seat and use of your baby's certified car seat.

Get the right seat. A CRS should be placed in a window seat so it will not block the escape path in an emergency, but it may not be placed in an emergency exit row.

Check the width of your CRS. Plane seats vary, but a CRS no wider than 16 inches should fit in most coach seats. (Check with the airline when you reserve to see if your seat will fit.) If your seat is wider than 16 inches, it won't fit properly, even with the arm rests raised out of the way. Reclining the plane's seat back during child-seat installation can make the job easier. The plane seat must be upright for flight, though.

Allow enough time. If you must change planes for a connecting flight, remember that hauling a car seat, a diaper bag, purse, and hand luggage through a busy airport can be a real challenge. Book your connections with enough spare time to get to the other gate without a problem. You can also ask flight attendants to arrange for a ground employee with a cart to meet the plane and help you get from here to there.

Airlines now board half an hour early. But arriving at the airport an hour and a half in advance saves a lot of hassle—racing down airport hallways with your baby in your arms, standing in long lines at the ticket counter, and making it to the gate before the doors close. And you'll be in plenty of time for the early boarding often allowed for parents with young children.

Reserve a car seat at your destination

You may not be allowed to drive a rental car without a safety seat for your baby or child under age four. Most large car rental companies offer safety seats for rent, but you can't always count on an available seat when you arrive.

When you reserve your car, ask the rental company customer service representative about their car seat policy, so you'll know for sure that they have an appropriate one for you to rent. Then call the airport rental desk a day or so before your arrival to make sure a seat is held for you.

SPECIAL REPORT

TESTS OF CHILD CAR SEATS

How Consumer Reports tests the seats

Consumer Reports had 28 seats for infants, toddlers, and children crash tested by an outside laboratory. The infant models were all part of "travel systems"—seven came with a companion stroller; another had wheels and a handle and could be converted into a stroller.

The laboratory performed crash tests similar to the government's, strapping dummies of various sizes into seats placed on a rig that was then run through a simulated head-on collision. Using high-speed cameras, we could see, for example, if a dummy's head moved forward so far that in real life a child might have been injured by hitting the seat in front. In our labs, we also judged ease of use for each seat and whether it could be installed correctly in vehicles with different safety-belt systems and seat configurations. Results were published in Consumer Reports in January 1999.

One problem with government car-seat crash tests is that they often use a

1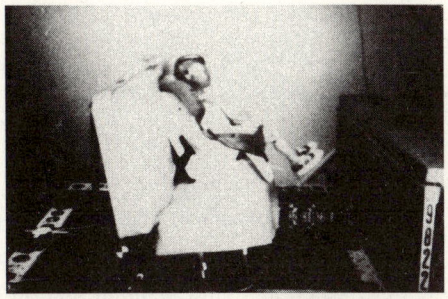

2

3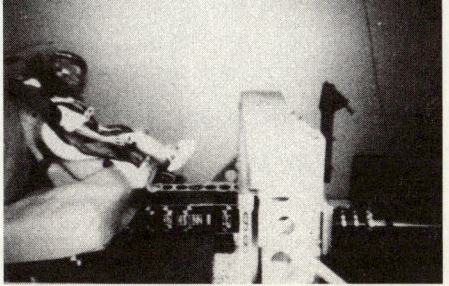

The tests in action.
The Evenflo Scout in our crash test. The seat is successful in holding back the 40-pound dummy so its head doesn't hit the seat in front.

Traveling in the Car ■ **75**

dummy weighing less than the maximum the manufacturer specifies as appropriate for that seat. And though the standard specifies a 30-mph test, government tests can be run as low as 28 mph.

We first tested each seat with a dummy weighing the maximum listed on the label, at 30 mph. All but five seats did fine. With four convertible seats—the Britax Roundabout, Century Smartmove XT 4720, Cosco Touriva 02-584, and Kolcraft Automate 13207—the head of the toddler dummy moved forward farther than the government standard allows. We downrated those seats and retested them at 28.5 mph. All but the Kolcraft, whose harness loosened, passed the second test. The Kolcraft also performed poorly in a third, 28.5-mph test using the lighter government dummy. We rated the seat poor for use with a toddler.

The Evenflo Two-in-One 636 toddler seat/booster also gave mixed results. Tested at 30 mph with a 40-pound dummy (the maximum child weight specified for use with its harness), the base cracked and the seatback tore away. This problem is similar to one that triggered a company recall of the seats last year (see Product Recalls, page 267). Our models, manufactured after the dates of the recalled models, appear to have undergone only a borderline improvement. We recommend against using the seat with its harness.

Test results

Infant seats are placed in a semireclined, rear-facing position so a baby's head, neck, and back are supported. They can be used until a baby is 20 to 22 pounds (a typical 9- to 12-month-old). Many infant seats can be used with or without a base that stays in the car, while the seat itself snaps in and out of the base and doubles as an infant carrier. Some can also snap into a stroller frame.

All eight infant seats we tested performed satisfactorily in our crash tests, with and without their base. But in terms of security of installation and convenience, the models differed a lot. Babies should stay rear-facing as long as possible, but at least until their first birthday. For heavier infants, a convertible seat, used in the rear-facing position, is the answer. These are also an option as a first car seat for a newborn, though they can't double as a carrier.

After a toddler is at least one year old, face the seat forward and continue to use it until the child weighs about 40 pounds (the weight of a typical four-year-old). These seats will have one of three harness types; the five-point harness is best for infants.

Most convertible seats we tested come with a tether or offer an optional

SPECIAL REPORT

tether that secures the top of a forward-facing car seat to an anchor in the car. In our tests, seats used with a tether pitched forward less than seats used without one. But the Evenflo Horizon V420 cracked when used with its tether in our 30-mph crash test.

Toddler seat/boosters have a harness for 20- or 30-pound toddlers. When the child weighs 40 pounds, you remove the harness and use the seat to boost a child to a height where he or she can use the car's own safety belt. Regular boosters work without a harness and are used only after a child weighs 30 or 40 pounds.

All the booster seats provided excellent restraint in our crash tests when used with the car's own safety belt.

Recommendations

Until your child is big enough to use a regular safety belt, you'll need to buy at least two sizes of car seats. With a newborn, you can usually start with an infant or convertible seat. If you choose an infant seat, which you can also use as a carrier, you must graduate to a convertible seat when the child reaches 20 to 22 pounds. If you select a convertible seat, get one with a five-point harness, which won't obstruct a small baby's head. When the child outgrows the convertible, move him or her into any type of booster seat.

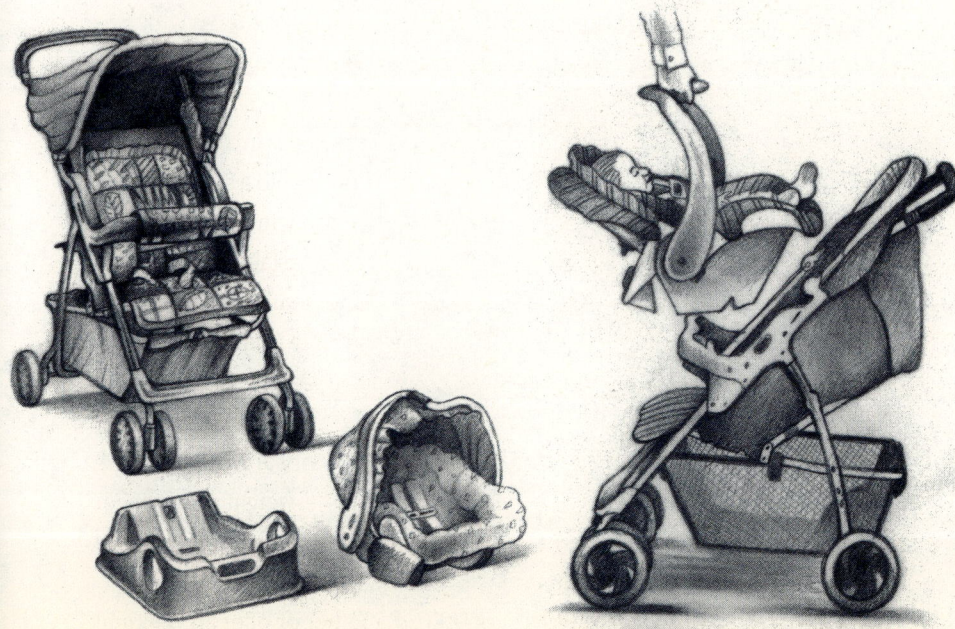

A **travel system** typically consists of a **stroller,** a **seat,** and a **base** that stays in the car. The seat snaps into the stroller and the base, making transitions especially easy. The stroller with the seat attached can be heavy, but the convenience may be worth the extra pounds.

Traveling in the Car

SPECIAL REPORT

In the infant seat class, the Graco 7497 Travel System, $160, is easy to use and should install securely with a range of safety-belt types. However, the car seat can't be purchased separately from the stroller, so if you're looking for a cheaper option, consider one of the very good infant seats we tested.

Among convertibles with top crash-test performance, two models from Century—the 1000 STE Classic 4161, $50, and the 2000 STE Classic 4261, $60—are easy to use and should install securely in many types of vehicles. If you have a heavy infant, choose a model that can be used facing rear until a baby weighs 30 pounds.

The Cosco High Back Booster 02-442, $40, and the Century Next Step 4920, $100, are good toddler seat/boosters. For children who outgrow a convertible seat and don't need a harness, most regular boosters should be simple to install and use, and should offer excellent crash protection. At $25, the Evenflo Right Fit 245 is A CR Best Buy, but a child must weigh at least 40 pounds to use it, and your car must have a high seat back or a head restraint.

Built-in car seats (discussed on page 60, "Car-seat options") were not crash-tested. But because they're tightly secured and the child sits further back than in a separate car seat, they should perform very well.

Never use a seat that's been in an accident. And don't buy a secondhand seat: You can't be sure it wasn't damaged or recalled.

RATINGS & RECOMMENDATIONS

CONVERTIBLE CAR SEATS

THE TESTS BEHIND THE RATINGS Overall score is based mainly on a seat's performance in crash tests and on our judgments of security of installation and ease of use. **Crash protection** reflects results of tests simulating a head-on crash at about 30 mph. If a seat performed poorly in our tests, which were slightly tougher than what government standards call for, we retested according to the government's criteria. Separate scores are given for **infant** and **toddler** protection, based on tests without tethers and with dummies of different weights in a rear-facing position (for infants) and a front-facing position (for toddlers). **Ease of use** includes the ease with which straps and harness were adjusted. **Installation** indicates how securely a seat could be installed in three different cars with different seats and safety-belt types. **Price** is the estimated average.

TYPICAL FEATURES FOR THESE MODELS • Adjustable five-point harness with three height positions. • Tether or optional tether kit that improved the seat's crash protection. • Can be used rear-facing with infants (birth to 22 lb.), forward-facing with toddlers (20 to 40 lb.). • Removable machine-washable cloth cover. • Certified for use in aircraft. • Lack warranty information.

RECOMMENDATIONS Most convertible seats tested rated at least very good. Two models from Century—the 1000 STE Classic 4161, $50, and the 2000 STE Classic 4261, $60—are easy to use and should install securely in many types of vehicles. The Britax Roundabout, $200, was the top-rated model that can be used rear-facing until an infant weighs 30 pounds, making it a good choice for a heavy infant.

RATINGS CONVERTIBLE CAR SEATS

OVERALL RATINGS
Listed in order of overall score

Ratings key: E (Excellent), VG (Very Good), G (Good), F (Fair), P (Poor)

Key no.	Brand and model	Price	Overall score (0–100, P F G VG E)	Crash protection INFANT	Crash protection TODDLER	Ease of use	Installation INFANT	Installation TODDLER
1	Century 1000 STE Classic 4161	$50		⊖	○	⊖	⊖	⊖
2	Century 2000 STE Classic 4261	60		⊖	○	⊖	⊖	⊖
3	Century 3000 Room-to-Grow Classic 4331	70		○	○	⊖	⊖	⊖
4	Fisher-Price Safe Embrace 79700	130		⊖	○	⊖	⊖	⊖
5	Evenflo Scout 217	50		○	○	⊖	⊖	⊖
6	Britax Roundabout	200		○	◐	⊖	⊖	⊖
7	Cosco Touriva 02-584	60		○	◐	⊖	⊖	⊖
8	Guardian Folder 1231-16	120		○	○	⊖	⊖	⊖
9	Century Smartmove XT 4720	125		○	◐	⊖	⊖	⊖
10	Evenflo Horizon V 420	80		○	○	⊖	⊖	⊖
11	Safeline Sit n' Stroll 3240	160		○	○	◐	●	⊖
12	Kolcraft Automate 13207	80		○	●	⊖	⊖	⊖

DETAILS ON THE MODELS

1 Century 1000 STE Classic 4161 $50
Optional $22 tether kit. **Similar seat model:** 1500 STE 4177, $70. **Recommendation:** Very good.

2 Century 2000 STE Classic 4261 $60
Has a T-shield harness. Optional $22 tether kit. **Recommendation:** Very good; better for older infants and toddlers.

3 Century 3000 Room-to-Grow Classic 4331 $70
Uses an overhead harness to restrain infant. Optional $22 tether kit. **Similar seat model:** 3500 Room-to-Grow Prestige, $70. **Recommendation:** Very good; better for older infants and toddlers.

4 Fisher-Price Safe Embrace 79700 $130
Labeled for an infant weighing at least 6 lb. Has built-in safety-belt clips that are easy to use with emergency-locking-retractor car safety belts. Includes top tether. Some were recalled because the harness adjuster may malfunction. **Recommendation:** Very good, but avoid recalled seats, produced between May 19, 1997 and March 29, 1998 (production date is labeled on the seat).

5 Evenflo Scout 217 $50
Labeled for an infant weighing at least 5 lb. Can be used rear-facing with an infant weighing up to only 20 lb. Optional $8 tether kit. Padded seat cover is harder to remove than others. 1-yr. warranty. **Recommendation:** Very good.

6 Britax Roundabout $200
Labeled for an infant weighing at least 5 lb. Has built-in safety-belt clips that are easy to use with emergency-locking-retractor car safety belts. Can be used rear-facing with an infant weighing up to 30 lb.; only model that can be used with top tether in that position. In 30-mph, front-facing crash test, dummy's head moved farther forward than the standard allows, but the tether improved performance. (When seat was used in rear-facing position, tether routed toward the rear of the car improved performance; tether routed toward the front of the car worsened performance.) 1-yr. warranty. **Recommendation:** Very good; suitable for heavy infants in a rear-facing position.

7 Cosco Touriva 02-584 $60
Labeled for an infant weighing at least 5 lb. In 30-mph, front-facing crash test, dummy's head moved farther forward than the standard allows. No tether available. **Similar seat model:** 02-514, $45. **Recommendation:** Very good. **Note:** Models made 8/9/97–8/22/97 have been recalled. See Product Recalls for specifics.

8 Guardian Folder 1231-16 $120
Labeled for an infant weighing at least 7½ lb. Can be used rear-facing with an infant weighing up to only 20 lb.

Guide to Baby Products

No tether available. Folds for storage. **Recommendation:** Very good.

9 ▶ Century Smartmove XT 4720 $125

Can be used rear-facing with an infant weighing up to 30 lb. In 30-mph, front-facing crash test, dummy's head moved farther forward than the standard allows, but the top tether improved performance. Hard to thread the car's safety belt through the seat. **Similar seat model:** Smartmove 4712, $120. **Recommendation:** Good; suitable for heavy infants in a rear-facing position.

10 ▶ Evenflo Horizon V 420 $80

Labeled for an infant weighing at least 5 lb. Can be used rear-facing with an infant weighing up to 30 lb. When the seat was used front-facing with its tether in 30-mph crash test, the tether cracked the back of the car seat shell. 1-yr. warranty. **Recommendation**: Good; suitable for heavy infants in a rear-facing position. Very good when used without its tether.

11 ▶ Safeline Sit n' Stroll 3240 $160

A convertible car seat with wheels that fold out and a handle that telescopes for use as a stroller. **Seat:** Can be used rear-facing with an infant weighing up to 25 lb. Has adjustable canopy. Harness is hard to adjust. No tether available. **Stroller**: Seat faces away from parent. 15 lb. Only 18½ in. wide. Canopy affords only partial protection. **Recommendation:** Good seat, good stroller.

12 ▶ Kolcraft Automate 13207 $80

Labeled for an infant weighing at least 7 lb. In every forward-facing crash test, dummy's head moved farther forward than the standard allows. No tether available. Padded seat cover isn't removable. 1-yr. warranty. **Similar seat model**: 13205, $50. **Recommendation**: Poor; shouldn't be used with toddler in forward-facing position.

Traveling in the Car

RATINGS & RECOMMENDATIONS

BOOSTER CAR SEATS

THE TESTS BEHIND THE RATINGS Overall score is based mainly on a seat's performance in crash tests and on our judgments of security of installation and ease of use. **Crash protection** reflects results of tests simulating a head-on crash at about 30 mph. If a seat performed poorly in our tests, which were slightly tougher than government standards call for, we retested according to the government's criteria. For toddler seat/boosters, separate scores are given for **toddler** protection (with a harness) and **child** protection (without a harness), based on tests without tethers and with dummies of different weights. **Ease of use** includes the ease with which straps and harness were adjusted. **Installation** indicates how securely a seat could be installed in three different cars with different seats and safety-belt types. **Price** is the estimated average.

TYPICAL FEATURES FOR THESE MODELS • Easily installed when using the car safety belts. • Adjustable five-point harness with three height positions. • With the harness, suitable for use in an airplane. • Have removable, machine-washable cloth cover. • Lack warranty information.

RECOMMENDATIONS Toddler seats convert into boosters for older children. The three we tested are rated very good. The Cosco High Back Booster 02-442, $40, and the Century Next Step 4920, $100, are the top picks. The Cosco wasn't as easy to use with toddlers as it was with larger kids. Regular boosters are for children large enough to use a safety belt instead of a harness. At $25, the Evenflo Right Fit 245 is **A CR Best Buy**. But a child must weigh at least 40 pounds to use it, and your car must have a high seatback or a head restraint. Other models that we tested offered excellent protection.

BOOSTER CAR SEATS

OVERALL RATINGS Listed in order of overall score

Legend: E VG G F P

Key no.	Brand and model	Price	Overall score 0–100 (P F G VG E)	Crash protection TODDLER	Crash protection CHILD	Ease of use TODDLER	Ease of use CHILD	Installation TODDLER	Installation CHILD
	TODDLER SEAT/BOOSTERS								
1	Cosco High Back Booster 02-442	$40		⊖	⊖	◐	⊖	⊖	⊖
2	Century Next Step 4920	100		○	⊖	○	⊖	⊖	⊖
3	Century Breverra Classic 4865	60		○	⊖	○	⊖	◐	⊖
	REGULAR BOOSTER SEATS								
4	Fisher-Price Safe Embrace 79750	60		—	⊖	—	⊖	—	⊖
5	Evenflo Right Fit 245 **A CR Best Buy**	25		—	⊖	—	⊖	—	⊖
6	Kolcraft Prodigy 53000	50		—	⊖	—	⊖	—	⊖
7	Guardian Double-Up 1300-05	60		—	⊖	—	⊖	—	⊖
	CONDITIONALLY ACCEPTABLE Don't use this toddler seat with a harness, or with a child weighing less than 30 lb.								
8	Evenflo Two-In-One 636	80	Not scored	●	⊖	⊖	⊖	⊖	⊖

DETAILS ON THE MODELS

TODDLER SEATS/BOOSTERS

1 Cosco High Back Booster 02-442 $40
Labeled for children weighing 22-65 lb. (with the harness, for children weighing 22-40 lb.) Has only two harness positions; harness tension and height are hard to adjust. **Recommendation:** Very good.

2 Century Next Step 4920 $100
Labeled for children weighing 20-65 lb. (with the harness, for children weighing 20-40 lb.). Optional $22 tether improved crash protection. Has built-in recline adjustment. Harness tension is relatively hard to adjust. **Recommendation:** Very good.

3 Century Breverra Classic 4865 $60
Labeled for children weighing 30-60 lb. (with the harness, for children weighing 30-40 lb.). Optional $22 tether kit significantly improved crash protection for front-facing dummy. Has only two harness positions. Harness tension is hard to adjust; shoulder-belt height is not adjustable at all. Confusing installation instructions refer to features in a different model. **Similar seat model:** Breverra Premiere, $60. **Recommendation:** Very good.

REGULAR BOOSTER SEATS

4 Fisher-Price Safe Embrace 79750 $60
Labeled for children weighing 30-60 lb. Seat cover is easy to remove. Easy to adjust car's shoulder-belt position. **Recommendation:** Excellent.

5 Evenflo Right Fit 245 $25
Labeled for children weighing 40-60 lb. The backless design requires a car with a high seatback or a head restraint. Seat cover is easy to remove. 1-yr. warranty. **Recommendation:** Excellent. A CR Best Buy.

6 Kolcraft Prodigy 53000 $50
Labeled for children weighing 30-60 lb. Easy to adjust car's shoulder-belt position. 1-yr. warranty. Seat cover isn't machine washable. **Recommendation:** Excellent.

7 Guardian Double-Up 1300-05 $60
Labeled for children weighing 30-60 lb. Seat cover relatively easy to remove. Make sure you have instructions and product registration card; none were provided with the seats we bought. **Recommendation:** Excellent.

CONDITIONALLY ACCEPTABLE

8 Evenflo Two-in-One 636 $80
In a 30-mph crash test with a 40-lb. dummy strapped into the harness, the base cracked and the seatback tore away. Labeled for children weighing 22-65 lb. 1-yr. warranty. **Recommendation:** Don't use it as a toddler seat; for booster seats, there are better values in the group above. **Note:** Models made 1/7/98–3/20/98 have been recalled. See Product Recalls for specifics.

RATINGS & RECOMMENDATIONS

TRAVEL SYSTEMS: INFANT SEATS

THE TESTS BEHIND THE RATINGS Overall score is based mainly on a seat's performance in crash tests and on our judgments of security of installation and ease of use. **Crash protection** reflects results of tests simulating a head-on crash at about 30 mph. If a seat performed poorly in our tests, which were slightly tougher than government standards call for, we retested according to the government's criteria. Separate scores are given for the seat used **with** and **without** its base. **Ease of use** includes the ease with which straps and harness were adjusted. **Installation** indicates how securely a seat could be installed in three different cars with different seats and safety-belt types. **Price** is approximate retail and, except for #1, does not include stroller.

TYPICAL FEATURES FOR THESE MODELS • Accommodate babies from birth to 20 lb. • Can be used as an infant carrier. • Can be bought with a stroller. • Separate base that can be left strapped in the car. • Leveling indicator to help install the seat at a safe angle that's comfortable for the infant. • Adjustable three-point harness. • Attachment to use with a shopping cart. • Weigh 6 to 8 lb. **Most strollers:** • Must have the car seat snapped in when used with infants. • Face the car seat toward the parent. • Have a backrest that reclines to be nearly flat. • Have a canopy viewing port so the parent can see the child. • Have rear-wheel brakes. • Have front wheels that swivel. • Weigh 18 to 24 lb. • When open, are 35 to 39 in. long, 37 to 42 in. high, 21 to 25 in. wide. • When folded, are 34 to 38 in. long, 15 to 19 in. high, and can stand upright and be rolled. • Use T-buckle restraints with straps at the crotch and waist.

RECOMMENDATIONS Although an infant seat won't work for as much of your child's life as a convertible seat, it will take him or her more places. Infant seats can also be used as carriers. All the seats tested rated at least very good. The Graco 7497 Travel System, $160, is easy to use and should install securely with a range of safety-belt types. The price includes a stroller. See page 86 for information about these models as strollers.

See also Ratings of strollers, page 86.

OVERALL RATINGS Infant seats
Listed in order of overall score

Ratings key: E VG G F P

Key no.	Brand and model	Price	Overall score (0–100) P F G VG E	Crash protection W/ BASE	Crash protection W/O BASE	Ease of use	Installation W/ BASE	Installation W/O BASE
1	Graco 7497 Lite Rider All Terrain Travel System	$160		○	⊖	⊖	⊖	⊖
2	Evenflo On My Way 207	55		○	⊖	⊖	⊖	●
3	Century SmartFit Plus 4529	60		○	○	⊖	⊖	⊖
4	Kolcraft Secura 43834	75		○	⊖	⊖	○	⊖
5	Evenflo Discovery 209	50		○	○	⊖	○	◐
6	Fisher-Price Safe Embrace 79725	70		—	○	⊖	—	○
7	Cosco Arriva 02-751	40		○	⊖	⊖	●	●
8	Cosco Turnabout 02-764	55		○	⊖	○	●	●

DETAILS ON THE MODELS

1 Graco 7497 LiteRider Travel System $160
Seat: Carrying handle is very comfortable. Can't be attached to a shopping cart. **Stroller:** Opens to 41 in. long. Swivel wheels are lockable. Brake is easy to use. Seat attachment to stroller is less secure than most. **Recommendation:** Excellent seat and very good stroller (can't be purchased separately).

2 Evenflo On My Way 207 $55
Seat: Carrying handle is very comfortable but harder to adjust than others. Harness height not adjustable. 1-yr. warranty. **Stroller:** Trendsetter Travel System 495, $170 (includes seat). Has tray for toddler. **Recommendation:** Very good seat and stroller. **Note:** Seats made 12/15/95–7/27/97 may have handle flaws. See Product Recalls for specifics.

3 Century SmartFit Plus 4529 $60
Seat: Harness is harder to adjust than others. **Strollers:** 4-in-1 System Adventure 11-770, $170 (includes seat), or 4-in-1 Pro Sport Plus 11-750, $150 (includes seat). Seat attaches with an adapter, which broke in our durability test with a 20-lb. dummy. Faces toward or away from parent. The System Adventure's front wheels are lockable. When folded, the Pro Sport Plus rolls but will not stand upright. **Similar seat models:** SmartFit 4541, $50, Century Assura 4551, $40. **Recommendation:** Very good seat, good strollers.

4 Kolcraft Secura 43834 $75
Seat: Difficult to install and to remove from base. Harness height is not adjustable. Padded seat cover is not machine washable. Handle is harder to adjust than others. Can't be attached to a shopping cart. 1-yr. warranty. **Stroller:** Travel System 36851, $140 (includes seat). Folds up smaller than most. Can also be used with an infant without snapping in the car seat. Waist buckle is less effective than T-shaped buckle system. **Similar seat models:** 43964, $60, 43924, $50. **Recommendation:** Very good seat and stroller.

5 Evenflo Discovery 209 $50
Seat: Carrying handle is very comfortable. No leveling indicator to ease installation. 1-yr. warranty. **Stroller:** Travel System 497, $150 (includes seat). Opens to 41 in. long. Viewing-port visibility for the Travel system 497 is better than most. **Recommendation:** Very good seat and stroller.

6 Fisher-Price Safe Embrace 79725 $70
Seat: Labeled for an infant weighing up to 22 lb. Uses a five-point harness. Can't be secured well when used with emergency-locking-retractor car safety belts. No base. **Stroller:** None available. **Recommendation:** Very good seat.

7 Cosco Arriva 02-751 $40
Seat: Labeled for an infant weighing up to 22 lb. Harness tension and seat handle are hard to adjust. **Stroller:** Complete Voyager 01-851, $80 (includes seat). 14 lb. Folds up smaller than most. Rolls when folded, but won't stand upright. Requires adapter to secure car seat; awkward. Canopy has no viewing port and doesn't lock in place. Waist buckle is less effective than T-shaped buckle system. **Similar seat models:** 02-733, $30, 02-750, $40, 02-771, $50, 02-772, $60. **Recommendation:** Good seat and stroller.

8 Cosco Turnabout 02-764 $55
Seat: Labeled for an infant weighing up to 22 lb. Harness tension is hard to adjust. Carrying handle is very comfortable but hard to adjust. No leveling indicator to ease installation. **Stroller:** Rock N Roller 01-654, $140 (includes seat). Converts to bassinet. Viewing-port visibility better than most. Harder than others to open and fold. Inserting the car seat requires adapters, but stroller can also be used with an infant without snapping in the car seat. Rivets sheared off during durability tests. **Model availability:** Discontinued. **Recommendation:** Good seat and stroller.

Traveling in the Car

RATINGS & RECOMMENDATIONS

TRAVEL SYSTEMS: STROLLERS

THE TESTS BEHIND THE RATINGS Overall score is based on convenience, durability, and safety. Trained staffers judged **convenience** of functions such as opening and folding, inserting and removing the car seat, operating the brakes, steering, and using buckles. **Durability** reveals how well each stroller handled loads of 100 pounds on the seat and 10 pounds on the foot rests, as well as repetitive opening and folding and an endurance track test the equivalent of 50 miles of bumpy sidewalks or rough road surfaces. The **safety** scores indicate areas where the standards are inadequate—protecting an infant sleeping in the stroller (without the car seat) or the instability when force is applied to the handle. **Price** is approximate retail and includes the car seat. Models (1) to (8) are paired with infant seats; (9) is a convertible seat.

TYPICAL FEATURES • Canopy for stroller and car seat. • Brake(s) that can lock two rear wheels and engage using levers. • Relatively large wheels. • Crotch-strap or waist-belt restraint system with T-type buckle. • Backrest that reclines to a near horizontal postion. • Fabric that can be cleaned by damp-wiping. • Canopy that locks when positioned. • Swivel wheels that don't lock. • Handle with padded cover. • Shock-absorption at frame and wheels. • Padding for child.

RECOMMENDATIONS You won't go far wrong with any of these travel systems. All were judged at least as good as strollers. The top three—Kolcraft 36851, Evenflo 497, and Evenflo 495—earned the highest scores in convenience, durability, and safety.

See also Ratings of infant seats, page 84.

OVERALL RATINGS Strollers
Listed in order of overall score

E VG G F P

Key no.	Brand and model	Price	Overall score 0–100 (P F G VG E)	Convenience	Durability	Safety	Stroller weight
1	Kolcraft Secura Travel System 36851	$140		⊖	⊖	⊖	23 lb.
2	Evenflo Discovery Travel System 497	150		⊖	⊖	⊖	19
3	Evenflo Trend Setter Travel System 497	170		⊖	⊖	⊖	21
4	Graco LiteRider Travel System	160		⊖	⊖	○	22
5	Cosco Rock N Roller 01-654	140		○	○	⊖	24
6	Century 4-in-1 System Adventure 11-770	170		⊖	◐	○	22
7	Century 4-in-1 System Pro Sport Plus 11-750	150		⊖	◐	○	18
8	Cosco Complete Voyager 01-851	80		○	⊖	○	14
9	Safeline Sit 'n Stroll 5-in-1 3240	160		○	○	○	15

DETAILS ON THE MODELS

Dimensions are in inches. Stroller weight and dimensions are without the car seat. Length and width are given for the stroller in the open and closed position. Handle height gives two measurements for curved handles.

1 Kolcraft Secura Travel System 36851 $140
• 23 lb. • 36½x11, folded • 37x22, open • 38/40 handle height Stands and rolls folded. Medium-size basket. Fair viewing port canopy. Does not require an adapter for car seat attachment to stroller. Single buckle at waist belt judged less effective than T-type buckle system. **Recommendation:** A very good stroller at an average price.

2 Evenflo Discovery Travel System 497 $150
• 19 lb. • 34½x15 folded • 41x22, open • 39/42 handle height Stands and rolls folded. Large basket. Storage console at handle poses danger of spills onto child. Tray for toddler. Does not require an adapter for car seat attachment to stroller. Excellent viewing port in canopy. **Recommendation:** A very good stroller.

3 Evenflo Trendsetter Travel System 495 $170
• 21 lb. • 34x16, folded • 22x37, open • 40/42 handle height Stands and rolls folded. Large basket. Storage console at handle poses danger of spills onto child. Tray for toddler. Does not require an adapter for car seat attachment to stroller. Very good viewing port in canopy. **Recommendation:** A very good stroller.

4 Graco LiteRider Travel System 7497 $160
• 22 lb. • 36½x16, folded • 41x25, open • 40/41½ handle height Stands and rolls folded. Large basket. Single action operates brakes at both wheels. Very good viewing port in canopy. Swivel wheels are lockable. Car seat attachment to snap-on tray on stroller is less secure than most. **Recommendation:** A very good stroller.

5 Cosco Rock N Roller 01-654 $140
• 24 lb. • 38x18, folded • 38x24, open • 38/39½ handle height Not as easy to open and fold as others. Car seat placement and removal judged cumbersome. Stands and rolls folded. Large basket. Requires adapters for attachment of car seat to stroller. Excellent viewing port in canopy. Rivets sheared off in durability test. Converts to bassinet. With backrest reclined, stroller's openings pose no danger of strangulation to the infant. **Model availability:** Discontinued. **Recommendation:** A very good stroller.

6 Century 4-in-1 System Adventure 11-770 $170
• 22 lb. • 35x19, folded • 37x25, open • 40½/42 handle height Stands and rolls folded. Large basket. Good viewing port in canopy. Swivel wheels are lockable. Single action operates brakes at both wheels. **Recommendation:** A good stroller.

7 Century 4-in-1 System Pro Sport Plus 11-750 $150
• 18 lb. • 36½x13, folded • 36x22, open • 39/40½ handle height Rolls but does not stand folded. Large basket. Good viewing port in canopy. **Recommendation:** A good stroller.

Continued

Continued

8 ▶ Cosco Complete Voyager 01-851 $800
• 14lb. • 35½x13, folded • 35x21, open • 39 handle height
Rolls but does not stand folded. Large basket. Requires adapters for attachment of car seat to stroller. Lacks viewing port in canopy. Canopy does not lock in place. Single buckle at waist belt judged less effective than T-type buckle system. Car seat placement and removal judged cumbersome. **Recommendation:** A good stroller.

9 ▶ SafeLine Sit n' Stroll 5-in-1 3240 $160
15 lb. • 25x19, folded • 39 x18½, open • 37/38 handle height
Unique model that is essentially a car seat for infants to 25 lbs. and for toddlers to 40 lbs. with wheels and handle that fold out to convert to a stroller. Small storage bin. Relatively small wheels. Five-point harness judged excellent as a restraint in stroller use. Canopy protects only partially. No assembly required. **Recommendation:** A good stroller.

Chapter 4

THE LATEST BABY WHEELS

Strollers offer convenience for you and comfort for your baby. Check safety features and don't be tempted by extras you don't need.

Picking the right set of wheels for you and your baby can be quite an undertaking—not unlike searching for a new car. Your choices range from a simple, inexpensive, "umbrella" stroller (a lightweight model with a "pouch" seat) to a luxurious, expensive European-style vehicle. Model names even sound like classy vehicles: "Legacy," "Explorer," and "All Terrain." And, of course, you'll want to take a test drive. In spite of innovations, most parents are sticking to tried-and-true domestically made reliables—the Fords of the baby world—dependable midweight models from familiar companies that keep on rolling, baby after baby.

Specialty strollers are a whole other category. Every major manufacturer in the country now offers car seat/stroller combos, virtually unheard of only a few years ago. Tandems and side-by-side strollers with dual or triple seats can cart more than one child. Three-wheeled sports strollers are made to appeal to runners who want to take their babies along for the ride or parents who like the look and the ease of handling on rough terrain.

THE MANY STROLLER CHOICES

Strollers are indispensable baby gear. They're the third largest seller in the juvenile product world, second only to cribs and mattresses. And for good reason—with a stroller, you can take a baby just about everywhere

Contents
- **Stroller choices,** page 89
- **Doubles and triples,** page 103
- **Sports strollers,** page 105
- **Bicycle trailers,** page 108

you go. But finding the model that really works for both you and your baby may take some looking.

There are advantages and disadvantages to each type. For example, umbrella strollers are inexpensive and easy to push but may prove fragile. Carriage/stroller combos adapt to your growing child but can be heavy and cumbersome. Sports strollers roll along outside but are unwieldy in close quarters and take up considerable trunk room. Detailed descriptions begin on page 100.

SHOPPING SAVVY Strollers

The close resemblance of one stroller to another—especially in the mid-priced range—makes it hard to single out one model from the herd. Most strollers have navy blue seat covers—navy and white dots, navy with white stripes, navy checks—because these are the biggest sellers. No one really knows why parents prefer navy. Does navy show less soiling? Does it emanate quality? Or is it a good "Daddy" color?

As you shop, aim to look beyond the remarkable surface similarities to the sound construction, performance, and price you want.

A model for your lifestyle. If you live in a big city, you'll appreciate a sturdy, lightweight model with good shock absorbers. You'll be jiggling it across uneven sidewalks; opening and folding it repeatedly as you get in and out of cars, taxis, or buses; and probably lugging it up and down staircases (without baby inside, please).

If you're a suburban dweller and anticipate long, leisurely strolls with baby, then consider a midweight model with its plush seat padding and big, easy-rolling wheels. You might also consider a travel system that combines a midweight stroller with a snap-in infant car seat and base. (See our stroller/car seat combo Ratings starting on page 84.)

If you'll be spending most of your out-of-the-house time with baby walking through stores and shopping centers, get a model slender enough to roll through aisles or squeeze into crowded elevators. (Never ride escalators with baby inside a stroller.) A big storage bin is a must, too.

Vacationing and air travel demand a truly compact model you can squeeze into a loaded trunk or a plane's overhead storage compartment, or box and check as luggage.

If you've got more than one child, you may want a two-seater to wheel them both at once. The model should be lightweight and maneuverable and not so wide that it can't fit through doorways or in the back of your car.

Fitness fans may want a large-wheeled sports stroller that will roll you and baby beautifully along trails, tracks, and paths. (It's good for the open road but a liability in a mall.)

You could decide, as some parents do, to purchase two strollers. A combination carriage/stroller will recline flat for the child's first six months to a year. The second, a more compact model, would carry you through the toddler and early preschool years, providing wheels for errands and trips that won't take up too much space.

Price and quality don't always match. As with most big-ticket baby products we discuss throughout this book, high price and good quality don't always go together. Over the years, rigorous stroller tests conducted in CONSUMER REPORTS' labs have shown that some economical strollers can perform equally as well or, in some cases, even better than models priced hundreds of dollars higher.

Even the most sophisticated models—regardless of how costly or ingenious—are prey to typical stroller flaws: malfunctioning wheels, frames that bend out of shape, locking mechanisms that fail, seat belts that come loose, or buckles that lose their holding power.

There are two kinds of lightweight strollers. A mini marvel, left, is light and packed with with features. Umbrella models are light and inexpensive, but can sometimes be flimsy.

The Latest Baby Wheels

Safety testing. The Juvenile Products Manufacturers Association (JPMA) sponsors a stroller certification program. Strollers are certified by an independent testing laboratory if they meet all of the requirements of a safety standard by the American Society of Testing and Materials (ASTM). (For testing specifics, see Product Recalls, page 259.)

Not all strollers on the market are certified. Uncertified models might be as safe as certified models, but there is no verification of that. All things being equal, go for the certified model.

You'll find the certification sticker on the stroller's frame or the carton. The sticker will state that the stroller has been tested "for compliance to ASTM F-833 safety standards for carriages/strollers." You can also call for a copy of JPMA's most recent directory of certified products (see the Resource Guide).

Judging a stroller. When you begin your stroller shopping, start with the inexpensive strollers and move along toward the plusher, more costly ones to see how additional features affect the price.

The difference between a high-quality stroller and a flimsier model isn't always easy to figure out. Here are some of the signs that a stroller has been poorly constructed:

The frame will feel rattley when you give the handlebar a good shaking. Metal components may be thin and have sharp, unfinished edges. You may spot roughly welded seams or uneven paint. The folding, opening, and reclining mechanisms may be stiff and uncooperative. The axle rod connecting the back wheels will appear thinner and thus be more apt to bend than the thick axles on better-quality models.

Thin, cheap fabric coverings have an insubstantial, rough feel. Interior padding, rather than thick and plush, will be loose and lumpy. Seat covers may sag because they don't fit the seat securely, and you may spot loose strings or uneven stitching.

Thin plastic components, such as the foot rest or brake tabs, may be uneven and warped or have ragged, unfinished edges left over from the molding process.

If there's a canopy, it will be thin and shallow. There may be little springiness or shock absorption from the wheels. Tires, instead of thick and cushioned, will be blown plastic or without treads.

Wheels may not contact the floor uniformly. The storage bin will appear flimsy and have thin, poorly attached flooring. The bottom of the bin may bow especially when filled, causing it to drag on the ground or scrape over curbs.

The safety belt and belt latch may appear weaker or do a poorer job of contacting baby's waist and crotch than those on well-designed models.

Taking a test drive. If you find models that appeal to you, don't hesitate to lift them off the shelves so you can examine each version more closely.

Next, take a few models on a brief test drive, steering with one hand for part of the trip. Check to see that the tires on all four wheels contact the floor and that the stroller rolls straight, with no veering, even with one-handed pushing. Press down on the handlebars to test how easily the model might tip over backward.

Locate the reclining mechanisms behind the seat and check the number of positions. Find the locks on the folding mechanisms (usually on both sides of the stroller), then try shutting the stroller down and latching it in the folded position. The task should at least be doable. (Tip: Fold back the canopy and make sure the seat back is in an upright position.)

Lift the stroller a few times to see if the weight is comfortable for you. Now open the stroller and lock it into position. Then press into the seat

Large strollers have deep canopies, wide seats, generous storage bins, but all these extras, plus the large wheels, can make these models cumbersome to use. **Midweights,** such as the one at right, are the typical workhorse stroller. **Carriage/ strollers** let a baby lie flat—but after a few months, you'll likely not need that feature.

padding, pinching to test thickness. Open and close the seat belts a few times, and pull on the belts when they're latched to test how well they hold.

Keep notes about your favorites, including the manufacturer's name, model name and number, and price. Give the model an informal grade—A+? B? F? Once you've rated about five models, you'll have a better idea of which features are important to you.

At this point in stroller shopping, many parents wade into deep waters. A salesperson may subtly (or not so subtly) try to steer you toward costlier models. And after spotting a lot of the flaws in poorer-quality designs, you may find yourself moving toward the strollers with the biggest price tags.

So it may be time for a reality test. Come back with a veteran parent and a good-sized tot and try out your favorites a second time. Some models may do well with very little weight inside but shimmy or be tough to steer with a real baby on board. And before you pull out your credit card, read on.

Stroller guarantees vs. warranties. A warranty is a promise to repair a stroller if it has any defects. A guarantee is something else entirely. It promises you'll be 100 percent satisfied with the stroller or get your money back. Most stroller manufacturers and retailers have warranties against poor workmanship and flaws inherent in the unit—but they won't guarantee to take the stroller back if you don't like it or if, say, a wheel falls off after a few months of wear and tear. So check the retailer's return policy before you buy.

Just as with crib mattresses, some manufacturers advertise huge warranties for their strollers—10 years, even a lifetime. Read the fine print. Most likely, the warranty is only for defects in workmanship, not for wheels that go bad, seats that tear, safety latches that fail, or axles that break after a year of use.

When parents try to cash in on their warranties, most manufacturers refer them back to the store for a replacement. Or the manufacturer may insist that you ship the stroller back for repair, at your expense. But repairs can take months, leaving you stranded without baby wheels. If the flaw is specific to the model, say, a weak component, you may face the same problem all over again with the repaired or replaced version.

Your best bet is to purchase the stroller from a store, catalog, or web site that stands firmly behind its products and has an open-ended customer-satisfaction policy, which gives you a better chance to return a lemon and get a satisfactory replacement.

Weight. Finding a stroller that will safely roll baby around with minimum discomfort for you isn't the only buying concern. There's also a "hidden discomfort factor"—the weight of the stroller itself. Remember, you'll be lifting, opening, and folding your child's stroller hundreds of times over the next four years. Stroller weights range from seven pounds to more than 50. You'll soon feel the stress of a too-heavy model.

A simple rule is to avoid any model that exceeds one-fourth your own body weight. Veteran parents warn newcomers to buy the lightest stroller you can afford without skimping on quality, safety, and comfort—either yours or your baby's. However, stroller lightness can be confusing. It can be a sure sign of weaker materials (a scrawny, no-frills umbrella stroller weighing seven pounds, $15), or it could signal extraordinary design sophistication (an option-packed, high-quality import—seven pounds, $150), so size up total construction along with weight.

Some manufacturers reduce stroller weight by molding the frame from more costly airplane-quality aluminum instead of readily available steel. Even though two strollers may appear identical, the aluminum-framed model, equally as sturdy as the steel, will weigh two to five pounds less—and cost more.

What adds weight? Frame size and a large, spacious seat both put on pounds. And every convenience increases not only the cost of a stroller but also the load you push: additional seat padding, front bar or tray with toys, bigger storage bin, larger wheels, handlebar cup holder, more intricate folding mechanism, reversible handles, bigger canopy.

Judging stroller weights in the store may not be easy. You can simply lift a folded stroller several times and compare one unit to another. Or sometimes a stroller's weight is printed as part of its description on the side of the shipping carton. You can also call the manufacturer's customer service number and ask. (See the Resource Guide, page 292.)

Sometimes, though, convenience can supersede weight issues. Most parents we've interviewed are very enthusiastic about infant car seat/stroller travel systems. The combos, which allow you to remove baby's car seat from the installed base in the car and snap it onto a specially adapted midweight stroller, make it possible to move your tot without waking him. Car seat, base and stroller are all sold as one unit for around $150. The stroller's weight with a car seat attached is 32 to 44 pounds. When baby is ready for a regular stroller, you can use it without the car seat attached. (For CONSUMER REPORTS' ratings of travel systems, see pages 84 to 88.)

However, there are lighter routes to travel. You could secure your baby in a tetherable convertible seat (around $100). It will stay fastened in the

Hands free

Invest in a fanny pack (or belt pack) to hold your absolute minimum needs so you'll have both hands available for your child and you won't have to carry a purse.

car, and offer crash protection until she's nearly age four. Outside the car, baby can ride in a reclining "mini-marvel" stroller ($150 and up) that weighs only 10 pounds and will leave you a lot more storage room in your trunk. It also puts less pressure on back and shoulders than a hefty midweight.

Umbrella strollers

In the bantam ring (under 12 pounds) are umbrella strollers available from companies such as Cosco, Delta, Baby Trend, and J. Mason. (Some have umbrellalike, curved handles.) Prices start under $20 for a simple no-frills model made with metal tubing and equipped with a pouchlike, suspended fabric seat. Seat belts may be just two straps attached to the stroller frame on either side. Rear-wheel brakes are simple but operational. For a few extra bucks, you get an ersatz canopy—a piece of fabric strung between two wires—and possibly a padded seat offering firmer back support for baby.

Umbrellas are inexpensive, lightweight, and fold easily and compactly, and you can roll one behind you in the folded position, an advantage for buses, malls, and airports. If you're going shopping, they fit in the fitting room. Many parents consider these strollers a stopgap measure. If something goes wrong—as it most likely will—they figure they can toss out the broken one and buy another.

Poor durability is the biggest disadvantage—it may take several umbrellas to get through one baby's stroller phase. Wheels wobble out of line or fall off. Frames bend under everyday stresses. Fabrics can stretch or tear, and seat belts fray or pull loose.

Instability can be a problem. Pressing down too hard on the handles or looping a pocketbook or shopping bag over them can tip the stroller over backward with baby inside. Some models have frames with dangerous X joints (where metal tubes cross each other), which could capture and bruise a child's hands during folding.

Most seats simply aren't comfortable for any length of time. Pouch models cause young babies to slump forward, and without a foot rest, children's legs hang suspended from a thin fabric rim that leaves a noticeable pressure stripe.

What's available

The following are a few examples of economical lightweights offering adequate back support or other niceties. However, stability and durability may still be a problem.

Delta Enterprise (Delta Luv) makes the Road Runner (Model 113-17, $25) with umbrella-style handlebars, a steel frame, swiveling front wheels, a soft front bar for baby and an underseat storage bin.

J. Mason Skedaddle (Models 3850 and 3953, $20 to $25, 8 pounds) also has swivel wheels and a larger underside storage bin than the other models. It's easy to open and fold, and can fit into a plane's overhead luggage bin.

Kolcraft Reclining Umbrella Stroller (Model 36506, $35, 12 pounds), a typical X-frame, has umbrella-style handles. The seat offers firm back support for baby, can be reclined 45 degrees, and has a small canopy.

The mini-marvels

Highly sophisticated lightweights—all imports—weigh the same as umbrella models but are in an entirely different design league. Name brands are Combi, Peg Perego, Aprica, and Maclaren. Most have 40 or more interacting parts and price tags that reflect the complexity—$150 to $350 each.

They have numerous special features: thick padding, reclining seats, adjustable sun canopies, strong seat belts with crotch straps, sturdy buckles, and easy-to-operate brakes. Most wheel assemblies have built-in, spring-action shock absorbers. Dual front wheels swivel for quick turns and can also be locked into a forward-facing position for uneven terrain.

But perhaps the greatest feature is the spring-action folding mechanism. A quick release of the safety locks and a squeeze of the frame, and everything is locked compactly for trunk, luggage bin, or closet. Opening is equally impressive—release the safety catches, jerk back the frame using the handles, and the unit is ready to ride.

Their biggest drawback is the aforementioned price. Handling takes some practice—their "loosey goosey" frames make them feel more fragile than they really are. The small wheels don't perform well on uneven sidewalks or rough terrain. One downside of their compact size is the narrow shoulder and seat dimensions of some that can cramp preschoolers, particularly in bulky winter wear. Plus, their underseat bins offer less storage than larger strollers.

What's available

The following examples have particularly useful options. (No Maclaren models were included, as the company is renegotiating its U.S. distribution arm.)

Aprica's Sprint Royale (Models 746, 747, and 843, $219, 9 pounds) offers

Records

Use the back of a copy of your child's birth certificate to record childhood diseases and their dates of occurrence.

easy one-handed opening and closing. It has a handlebar rather than umbrella handles, and its swivel wheels can be locked into a forward-facing position. The reclining seat is fully cushioned; and there's a large fold-down canopy, a small mesh storage bin underneath, and a removable front arm rest. The stroller stands by itself when folded.

Combi Savvy strollers (Ultra Savvy, $279, 9 pounds) fold with one hand using a handlebar release, and offer a fully reclining three-position seat, canopy, removable front guard rail, and swiveling front wheels. These strollers are compact, simple to fold, and open with a crisp, spring action.

Peg Perego PlikoMatic lightweight umbrella strollers (Models QP41, RC41, RN41, RI41, $200, 17 pounds) have a spring-assisted, easy-to-open chassis and a four-position reinforced backrest. They're wider than most of the lightweights—useful if you've got a large tot. The front wheels swivel or lock into a forward-facing position.

The midweights

Weighing between 17 and 35 pounds, these are the everyday workhorses of the baby world. They're moderately priced: Basic models run between $70 and $110, step-up features are added in increments of $20 or so.

Their overall feel is heavier, bulkier, and more stable than mini-marvels. Thanks to dual tires on both front wheels, rolling and cornering are smooth and predictable. Some models have hard plastic wheels, but most have dense foam tires to soften baby's ride. Front wheel assemblies have built-in, shock-absorbing springs, and upper-end models may offer shocks on all wheels. Swiveling front wheels can be locked into a forward-only position with foot tabs on most models, so they won't wobble over uneven sidewalks or rocky gravel.

At best, folding is awkward, usually requiring two separate actions—simultaneously squeezing two release mechanisms on the sides of the frame, or releasing first one latch, then another. (Two-step folding is designed to prevent accidental collapsing when baby's inside.) Some better-engineered types balance upright on wheels and frame when folded—handy for airport lines and closets.

Midweights' interiors are deeper and roomier than those of lighter-weight strollers. Even bottom-line models have padded seat coverings that are removable for gentle laundering. Reclining seatbacks offer two to three positions, from upright to nearly total recline.

Folding down the seat requires removing baby and then adjusting the release bar, usually found in back of the seat. In the reclined position, your baby's head and body should be completely enclosed by padding, with no gaps or exposed frame pieces that could lead to dangerous entrapment.

Unlike the two curved handles of umbrella-type handlebars, most mid-weights have a single crossbar, making single-handed pushing easier. Handlebar heights are comfortable for average-sized parents, but taller parents may have to bend over to push, or may find themselves accidentally kicking the wheels or back axle.

Seat belts securely enclose a baby's waist, and most include a between-the-legs crotch strap so baby can't slide out the front. Foot rests also fold up and lock, shutting off the leg holes and keeping small babies from sliding through and becoming entrapped.

Brakes are efficient, engaged by pressing down with your foot on tabs just above each back wheel, or on a bar on the back of the frame. Tiered canopies shield baby from sun or rain, and you'll find spacious, mesh-sided storage bins on the underside for baby paraphernalia or shopping bags.

The extras money can buy. Stepping up from the lowest price point, you get wider seats and deeper padding. Some models offer a removable front restraining bar or play tray; a handlebar cup holder and coin tray for parents; and a clear vinyl window in the canopy so you can check on baby.

A bigger investment buys larger wheels, which make it easier to push or maneuver over curbs, but add bulk to the folded stroller. Other add-ons include springier shock absorbers and thicker handlebar cushioning for parents. And some models from Evenflo, Graco, and Kolcraft have handlebars that can be extended or angled to fit different parent heights. These companies also offer models with reversible handlebars, which swing over the top of the stroller, then lock into a front position so baby rides facing you. But this option adds pounds to the stroller and is useful only when baby is less than a year old—toddlers usually prefer facing outward.

Top-of-the-line models exchange shallow, square-shaped canopies for deeper, rounded "European-style" versions with decorative fabric piping. The added ribs and extra fabric allow these canopies to shield almost the entire front of the stroller. Some models have boots in stroller-matching fabrics to snap over baby's legs for added warmth. A few have a weather bubble, which completely protects baby from rain and wind—but at a substantial price increase. You can buy generic boots and rain shields in baby

No Shocks

Take along a few electrical outlet covers as a traveling child-proofing measure if you'll be staying at a hotel or in the homes of others who might not have them.

boutiques and large baby retail chains, a much less expensive move than paying for a top-of-the line stroller to get them.

These mainstream models are sturdy, faithful, affordable performers, easiest to steer and roll of all weight categories. However, some parents regret not buying a lighter, more portable model. When folded, these units can completely monopolize a small car's trunk. Features may sometimes be hard to use, requiring you to bend, grope, and squeeze to make them work. Some safety problems have occurred: Accidental collapsing has caused baby hand injuries, and some babies have gotten caught by the neck in leg holes and died. Most flaws are being aggressively addressed through federal monitoring and voluntary safety standards. (See Product Recalls, page 270.)

What's available

These representative models have serviceable features and are mid-priced. (For detailed results of CONSUMER REPORTS' testing and rating of mid-weight strollers for travel systems, see pages 86 to 88.)

Century Products Euro Adventure All-Terrain Stroller (Model 11-325, $109, 25 pounds) has a wider seat than many midweights, making it suitable for bigger-than-average tots. But the nonremovable front tray sits too high for smaller children, although it does fold down to allow easier entry. The stroller's elongated, curved handlebar comes with a detachable cup holder. The seat offers a two-position recline and padded cushion removable for washing. The canopy is also removable. Swiveling dual wheels in the front can be locked in the forward-facing position, and there's spring suspension on all wheels.

Cosco Explorer All-Terrain Stroller (Model 01-875, $100, 24 pounds) has an elongated, curved handlebar with detachable accessory tray. The seat has two reclining positions, and padding removable for laundering. You'll find a large canopy with a zippered weather shield, and a storage bin below the seat, but no side arms, front bar, or tray. The large-sized wheels have swivel locks.

Graco LiteRider (Models 6955, 6957, 6959, $60 to $70, 20 pounds) has an ergonomically designed handle and large wheels with front swivel and suspension. The seat has a two-position recline and there's a large, rounded canopy with clear plastic viewing window for the parent to keep an eye on baby. This model includes an extra-large storage basket and relatively easy-to-operate folding mechanism.

Kolcraft Catalina (Model 46520, $80, 22½ pounds) has thickly padded seat and arms, padded front bar, and large underneath storage bin. Its telescoping and reversible handle makes pushing more comfortable for tall parents and allows baby to face Mom or Dad. The seat offers multiple reclining positions and a removable, washable seat pad. The stroller's large wheels have shock absorbers and swivel locks.

Baby Safe

Strollers must be gap-free and stable

Babies and toddlers face different injury risks in strollers. Tots under seven months old may get their arms, legs, or head captured in unprotected gaps in the sides of the stroller frame when the seat is reclined. They may also wriggle out one leg opening and get hanged in the process. Toddlers may try to stand up inside a stroller, resulting in a fall or a stroller tip-over. If the stroller accidentally collapses or if they're playing nearby when you fold the stroller, children of any age can catch and injure their hands at the juncture of frame parts.

• When the back of the seat is fully reclined, the inside of the stroller should be well shielded on all sides by a fabric covering. Most midweight and larger strollers offer a way to enclose leg holes, too, either by folding up and locking a foot rest or by snapping a fabric closure across the two holes.

• Test a stroller in the store to be sure it locks securely in the upright position.

• Get a model with a sturdy seat belt and a crotch strap, and fasten your child in every time. If you have a very active toddler, buy an extra harness, the kind that fastens over the shoulders too.

• Strictly follow weight limits set by the manufacturer, and never put two kids in a stroller meant for only one.

• Store the stroller when you're not using it, and keep tots clear of it when they're not riding. Children can injure themselves if they fall against the frame.

• Open and fold it away from your tot so there's no risk of caught or pinched fingers.

• Don't reverse the handle or recline the seat while baby's inside. The stroller could collapse or baby could get caught.

• Carrying the stroller with a child inside is dangerous; tripping is a real possibility.

• Be particularly cautious when pushing the stroller out in front of you into traffic—especially when you are emerging from between two parked cars.

• Never leave your baby or toddler unattended in a stroller, especially when she's sleeping. (Even in a stroller or carriage, babies should always sleep faceup.)

Dress up

Put a small treat such as a raisin or piece of dry cereal into your child's hand so he or she will make a fist to push through a sleeve.

Carriage/strollers

At the top of the weight chain are carriage/stroller combinations and carriage-only models. These posh sedans feature cozy, completely enclosed sleeping spaces for small babies. They can later be converted into upright seats for forward-facing toddlers and preschoolers. Some old-fashioned carriage models offer only the enclosed bed options without a seat, or they supply a separate seat that has to be fastened onto the frame once the bassinet portion of the carriage has been removed.

The generous bassinet portion of a carriage/stroller will be needed only during baby's first six months. (A baby shouldn't be allowed to sit up in the bed portion.) The freestanding bassinet feature of some models could come in handy when separated from the unit.

Some parents like the springy, soothing way big carriages can be rocked and rolled when baby is fussy—even indoors. Big wheels do make rolling a breeze, even over rough surfaces. But nonswiveling wheels on large carriages make maneuvering difficult in tight spaces, and raising them over high curbs can be a struggle.

Sometimes weighing in at over 50 pounds, these stroller/carriages are just too bulky and heavy for everyday use. You'll want only one if you're planning on long, leisurely strolls, have plenty of trunk and indoor storage space, and won't have to repeatedly heft the thing up and down stairs or in and out of your car. Plus, they carry huge price tags—hundreds of dollars more than mid- and lightweight strollers.

What's available

The following stroller/carriage combinations were chosen for their convenience features and well-padded bedding areas.

Aprica Super Zap EP/LX (Model 981, $345, 11 pounds) doesn't really belong in the heavyweight category as such. It offers the features of most carriage-style stroller giants but without the heaviness, because the Zap is made with an aluminum frame. Features include triple-layered head support; a double-padded seat with removable, washable cover; a removable front bar; and a height-adjustable handlebar. The unit opens and shuts from the handle. There are dual wheels on front and back, a full hood, and a removable cold-weather boot but a very small underside bin. The Zap stands independently when folded.

Evenflo Pacesetter Carriage Stroller (Model 4961F9, $130 to $140, 34 pounds) has an extendable handlebar with vertical handhold in the center for one-handed pushing, plus a cup holder for parent and a removable, front snack tray for baby. The seat has padding and a deep canopy, and the seat back completely reclines into a fully enclosed area for baby. The foot rest can be locked to shield leg holes during napping. An underneath storage bin slides out. Wheels swivel or lock in the forward-facing position.

Graco Carriage Stroller (Model 7855, $40, 35 pounds) has a three-position, height-adjustable handlebar. There's a padded, removable front arm rest for baby and a large canopy. The seat offers multiple reclining positions, including full recline; and the cushioned seat pad and head supports are removable for washing. There's a storage bin underneath. Double balloon tires both front and rear can swivel or lock into the forward-facing position. Also included is an all-weather boot.

Peg Perego Milano (Model 41, $359, 20 pounds) is a well-cushioned, roomy carriage/stroller with a lightweight aluminum chassis, swivel wheels, and a removable basket. It easily converts into a stroller.

DOUBLE AND TRIPLE SEATERS

Most companies that manufacture regular strollers also make a version with two seats. A couple of companies also offer giant three-seaters.

There are basically two kinds of two-seaters. Side-by-side models are like two strollers joined into one, with two seats next to each other on a single large frame. Tandem strollers, on the other hand, have long profiles, with one seat directly in back of the other. Parents usually prefer tandems because they are slim enough to go through standard 36-inch doorways, something most side-by-sides can't do.

While a side-by-side stroller works well for twins or children approximately the same weight, tandems can accommodate children of two different weights, with the heaviest in the front and the smaller one in the back.

Side-by-side features. Side-by-sides balance best when both children can sit upright. (Tandems work fine if the child in the back needs to be reclined—but not as well if the front child wants that, too.)

Although manufacturers may promise that the stroller is slender enough to go through doorways, measure for yourself. Get the dimensions from one side of the frame to the other, and also from wheel hub to wheel hub. Anything over 29 inches wide could cause headaches. As with any stroller, seat belts should securely contact each child at the waist, there should be good brakes, and the model should offer steering and folding ease.

Separate canopies, one for each seat, are a plus.

If you want a side-by-side stroller that can be separated—for carrying one child at a time or squeezing through tight spaces—consider separate brackets that can join two lightweights together. Prince Lionheart Stroller Connectors (Style #6550, $10 to $12) are three plastic brackets (two for the bottom, one for near the handlebars) that connect most strollers and can be removed with a squeeze release.

Tandem features. In contrast to side-by-sides, tandems are the same width as most single-passenger strollers—but they're definitely more difficult to steer than single models.

Different models vary substantially in quality, design, and durability. Usually the rider in the back seat gets the short end of the deal. Poorly constructed models will have virtually no leg room for the back seat and limited leg support. While the back seat can recline fairly well, the front seat can't tip back all the way without infringing on the space (and sometimes the safety) of the rear rider.

Some heavier and more costly tandems have completely removable

Two-seaters are handy when you've got two kids. This model is designed for putting the heavier child in front and the smaller baby in back. Tandems with **side-by-side** seats work better for children of roughly the same weight.

seats that can be faced child-to-child, toward the parent, or toward the front.

If you can't afford a tandem right away and need a simple solution for toting twins or a pair of young children, try putting the smaller of your two in a front or back carrier (see Chapter 5) and pushing the other child in a lightweight stroller.

SHOPPING SAVVY Tandems and side-by-sides

Weigh the pros and cons as you size up your choices. A tandem is easier to maneuver, particularly with one hand, but a side-by-side stroller goes over curbs more easily. A tandem will steer reasonably well with only one baby inside, but uneven weighting on a side-by-side may cause veering. A folded tandem takes up little more space than a single-occupancy model, while a folded side-by-side unit normally requires twice as much storage space. If you're into jogging, you might want to check out two-seater sports strollers as another option.

What's available

Cosco Two Ways Tandem Stroller (Model 01-644, $120, 31 pounds) has a reversible front seat so your kids can face each other. The padded back seat reclines for an infant. Each seat has its own individual canopy; the one over the rear seat has a vinyl see-through window, and the front seat canopy can be unzipped in the back to give the rear passenger a better view. The seats recline, and there's a storage bin under the rear seat. (Note: Some models may have a folding-mechanism flaw. See Product Recalls.)

Graco Lightweight DuoRider (Model 6555, $129.99, 27 pounds) is a side-by-side with individual reclining seats, extra-large separate storage baskets underneath, a large quilted canopy, and two removable padded arm bars. It has a large, curved handlebar and dual front swivel wheels.

Kolcraft Lil' Limo (Model 46640, $125, 28 pounds) is a tandem with a lightweight steel frame. Its two seat backs recline independently, the front bar is removable, and the two canopies are adjustable. There's a mesh storage bin underneath. There are swivel locks for dual front wheels, and the unit stands by itself in the folded position.

SPORTS STROLLERS

Sports or running strollers are large-wheeled (12 to 20 inches in diameter) strollers that are more closely related to bicycles than to traditional low-to-the-ground baby buggies. They're huge, don't fold readily, and aren't meant for maneuvering in malls or tight, crowded spaces.

Most buyers are fitness buffs who want to run with baby, introducing the child to fitness and the joys of the outdoors early on. A smaller percentage of parents buy one of these high-profile strollers just for taking brisk walks. Sports strollers are easier to roll than standard models, and can conquer snow piles, uneven sidewalks, and rocky trails.

Their cost, between $100 and $400, depends mostly on wheel size. The bigger the wheels, the easier they are to roll—and the higher the price tag. Models with the largest wheels are for dedicated runners willing to put up with their bulk for the rolling ease. Accessories, such as canopies or storage pouches, may be included in the purchase price or sold separately for some units.

Like bicycle frames, sports strollers are constructed from welded metal tubing. Their three large wheels with spokes—one wheel in front, two in the rear—have rubber, air-inflated bicycle-type tires with inner tubes, and some have ball bearings. Bicycle-style hand brakes, positioned on the rear

High bicycle-style wheels and a tall profile make a sports stroller a great way to cover ground outdoors. They're impractical for close quarters, however, and wheels have to be removed before the frame will fit in a typical car trunk.

handlebar, can be used to slow or stop the stroller. Most models also offer a solid locking mechanism to keep the stroller immobile, a safety advantage when loading and unloading your small passenger. The wheels are removable for stroller storage in a trunk or closet.

It makes sense to delay investing in a sports stroller until you know you're ready to return to former fitness routines. Some parents find they regret the purchase. Instead of the post-baby exuberance they anticipated, they feel zapped by around-the-clock baby demands. The giant stroller then becomes an onerous symbol of what they don't want to do anymore—at least for a while.

Postponing your purchase makes sense for your baby, too. Some safety experts recommend waiting until your child is at least a year old to run with him, because of the jarring and the lack of good seat support of most models. Even sports stroller manufacturers suggest waiting until your baby is at least a month-and-a-half old.

Once you start using the stroller, don't forget to dress your baby for the weather outside. Even though you'll heat up as you run, your baby's temperature will be vulnerable to the outside air.

SHOPPING SAVVY Sports strollers

Look for a deep seat with a sturdy, five-point seat belt (straps for a child's shoulders, waist, and crotch); responsive brakes; a sun-shielding canopy; a wrist strap to hold the stroller if you accidentally let go of the handlebars; and a storage pouch for diapers and other paraphernalia.

Some manufacturers of standard strollers have jumped into the sports stroller market with smaller versions of three-wheelers. These units may not be as stable, or as easy to run with, as the larger models produced by a handful of single-focus companies.

Check the comfort of the handlebar heights. Some knock-offs position theirs too low or too close to the back wheels for jogging comfort, or they may have a rear axle (the metal rod that connects the tires) like a standard stroller—which you could kick when in full stride.

The seat should be at a comfortable angle for both babies and young children and offer adequate leg support without cutting into the back of a child's legs. Check the welding of the frame and the mechanisms for removing the wheels, and be sure the overall weight of the unit isn't too heavy for your comfort when moving fast.

What's available

Below are brief descriptions of the sports stroller lines from the two main manufacturers in the field, whose products are most widely available. For retail shopping information and price updates, contact the manufacturers directly, using the Resource Guide on page 292.

The Kool-Stop Kool Stride line offers the option of steel wheels (stroller weight 22 pounds) or aluminum alloy wheels (stroller weight 19 pounds). Prices range from $250 to $400. The Senior model has a curved, cushioned handle for parent comfort and a hand brake for slowing or immobile parking. Kool Stride offers a retractable canopy with a peekaboo window as standard equipment and features a zippered reclining unit for the baby's seat. There's a tether wrist strap to prevent runaways. The Junior version is smaller. A two-seater is also available.

The Baby Jogger Co. models range in price from $225 for Baby Jogger II-12 with 12-inch wheels, to $277 for 16-inch wheels, to $292 for Baby Jogger II-20 with 20-inch wheels. The easy-rolling wheels have sealed bearings and are removed by a tab release. (Earlier jogger models had small wing nuts for the wheels that could be ingested by babies.) The brake features a lock button for parking. Baby Joggers continue to put in the miles with few quality problems. Accessories, such as canopies, may be priced separately. Models with 16-inch wheels, two seaters (the Twinner II), and triple seaters (the Triple Jogger) are also available.

BICYCLE TRAILERS

These two-wheeled carts, designed to be towed behind a bicycle, have two bicycle-type wheels and a long hitching arm that fastens onto the bicycle's chain assembly or seat post. Trailers give the impression of being safer than bicycle-mounted baby seats, since kids are seated, strapped in, and enclosed inside a zippered compartment. Bicycle-mounted seats can make a bike unstable and hard to mount and dismount.

However, several recent recalls by the U.S. Consumer Product Safety Commission have underscored the fact that bicycle trailers have safety problems, too. Using the trailer on streets with passing cars intensifies the typical risks of bicycling. The low, unfamiliar profile of the trailers may blind motorists to them, particularly in limited light.

On some trailers, metal fatigue has caused failure at the pivot bracket of the hitching arm, allowing the trailer to swing loose from the bicycle and causing passenger injuries. Trailers can be vulnerable to turning over, particularly when there are abrupt sharp turns or when one wheel goes over a bump during a turn. As a bike speeds up, braking becomes harder, especially on wet surfaces. The trailers can also get snagged by passing bushes and objects.

SHOPPING SAVVY Bicycle trailers

Although some sports stroller manufacturers have conversion kits for turning one of their heavy strollers into a trailer, we recommend purchasing a dedicated bicycle trailer rather than trying to rig a stroller to your bike.

Select a model with clear assembly instructions and follow them carefully. The hitching arm should have a secondary backup to prevent it from accidentally breaking loose. Check the wheel mounting to be sure that it will hold securely. The interior of the trailer should offer comfortable seating for children, and storage pockets are helpful. A zippered front shield can help to keep mud from splattering onto the passengers. But if the model has a rain shield that encloses the entire cabin, make certain there's some form of ventilation.

For safety's sake, trailers should be considered off-road vehicles, used only in parks and on safe trails without the risk of car/bicycle encounters. For maximum protection, all child passengers should wear a well-fitted hel-

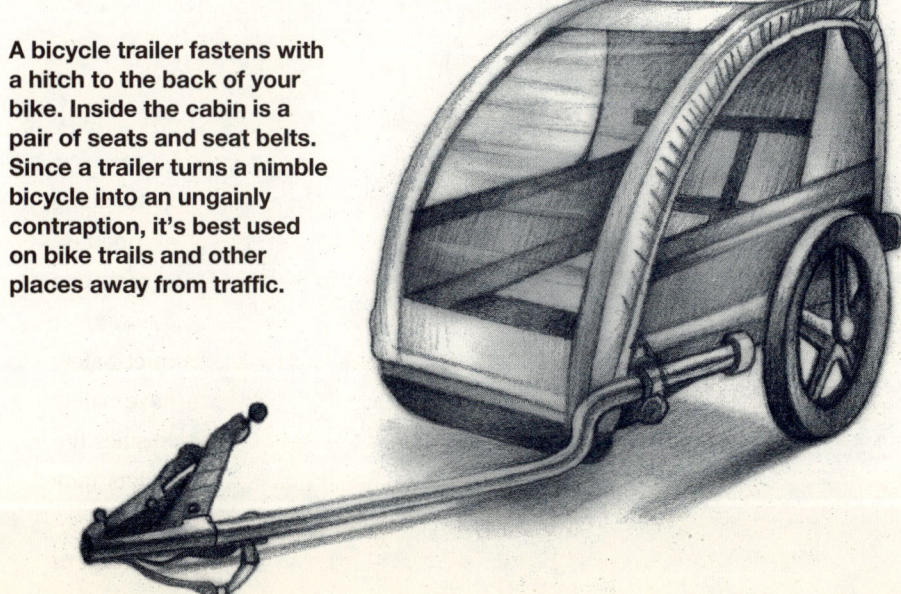

A bicycle trailer fastens with a hitch to the back of your bike. Inside the cabin is a pair of seats and seat belts. Since a trailer turns a nimble bicycle into an ungainly contraption, it's best used on bike trails and other places away from traffic.

The Latest Baby Wheels

met and harnesses. And follow the manufacturer's recommended weight and size limitations for passengers.

What's available

These represent the two best-known brands. As with the sports strollers, we suggest calling the companies directly (listed in the Resource Guide, page 292) to discuss model options and request printed literature. Some companies manufacture trailers especially for handicapped children as well.

Burley Solo ($265, 16 pounds) is lightweight and narrow (25 inches wide), designed for use with a single child weighing up to 60 pounds. It has a bolted aluminum frame with 16-inch plastic wheels. The inside seat offers a clear view from sides and front.

CycleTote Family ($395, 25 pounds) holds one or two children in fully adjustable 5-point seat harnesses. It has a welded aluminum frame and center-pull hitch; accepts 26-inch bicycle wheels; and has a low center of gravity, dual roll bars, a canopy, and a vinyl weather cover. This mail-order trailer can be a task to assemble. An automatic braking system and sports-stroller conversion are options available for $275 and $100.

Chapter

BABY-CARRYING CONVENIENCE

Baby carriers keep you and baby close—and keep your hands free. Check for baby safety and your own comfort.

All babies love and need to be carried. Carrying soothes them and offers the close physical contact and gentle walking rhythms they crave. But it's hard to get very much done when you're holding a baby all the time. So from ancient times until today parents have tied babies on their fronts or backs with animal skins or knotted pieces of fabric, and thus had their hands free.

Carriers can't make your baby any lighter but a well-designed model will help distribute your baby's weight more evenly on your shoulders and back. And thickly padded straps and a waist belt or other support features will ease the strain of carrying.

There are three basic types of baby carriers: slings, strap-on soft carriers, and framed back carriers. Slings, made of pleated fabric, are worn over one shoulder, forming a small hammock in front for holding baby. Strap-on soft carriers fasten to a parent's front or back with adjustable shoulder and waist straps. Framed back carriers are basically backpacks with a fabric baby seat.

Slings and strap-on soft carriers are especially useful during the early weeks and months after birth. Fussy babies can often be calmed by riding in a carrier as a parent walks. Framed carriers are great between the time babies can sit up and when they become secure walkers. The pack helps a

Contents

Shopping savvy, page 112

Slings, page 114

Soft carriers, page 115

Back carriers, page 118

tot feel close to you, and gives him a bird's-eye view of the world from over your shoulder.

Manufacturers have specific weight limits for babies riding in their carriers. Soft carriers are useful from birth, whereas backpacks require that a child be able to sit up unassisted (about six months of age). The upper limit of the carriers ranges between 20 and 40 pounds (around three years of age).

You'll probably find your child too heavy to carry long before he reaches the upper weight limit of most carriers. A simple rule is to stop using a carrier when a baby reaches approximately one-fourth of your own body weight. And by the time your child gets that heavy, she probably won't want to be confined on your back anyway. In fact, she'll demand to be put down to explore the world on her own.

Carrier designs vary from very simple with little padding and a few adjustment features to more elaborate models with extra padding, reinforced back supports for baby, foam-padded pelvic belts for parents (to help distribute weight from shoulders to the hip-girdle area), and numerous straps and latches for adjusting fit. Most have removable, washable flannel bibs. And some offer extra pouches or pockets.

Slings and soft carriers are made from a variety of fabrics—including cottons, corduroys, flannel-like materials, and moisture-resistant nylons—and in a large variety of colors and patterns. Backpacks are usually constructed of thicker materials that resemble canvas or suitcase fabrics and come in more muted colors, such as navy blue or dark green.

Expect to feel awkward the first few times you use any kind of carrier. First, you have to figure out how to put it on. Then, you've got to adjust the straps or fabric to fit your body comfortably. But the real test is safely getting your baby inside without upsetting her. Carrier manufacturers recommend practicing getting the carrier on and the baby inside by using a doll or teddy bear until all steps become comfortable.

Learning how to move with a carrier will take practice. You can't lean over, and you have to adjust to the extra weight on your back, shoulders, and legs. Plus, you've got to be mindful of your extra dimensions when you walk through doorways and around corners so you don't run baby into anything.

SHOPPING SAVVY Carriers

Comfort—yours and your baby's—is an important factor. Consider your baby's weight in comparison to your own size before purchasing a carrier.

A tall, strong parent will probably manage carrying a baby or toddler comfortably for a longer time than a short, slender parent. If you're carrying a too-heavy load, the carrier straps will cut into your shoulders, and you'll feel off-balance and achy when carrying—and even achier later.

All carriers tend to be awkward and difficult to put on until you get the knack of it. The only way to find out how your baby will respond to a carrier is to try one on with him inside, preferably before you buy it. (Read the directions carefully before you try to put baby inside.) Babies may hate being in certain carriers, usually because their heads are confined.

Shoulder straps should be thickly padded and close enough together to stay in place without slipping, but not so close together that they dig into your neck. If you're trying on a frame carrier, walk with it to make certain that the frame doesn't hit the back of your head.

Seats should have snaps that allow them to adjust to larger sizes and leg holes wide enough that they don't bind your baby's legs, but not so wide that a baby could slip through one hole. (See Product Recalls on page 271 for an example of overly large leg holes.)

Slings for the smallest infants carry them face in, close to your chest. When a baby is bigger, they can travel face out in a **soft carrier,** shown here, or a **framed carrier.** Good padding at the shoulders and extra support at the waist help make carrying baby more comfortable.

Baby-Carrying Convenience

Any latches or fasteners should be easy to use and hold securely without slipping. Since you'll probably have your baby in one arm when you're putting on or taking off the carrier, be sure that clasps, especially those that fasten in the back, can be opened with a single hand.

Front carriers should be completely washable. The fabrics on backpacks should be moisture-resistant and wipe clean with a mild detergent.

A SLING CREATES A BABY 'NEST'

A baby sling is an over-the-shoulder front "hammock" made from ample pleats of fabric. The sling's length typically adjusts with two O-shaped rings worn on one side, near the collarbone.

Veteran sling wearers often say they feel a sling carries a baby in a more natural, comfortable position than other soft carriers. Rather than sitting upright, the baby rides in a semireclined position with a rounded back—closer to a fetal position. And babies can remain in the sling for discreet nursing. Slings are also used by parents as an extra support for a toddler straddling one hip.

There's an art to adjusting a sling so both you and your baby are comfortable. The foam-padded section at one end of the sling isn't for the baby (as most parents assume) but for cushioning the mother's neck and shoulder area. And the rings aren't simple fasteners as they appear, but actually allow you to cinch or tighten various parts of the sling and release others, so baby is comfortably positioned and the sling doesn't pull on your neck and shoulders.

Coaching from an experienced sling wearer helps. Plus, sling makers give directions on how to use their product—how to put it on and adjust it, and where to put the baby. For maximum comfort, the baby should ride above the waist and below the bustline. You may want to cradle your baby with your arm while he's inside the carrier, until both of you get used to the feel of the sling. Walking around and talking to baby helps, too.

But mastering adjustment of rings, pleats, and rims so everything fits correctly takes time and patience. You may experience some back and neck discomfort from carrying most of a baby's weight on one side. Fabric can slip out of the rings unless there's a built-in stopper, such as another ring or plastic rod. The sling offers no safety straps or crotch to prevent a toddler from wriggling out. Once your baby can sit up on her own, you may decide you like a strap-on carrier or backpack better.

What's available

This list will help you compare features.

NoJo Original Baby Sling Soft Baby Carrier ($40) is made from cotton fabric with thickly padded edges and has a sewn-in shoulder/neck pad. The carrier adjusts by cinching one end of the fabric between two rings to tighten it. A small plastic rod at the end keeps the sling from accidentally coming loose.

Over the Shoulder Baby Carrier ($29 to $39) is made from soft cotton fabric in dozens of designer fabrics, and has padded edges. There's a double ring for adjusting the length and curvature of the sling to accommodate any size parent and baby. It has a third safety ring to prevent the sling from coming unbuckled. Directions are detailed and easy to follow.

Prenatal Cradle Natural Embrace sling ($50) has no latches or buckles to fiddle with. It's made from a single piece of soft, stretchy, fleece fabric. (It is also made in a cooler fabric for summer or warm climates.) The sling edges are sewn together at shoulder level, and the rims of the hammock are foam-cushioned. It's sized petite, small, medium, and large, and folds against the shoulder to form a soft, lightweight pillow. Some mothers of twins have used one on each side like saddlebags. Directions are clear.

Prince Lionheart Koala Sling (Model 0626, $39 to $44) is larger than other versions and constructed of a somewhat coarse, canvas-like cotton. Both the edges of the sling and the baby's hammock are padded. Rather than a cinching-fabric system like the Over the Shoulder and NoJo Original baby slings, the Koala has two long straps, which adjust the length by pulling on the strap that's doubled through the buckle. There's no stopper to prevent the strap from sliding loose.

Blankie

Cut a favorite blanket in half as soon as the child becomes attached to it, and whisk the dirty half away for laundering when the child's not around. With luck, the child will never realize there are two blankets.

STRAP-ON SOFT CARRIERS

Pouch carriers are designed for small babies and lightweight toddlers. Before you put one on, you might be intimidated by the octopus-like appearance of all the straps, sashes, and latches. So first look for the cushioning on the dangling straps—that's the shoulder padding. Most units have a strap for each shoulder; the two crisscross in the back. The other straps are for the parent's waist, or for securing the baby's seat in an upright position. Usually the carrier's packaging demonstrates how the carrier is worn. Printed directions and safety warnings are inside the box.

Some soft carriers are relatively easy to buckle or tie on, but others require practice and skill to use. Look for ease of use, a seat that adjusts to different baby sizes, leg-hole cushioning, a padded back and head support, and a removable and washable burper bib.

Carriers have two advantages over slings: The seat with a crotch is safer for tots—slings lack this built-in protection against slipping out or falling; and carrier straps and waist belts also distribute a baby's weight more evenly on your body than slings do.

But they hold young babies in an upright position, which the baby may or may not like, rather than a curled, semireclined position as allowed by slings. And they offer less structural support for babies over six months and for wearers than framed back carriers.

PACKS AND SLINGS ARE SECURE

- Examine the pack closely to be sure that it will fit your baby comfortably (it should not bind or scratch around the baby's legs). Packs for younger babies should offer firm, padded head and neck support that adjusts to the size of your baby.
- There should be a way to safely secure your baby into a backpack, such as a seat belt. All snaps and closures that adjust a baby's seat should be strong and not likely to give way.
- Check all buckles and other securing hardware to be sure seams won't tear and straps won't slip.
- If a framed pack has a kickstand, it should lock firmly into the open position, and the pack on the stand should be hard to tip over. But we and most manufacturers recommend that babies never be left in standing backpacks. Be sure the metal frame is padded around the baby's face to prevent bruises.
- Launder fabric slings and soft carriers a few times before use to soften them and remove any chemical odors in the fabric. Allow backpacks a few days to air out after you take them out of the packaging material, and launder the bib, if there is one.
- When carrying a baby in a pack, bend at the knees to stoop down rather than leaning forward from the waist.
- Never use a baby carrier or sling while in a car, on a bicycle, or while jogging or skiing. And don't use the carrier while cooking, or in other situations where baby might be injured.
- As with all devices that restrict a baby's movements, use of a carrier should not be a substitute for allowing your youngster natural freedom to crawl, walk, and explore under your supervision.

What's available

These models show features that are available. We suggest trying on models in the store to judge comfort and ease of use.

Baby Bjorn Baby Carrier (BB30, $83), a Swedish import, has won numerous awards for its elegant simplicity. The entire carrrier is softly padded. The seat portion adjusts with snaps, and is easily removed from the parent's harness assembly, which makes moving the baby on and off a simple process. The head support can be snapped down to allow a baby to ride facing outward. (Older models have been recalled—see Product Recalls—but models currently being sold do not have the flaw.)

Snugli by Evenflo includes five different models. The Double Take (Model 045, $20) and Double Comfort (Model 046, $20) carriers provide two carrying positions, face in and face out, along with head support and adjustable seats.

The Snugli Comfort Supreme (Model 078, $50) provides a padded waist belt and lower back support. The baby's head support and seat are both deeply padded. The seat snaps into three different height adjustments to grow with baby.

Snugli offers two soft carriers that can also be worn as backpacks—the Celebration Front & Back Pack (Model 076, $40) and 3-Way Front & Back Pack (Model 050, $29). Both offer three carrying positions; face in, face out, and back. A seat has three heights and a removable head bolster. The adjustable sternum strap and internal support panel offer comfort for parents.

Fisher-Price includes two soft carriers. The Natural Embrace Side-to-Side Carrier (Model 79472, $20) can be used as a carrier for a young baby. The pouch slides to either side to let larger babies ride on the top. In both models, the baby can face in or out. The pouch is adjustable, and a harness system distributes the weight across the hips. The Deluxe Perfect Support Carrier (Model 79471, $35) allows a baby to be carried facing inward, outward, or in a sling that doubles as a weather protector. The shell can also be adjusted for nursing privacy. The separate harness section means the baby's seat can be mounted after the parent has put on the harnesses. The seat mounts with an attachment button on the seat's crotch. Velcro closures allow seat width and height adjustments. Padding for the parent's shoulders and waist are thin. The sharp edges of the strapping material that secures the seat could be uncomfortable for baby's arms.

Kelty K.I.D.S. Kangaroo Child Carrier (Model 21959080, $70) is loaded with features. The parent's harness section can be put on separately before adding the baby's seat, and the parent's waist belt is reinforced for side and lower back support. It has a built-in bottle holder and key pouch, densely padded shoulder straps, and a removable storage pack. The baby's section has a zip-out hood to provide weather protection and a nursing cover. The padded seat offers gentle back and head support and adjusts with Velcro closures. Small, buckled straps on either side secure the seat from accidental opening. The seat opens into a flat surface for diapering on the go. The baby can face forward or toward the parent.

Prince Lionheart Koala Carrier (Model 0627, $70 to $80) is similar to the seat-within-a-pouch design of the Evenflo Snugli. The pack has adjustable, cushioned shoulder straps and adult waist belts that tie in the back. The baby's seat adjusts to three positions using a row of snaps.

FRAMED BACK CARRIERS

A framed carrier is for babies and children old enough to sit up independently—usually six months old and up. The frame helps to provide additional support for baby's weight, distributing it more evenly along the parent's back and hips, instead of concentrating it all on the shoulders as a soft carrier does.

Frames are constructed of lightweight aluminum, and seats and shoulder harnesses are sewn from moisture-resistant fabric. Some models have a U-shaped kickstand in the rear to allow the pack to stand on its own.

These carriers are difficult to put on without the help of another person. Hefting your baby or toddler around to the back in the carrier, or pulling the baby around from back to front for dismounting, is unwieldy at best.

Comfort varies with the fit of the pack, how practiced you are at wearing the carrier, and the type of walking you're doing. They feel the most comfortable when you're using long walking strides as you would during hiking, and the most uncomfortable when you do a lot of stopping and standing, like in the grocery store.

Most framed packs now come with built-in stands that help make back-mounting easier. However, the stands have caused numerous injuries when parents used the pack-and-stand combination as a baby seat. The baby's movements may cause the whole structure to topple over—stand, pack, and baby inside the pack. Fingers may also get pinched in the hinge mechanism of the stand if it hasn't got spacers to prevent a scissoring action.

Spotless

Carry a stain remover stick in a diaper bag (or keep one on hand near your changing area) to apply to spots before they set.

Top-priced carriers are designed for adult hikers—or dads, who may like them for travel or family outings. They're not usually found in baby stores but in camping stores and through direct mail. These models offer densely padded shoulder straps and hip belts to shift some of baby's weight to the adult's pelvic area, plus also extra storage compartments and add-on packs to help with diapers and other goods a baby needs on the trail.

Ample shoulder and hip padding and the supportive frame help make them the most comfortable for toting babies over six months old.

But packs are more cumbersome and expensive than soft fabric models. Some models have safety problems: no seat belts, unstable stands, or gaping leg holes that could allow a baby to fall through.

What's available

This review of framed back carriers will help you assess features. A good buy in a carrier depends on how much you'll use it. A bottom-of-the-line carrier may be fine for quick jaunts. If you plan serious, all-day treks with baby, a more luxurious model will be worth the cost. However, added features mean extra weight, too.

Kelty K.I.D.S. offers six hiking packs: Its Carrier Systems range in price from around $100 to $250. The lowest-priced model, Town (Model 21959040, $99), has many of the features of the company's more costly carriers: a spring-action kickstand with nonpinch hinges; an adjustable harness for baby and parent; densely padded shoulder and waist belts; and reflective tape to increase nighttime visibility.

Kelty's pricier models come with more features: padded adjustable harnesses, curved shoulder straps, foam back padding for the parent, and removable, zippered pouches. The Expedition (Model 21999078, $250) is at the top of the line. For serious trekkers, the pack has a multilayer foam waistbelt and shoulder straps, a detachable sun/rain hood, an upgraded suspension system, and two removable storage pouches.

Evenflo has four framed backpack carrier models. The Hiker (Model 074, $40) and Outbound (Model 093, $60) have similar lightweight, adjustable aluminum frames, padded shoulder straps, adjustable seat height, and over-the-shoulder support harness for baby. The Hiker and Outbound contain convenient storage packs. The Evenflo Trail Tech (Model 095, $70) and Trail Blazer (Model 770, $100) use a plastic frame that is elongated and provides a greater amount of adjustment. Each has additional padding and a sternum strap for greater support on longer hikes. The Trail Blazer—the top of the line—also offers a removable canopy to protect baby and provide lower lumbar support for the parent.

Baby Trend Compact Back Pack (Models 2309, 2310, and 2352, $39 to $49) offers a padded shoulder and face area for baby, a padded waist belt, and a pinch-resistant, spring-action support stand. The carrier can be folded in two and stored in a shoulder bag that fastens onto the back of the frame.

Tough Traveler offers different pack models for serious hikers, starting with the Montana (Model 1460, $99) and Colt (Model 1362, $88), both of which have densely padded shoulder straps and hip belts. Their high-backed baby seats offer head support and feature an underseat pocket. The Montana also offers lift/load straps to help control the fit of the pack to the parent and a sternum strap to further distribute weight across the upper chest. The Filly (Model 1350, $155) provides custom fit for parents from five to six feet tall, and the Stallion (Model 1385, $160) fits parents from five feet six to six feet six. Control straps distribute the load between shoulders and hips. A sternum strap adjusts the weight load on the upper chest and pulls the shoulder straps closer together. The shoulder pads and the hip belt have extra padding. The contoured frame and baby's padded, high-back seat offer back, neck, and head protection for the child. A sun/rain shield, extra pouches, and child's backpack are optional.

Chapter  6

SITTING PRETTY

All seats, swings, and play areas must be sturdy, safe, stable, and well-constructed. Look for secure seat belts.

In the early days of life with baby, you'll do a lot of carrying, rocking, and holding. Just about the time you'll want your sagging arms back, your baby will probably stop demanding to be held all the time.

That's when baby seats, swings, playpens, and other "baby containers" come in handy. (Walkers and stationary exercisers that also hold baby can be found in Playtime Gear, beginning on page 215. Soft carriers and backpacks are in Baby-Carrying Convenience, on page 111.)

BABY SEATS

It's important not to confuse baby seats with infant car seats. An infant car seat is a heavy, rigid baby holder with an arching handle and wide harnesses to protect a baby from a crash. However, baby seats have a lightweight frame covered with removable, quilted fabric sewn to conform to your baby's shape. They make a comfy, semi-upright nest for babies from birth to 20 to 30 pounds—or whatever weight the manufacturer suggests for a specific model. They aren't to be used in cars, ever.

The rounded back of a baby seat will support baby's yet-to-be-strong spine, while the semi-upright tilt lets him keep his eyes on you and everything else around him. This seat angle appears to make some babies more comfortable after a big meal than being plopped on their backs in cribs. (As

Contents

Baby seats, page 121

Shopping savvy, page 123

High chairs, page 124

Shopping savvy, page 125

Booster seats, page 130

Hook-on chairs, page 131

Baby swings, page 134

Shopping savvy, page 134

Traditional playpens, page 137

Travel play yards, page 141

with all baby holders, you should keep a constant eye on a baby in a seat, even when she's asleep.)

The supporting frame of a baby seat can be constructed from metal wire, tubular metal, or heavy-gauge plastic. Most frames are curved underneath to make the seat rock, and most are designed to add extra springiness with baby's every move—why they're often called bouncers.

The seat belt is typically a single waist strap that threads through a wide fabric crotch fitting between baby's legs. Most models have attachable U-shaped bent-wire bars that suspend toys in front of baby so he can bat them with his fists. Some upper-end models have add-ons, such as folding canopies to shade baby from the sun, extra-thick padding, or mosquito netting.

The top-priced seats are a completely different breed. Instead of frames from which the seat is suspended, they have molded, hard shells. Their covers are thickly quilted, and they feature built-in battery-operated motors to

Baby Safe

GUARD AGAINST SEAT FALLS

The biggest baby-seat problem is slipping off tabletops, counters, washers, and dryers. A baby's vigorous movements or hard rocking by a sibling can cause flip-overs or fall-downs. Slip-resistant pads on the base add some traction, but don't guard all that well against falls.

• Position the seat in the middle of a large table, rather than near the edge, and place a terrycloth towel or a strip of nonslip shelving material under the seat as a safety precaution. The best protection of all is to put the seat on the floor, far enough out of the way so that no one trips on it in passing.

• As with strollers and other baby holders, it's not a good idea to carry the seat with your baby inside. You could trip and fall, the seat frame could give way, or baby could slip.

• A car seat should not be used as a freestanding baby seat in your house. Even though the seats have rounded backs and manufacturers claim they can be used as baby rockers indoors, don't do it. Car seats are very heavy, and their rocker base allows them to work their way off the edges of tables and counters, or to be knocked over by siblings or family pets. Some babies have died when trapped underneath the weight of the overturned seat.

• If you carry your sleeping baby inside in his car seat, be very cautious and vigilant. Place the seat on the floor only. Test to be sure that the carpeting doesn't make the seat tippable, and stay nearby and watch baby all the while.

jiggle baby with a vibrator-type motion. In fact, these models could be used as a more compact alternative to a floor space-hogging automatic baby swing (see our discussion of automatic swings on page 134).

SHOPPING SAVVY Baby seats

Most large multiproduct baby manufacturers, including Fisher-Price, Kolcraft, and Playskool, have baby seats in their lines. Smaller companies, such as Summer Infant Products and Hoohoobbers, offer one style of frame with a variety of fabric choices and toy-bar options. Prices range from $35 for a simple, no-frills seat to $70 and more for a large vibrating model. You're more likely to find baby seats in baby specialty stores and children's megastores (Babies 'R' Us, for example) than in the baby departments of discount chains such as Wal-Mart or Kmart.

Seats vary in depth, leg room, and responsiveness to a baby's movements. Models also vary in stability. For maximum steadiness, look for a base or rear support that's wider than the seat itself. Without baby inside, press down on the unit from different positions to make certain it cannot be tipped sideways and will stay in place when rocked front to back.

If the seat's primary stabilizer is a flip-back handle, press down on the handle when it's in the rear support position. The locking mechanism should hold securely, and side movements shouldn't cause the unit to flip over. Check under the base for rubber pads or other nonskid surfacing that help prevent the seat from "walking" off smooth surfaces when baby's active.

Be sure to fasten the seat belt. It should fit around your baby's waist, not simply be strung from one side of the seat to the other so it only contacts baby's front. Look for a crotch belt, too. The wide fabric crotch pieces of most units appear to be comfortable and to secure baby well.

Check the stitching and seams all around the unit. There should be no loose threads or gaps where the sewing machine missed its mark. Since baby's wet diaper is bound to contact the fabric covering, make sure the fabric is removed and laundered.

What's available

The following representative models offer positive features, such as good seat belts, sturdy frames, and easy folding.

Both Evenflo Snugli Bouncer (Model 301, $20) and Snugli Car Ride Bouncer (Model 304, $60) have a folding rear support with slip-resistant

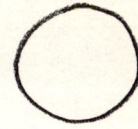

Target

Draw or tape a circle on the high-chair tray to show your child where the cup goes. (Not too close to the edge!)

pads. Large, colorful toys, including a rattle, are mounted in front of baby on a removable wire frame. Both these seats are made from a flexible tube frame that gives baby a solid, but springy, response, and both have an adjustable seat belt with a sturdy, locking buckle that threads through a wide fabric crotch belt and securely contacts baby around the waist. The stand has nonskid pads on the back. The Folding Bouncer offers additional padding in the seat and around baby's head. Both have removable seat pads for washing, and the frames can be folded flat for storage.

Kolcraft Rock 'n' Play Infant Seat & Rocker (Model 65205, $20, babies to 18 pounds), constructed from sturdy tubular steel rather than the bent wire of some seats, is a baby-sized rocker, rather than just a jiggler like the Evenflo models mentioned above. A kickstand in the back allows it to be used as a stationary seat. As with Evenflo's seats, there's a securely-locking seat belt threaded through a fabric crotch belt. Seat padding is plush and removable for washing. The seat comes with a retractable ruffled canopy and a row of spinnable, baby-sized toys. The unit folds flat for travel and storage.

Several baby seats vibrate as well as jiggle. The Fisher-Price Soothing Bouncer Seats (Models 79387, $30, and 79346, $35, 4 months to 25 pounds) combine springiness and a switch-operated, battery-powered vibration unit. Seat belts thread only from the side of the frames—not as effective as Evenflo's and Kolcraft's belts, but adequate if you watch baby carefully. The thick, removable seat pads are machine washable and dryer safe, and both models have detachable canopies, plus small slip-resistant pads on the base. Model 79346 comes with a front toy bar to help keep baby entertained.

Early Development Hammock Swing (Model 1400, $155) isn't a hammock at all, but a large seat with a bigger frame than other seats mentioned here. There's a battery-powered, switch-operated vibrator. Or, baby can make the seat jiggle with a bungee cord–like action. The seat can be reclined, the fabric seat pad is washable, and the crotch/waist belt firmly latches around baby's waist.

HIGH CHAIRS

Once your tot starts eating baby food and can sit up solidly on his own (usually about six months of age), it's time to think about a high chair. Since the chair must bear two or three years of grueling, everyday use plus lots of heavy scrubbing, choose the device carefully.

High chairs are usually found wherever other baby equipment is sold. Lower-priced models are available in the baby departments of Wal-Mart, Kmart, Cosco, and other large discount chains. Baby megastores often offer a choice of seven to 10 models. The highest-priced imports can be found in baby specialty stores, in the baby megastores, and on web sites selling baby equipment.

The high chair market is dominated by large, multiline baby product manufacturers, including Graco, Playskool, Cosco, Evenflo/Gerry, and Kolcraft, with imports such as Peg Perego and Chicco getting a portion of high-end sales. Prices range from $50 for bottom-of-the-line models to over $100 for many imports.

High chairs have been around since our great-grandmothers' day. Back then, they were simple wooden chairs on stilts with a wooden tray in front that flipped behind the chair. Most of today's high chair models are constructed from metal tubing, and all come with adjustable plastic trays with tall rims that hold back spills. Major options include a reclinable seat and a height adjuster that allows the chair to move up and down its frame. Thus, the chair can be lowered for pushing up to the table without the tray. Some models aren't really high chairs, but toddler-sized seats stacked on a play table. The pieces can then be converted into a floor table and chair. Some newer chairs offer seats that completely lift off their bases to serve as a booster seat or floor chair.

SHOPPING SAVVY High chairs

Higher-priced high chairs may have reclining features, height adjustments, tray sophistication, and padding thickness for the seat. Some features are worth paying for, others aren't important.

Huge footprints stabilize larger chairs. Those big footprints on midpriced chairs (up to 28 inches front to back, and 25 inches side to side) stabilize large, molded seats as they recline or move up and down. However, seat dimensions and footrest lengths on most midline chairs are better suited to two- and three-year-olds than the six- to eighteen-month-olds who are the main users of high chairs.

If you have a small kitchen, measure floor space before you shop. The most compact chairs can be found at the bottom end of the price spectrum and at the very top, where chairs become more streamlined. Just be careful not to sacrifice stability for compactness. Try tipping the chair over side to

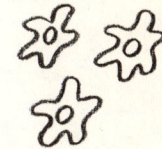

Get a grip

Keep the baby from sliding down in a high chair by putting a rubber sink mat or stick-on, nonslip bathtub daisies or strips on the seat.

side and front to back to test how well it holds its ground.

Sturdy seat belts are a necessity. Thousands of high chair–related accidents annually are serious enough to send babies to hospitals—mostly when they stand up and fall out (sometimes from the top of a poorly secured tray) or when they try to slide out underneath the tray and get caught.

The belt should hold baby securely in place, with no leeway for scrambling up or under. The safest belts are anchored to the seat or attached low on the backrest frame. Some belts require your baby to actually sit on a crotch strap that loops into the waist belt. Although this system presents a cleaning challenge, it also holds a baby in place. Belt buckles should be secured to the chair, and components shouldn't slip or separate when you tug on them. Standards for high chairs are changing to include a center post that helps keep baby safely in the seat; see page 129.

Some clean up better than others. Keeping a high chair clean is a big hassle. Crumbs and dried baby food get caught in crevices and small indentations. Some models have removable seat coverings—or entire seat panels—for easier cleaning. Be sure fasteners don't cause upholstery to tear when you pull off the seat or coverings. Solid light or

Baby Safe

HIGH CHAIRS HAVE HAZARDS

High chairs raise baby above the floor, so you must watch out for falls and tip-overs.

• Buy the most stable model you can. If the chair tips easily in the store, pass it up.

• Effective seat belts with firm buckles hold baby securely in the seat so she can't climb or stand up, either tipping the chair or falling out. They also help to prevent her from "submarining"—slipping under the tray and either falling to the floor or catching her neck on the tray.

• Fasten baby in as soon as she's in the chair and don't unfasten the safety belts until you're ready to take baby out of the seat.

• Keep an eye on your tot the whole time he's in the chair. He can get into trouble in the time it takes to answer the phone or door.

• Supervise baby's meals to guard against choking. (See page 214 for foods that pose choking hazards.)

• Check the chair regularly to be sure folding legs are securely locked and that no small parts that could cause choking, such as caps or plugs on metal tubing, have come loose.

dark seat colors show stains and grime more than patterns do.

A "one-handed" tray is easiest. Look for a lightweight tray that moves smoothly so you can remove it with one hand. Try it forward and backward, and remove and replace it a couple of times. (Some chairs allow the tray to swing to the side and back when not in use.) Check out handy features. Trays that wrap all the way around the baby help keep food and toys from going overboard. A tall rim can contain spills, and a tray angle that tips spills away from the baby is useful. Some manufacturers claim their high chair trays are "dishwasher safe"—but these trays are really too large to fit into most dishwashers.

Folding legs should lock. If the chair's legs fold, test them out. There should be a secure locking system to prevent accidental collapsing. When the chair is opened, the locking system should automatically engage to hold the chair in the open position.

Chairs need a safe-parts check. Before you buy, check to see that small parts, such as caps or plugs that cover the ends of metal tubing,

Modern high chairs take a broad, stable stance. Look for an easy-to-remove tray with a deep rim, wipe-clean upholstery, and a sturdy seat belt. Newest designs feature a "crotch post," which allows just enough space for each leg, preventing baby from slipping under the tray.

are well-secured. Parts small enough for a child to swallow or inhale are a choking hazard. Look at the underside of the tray to be sure there are no sharp edges that could scratch, or small holes or hinges that could capture a child's fingers. The whole underside of the tray should present a smooth, nonhostile surface in case a child falls on an overturned tray.

Reclining features aren't worth the extra cost. Babies under six months of age, who might benefit from the feature, aren't ready for being fed anything but mother's milk or formula. And feeding young babies shouldn't be done with baby lying in a chair, but in your loving arms and with your undivided attention to make sure baby doesn't choke.

Seat-cover thickness doesn't matter. Diapers, clothing, and baby's natural padding keep him comfortable—and thickness differences are minimal. But vinyl quality is important. Test vinyl by pinching it between your fingers and then rubbing it back and forth between your forefinger and thumb. You'll immediately feel the difference between thin, stretchy vinyl and higher-quality coverings that last. While you're at it, take a look at the heat-sealed seams, especially along the front rim of the seat where your baby's legs will hang down. Sharp seams on the seat could scratch the back of baby's legs.

Wheels aren't necessary. In fact, they can be a pain when you're trying to pull a tray off, or put a baby in. If there are other children in the house, they'll be tempted to give baby joy rides. And wheels on some models appear to make the chair less stable. If a tot tries to mount the chair using the foot rest as a ladder, the whole chair could turn over. If you decide to buy a wheeled model, test the chair's stability by pressing down firmly on the foot rest to see how easily the chair tips over. Look for locks on the rear wheels, preferably on all four.

What's available

Just as with strollers, cribs, car seats, and other big-ticket baby items, the more you pay, the more extras you get. With high chairs, higher prices bring giant seats, huge wrap-around trays, and wide frames that eat up floor space.

Chairs at the high end feature big, white, molded seats covered in patterned vinyl. Some seats have extensions on the side and recline for infants. Seats are also height-adjustable, moving up and down two posts, then locking into a given position. Heights range from nearly floor level to standard high-chair level, with a middle height low enough to allow the seat to be pushed under a dining room table (with the tray removed).

Many chairs in this price range offer molded center posts, which fit between baby's legs at the front of the seat. They act as an extra safety precaution against a baby's slipping under the tray and getting his head caught between a chair's leg holes and tray. This design is expected to be mandated by new voluntary safety standards (see box below).

Cosco Options 5 High Chair (Model 03-286, $50) has a center post attached to the tray that snaps into place when the tray is put on the chair. The dishwasher-safe tray can be removed with one hand from either side. The seat has seven height positions, reclines, and can be removed for use as a separate play chair or booster seat.

Graco offers two Height-Adjustable High Chairs (Models 3630, $50; 3635, $60). They enclose baby in a long, wide seat with the crotch bar molded on. The tray mounts onto the seat on top of the shell. The seats recline in three positions and adjust to five heights using back lock-release mechanisms. Graco's top-of-the-line Reclining High Chairs (Models 3845, $70; 3855, $80; and 3865, $90) feature synthetic leather chair pads and six height adjust-

Baby Safe

HIGH CHAIRS ARE CHANGING

Current high-chair safety standards have been in place for nearly 25 years. Products that pass the safety tests will have a sticker on the tray or frame carrying the word "certified" and the names Juvenile Products Manufacturers Association and American Society for Testing and Materials, the organization that sets these industry standards. Currently, the following high-chair manufacturers offer certified high-chair models: Century, Cosco, Evenflo, Gerry Wood Products Company (now part of Evenflo), Graco, Kolcraft, Playskool, and Rochelle Furniture.

New standards are expected in 1999 to prevent a situation where a baby slides out under the tray and gets her head stuck, an accident that has led to some deaths. In most cases, chairs that meet the new standard have a "crotch post" and seat dimensions appropriate for the age group so that babies can't slide through. Look for the new design (and for the certification sticker that shows the chair meets the revised ASTM F404-97).

For more on certification standards, see Product Recalls. Compliance is voluntary, but most manufacturers choose to comply.

ments. Each chair has two trays. The larger tray comes off, leaving a removable, smaller "snack" tray.

Evenflo Phases High Chair (Model 280, about $80) and the Evenflo Baby Looney Tunes Phases High Chair (Model 2802C5, about $90) have a restraining center post fastened to the bottom of the large, high-sided trays, and two seat-height adjustments. The chairs can be used with Evenflo's On My Way infant car seat/carrier (not included). The high chairs adapt into booster seats or play tables and chairs.

Kolcraft Perfect Recliner Adjustable High Chair (Model 19538, $60) and Perfect Height Adjustable High Chair (Model 19532, $40) both have center posts permanently attached to the high-chair tray. The Perfect Recliner has a three-position reclining seat; the Perfect Height, a contoured seat. Both have six seat-height adjustments and easy to release trays.

Playskool Three for Me High Chair (Model 30749, $40) has a permanent restraint bar molded into the seat base and a positive-contact waist and crotch belt. The adjustable, three-position tray remains upright even when the seat's back is reclined. The one-piece seat pad removes for cleaning, and the seat's legs come off so it can be used on the floor as a toddler-sized chair.

BOOSTER SEATS FOR CHAIRS

In decades past, a telephone book did the job of boosting a toddler too short to reach the table. Now, special booster seats are available to lessen the possiblity that a child will fall off the chair. Typically, the seat is made of molded plastic and designed to be belted to the seat of a regular adult dining chair. Although some manufacturers claim their seats can be used by six-month-olds, we suggest postponing the use of any booster until your child becomes very skilled at sitting alone—closer to a year of age.

These dining-chair boosters aren't to be confused with car restraints for children weighing 40 to 60 pounds. Car seats can be identified by the channels on the sides, which direct adult seat belts through the unit. (You can read about them on page 65.) Dining room boosters are simple, plastic risers, some with trays, and most with two sets of straps: one set to keep the child in place, the other to secure the booster to the chair.

What's available

Manufacturers of booster seats include Cosco, First Years, Kids II, and Safety 1st. Prices range between $12 and $25.

Safety belts are critical for holding babies in boosters and preventing falls, yet some seats we examined—Safety 1st 3 Level Booster Seat (Model 41752, $13) and Fisher-Price Grow-With-Me Booster Seat (Model 79118, $12)—had no belts.

Safety 1st Fold-Up Booster Seat (Model 173, $20 to $25) adjusts to accommodate children from six months to about three years of age. Two sets of webbed straps attach the seat to the adult chair. A safety belt with a crotch strap holds the child in. Skid-resistant bumpers on the seat base help keep it from sliding off the chair. The seat comes with a removable front tray, and the unit folds flat for storage.

First Years Portable 3-in-1 Booster Seat (Model 4200, $20) adjusts to different heights as the child grows. The manufacturer claims the seat is dishwasher safe, but its components would be prohibitively large for most washers. The seat comes with a removable tray, lap belts for the child, and a latching belt to go around the adult chair.

HOOK-ON CHAIRS

A hook-on high chair is a seat and back rest attached to a metal frame. Rather than sitting on the floor, the chair's frame slides onto a tabletop bracket-style and is held in position by friction and the weight of the child. Most chairs have locking mechanisms, suction cups, or spring latches designed to enhance the chair's holding ability. A typical chair has seat belts similar to those on a full-size high chair.

Baby Safe

BOOSTER SEATS SHOULD BE WELL-FASTENED

Booster seats are not specifically covered by either a mandatory federal standard or voluntary industry safety standard.

• Use a booster that can be belted onto a standard chair. Strap the booster seat firmly onto the chair before you put your baby in it.

• To accommodate a booster, the adult chair should have a seat area at least a few inches wider than the booster base.

• Pedestal-base chairs, swivel chairs, rocking chairs, bar stools, benches, or heavily padded chairs or seats with cushions aren't suitable for boosters, posing a danger that the booster will slip or fall off.

Hook-on chairs were introduced in 1969 by the Kantwet Company, with its Feed-N-Play unit. At first glance, they appeared to be a handy alternative to high chairs. They were very lightweight and folded compactly, making them immensely portable. They also allowed a baby to join the rest of the family at the table for meals. But the design concept itself is flawed, posing serious safety risks. Companies have ceased making them as a result of safety problems and the liability issues that arise.

When CONSUMER REPORTS tested a variety of hook-on chairs several years ago, we found the whole construction unsafe. The seats could be readily dislodged by the child in the chair, if he planted his feet in the right place and pushed back.

We also found that hook-on chairs couldn't be safely attached to every table. The tabletop had to be at least a half-inch thick; anything thinner was too flimsy to support the chair and the baby. Neither glossy surfaces nor breakable glass was safe. The table had to be stable, with a design that prevented easy tipping—which rules out all pedestal tables but big heavyweights. Smaller tables are likely to tip from the weight of the baby.

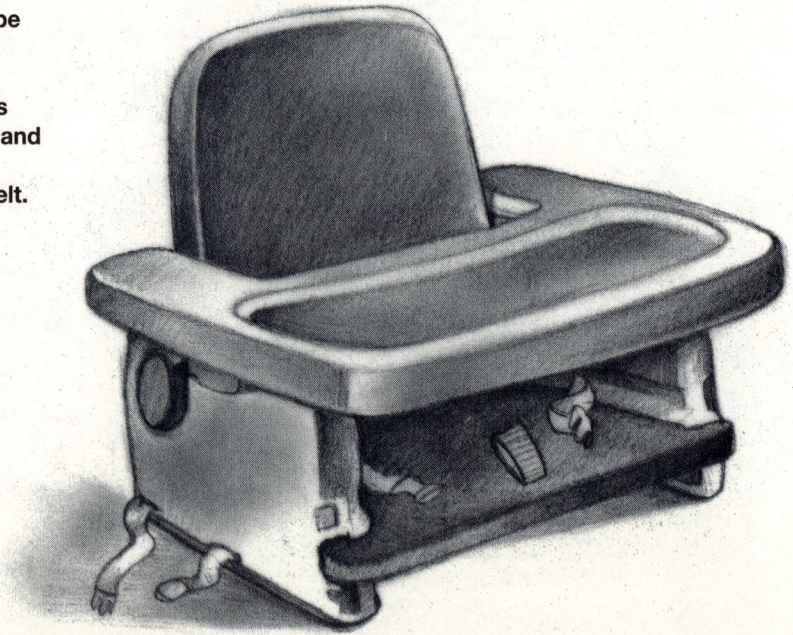

A booster seat can be strapped onto any sturdy, wide-based chair. Most boosters fold down for travel and storage. Look for a model with a seat belt.

Countertops don't work well, either—a child could easily push against the base of the counter and work the chair free.

Those tests also showed that hook-on chairs didn't score well in durability either. End caps and other small parts fell off, pieces bent, and plastic parts came loose.

Manufacturers of hook-on chairs may participate in a voluntary JPMA/ASTM certification program. Certified chairs must have a latching device to minimize accidental folding and be constructed without sharp edges, protrusions, or points. The seats must offer protection from scissoring, coil springs, holes, and openings. To be certified, chairs undergo drop tests, load tests, and push-pull tests, as well as disengagement and bouncing tests.

Warnings must appear on the unit against leaving a child unattended or out of view. Parents are instructed not to use the seat on glass or single pedestal tables, a loose tabletop or table leaf, or with a tablecloth or place mats, and are advised to check table stability. The standard recommends table thickness according to a child's weight and stipulates the table should be clean.

Other cautions include not placing an ordinary chair under the hook-on chair; keeping pets and other children away from the chair; making sure the child's legs are free from the chair supports; and not using the chair unless all suction cups are securely attached to the table's surface.

What's available

The Graco Tot-Loc Chair (Models 3000 and 3045, $25 and $30) has a plastic seat and two extended, padded arms on each side—the top arm to rest on top of a table, the lower to press into the underside of the table to hold the chair on the table's rim. The seat folds for storage. The 3045 has a higher back and a tray attached on the top arms.

Chicco's Pratique (Model 67650, $40) is constructed from fabric and has top and lower pressure arms.

Baby Trend makes a wheeled Home & Roam High Chair (Model 8206R, $119) with a seat unit that can be removed from the high chair stand and positioned on a table ledge. The seat has a crotch strap and a large wrap-around tray.

Both of the Graco models are certified. But frankly, we can't recommend that any hook-on chairs be bought or used. Their hazards are just too serious.

AUTOMATIC BABY SWINGS

Automatic baby swings, designed for indoor use, are baby seats suspended by rigid arms from a supporting frame. The frame's tubular legs have a wide stance. The swinging motion is controlled by winding a handle at the top of the frame or, with a battery-operated version, by flicking a switch.

Some companies manufacture swings with interchangeable baby seats and bassinetlike beds—both using the same support arms and rocking mechanisms. And at least one model has a stand to accommodate an infant car seat. Manufacturers set different upper weight limits for users, ranging from 16 to 25 pounds.

Hand-cranked swings run usually 15 or 30 minutes on a single wind. Battery-powered models will go as long as 250 hours on a set of batteries.

Extra features—multiple recline positions; front trays with toys; removable seats and bassinets that can be used on their own; frames without a top crossbar for ease in putting in and taking out baby; an electronic music option; two swinging directions, either head to toe or side to side—cost more.

SHOPPING SAVVY Baby swings

Before purchasing a swing, remember that its window of usefulness is very narrow: from birth until about six months, with most heavy-duty use during the first three months, when babies are more apt to be fussy. Nonetheless, parents are enthusiastic about the power of swings to lull babies into a sleep-like stupor. Some call their baby swings "supper savers," which calm babies during the frequent fussier early evening hours.

The footprints of automatic swings are large—about three feet wide and deep—so you'll sacrifice about nine square feet of floor space. Some parents find that the device takes up too much room to be practical. If you live in cramped quarters, you may want to consider acquiring a compact battery-operated vibrating baby seat for soothing baby instead (see the discussion of baby seats on page 121).

A bassinet attachment really doesn't work all that well. It causes the baby to roll back and forth from one side of the bed to the other. According to some experts, head-to-toe rocking is more natural and soothing to babies.

Windup swings with at least 30 minutes of run time offer some advantages over battery-operated versions. For one thing, they're quieter. Battery-operated models emit a low churn with each pass of the swing.

Battery-powered models are usually more expensive than hand-wound counterparts. They may appear more convenient on the surface, but there have been problems with motors in the past. Typically, the swing gets out of sync and slows down almost to a standstill from the weight of the baby. Plus, you may run out of battery juice just when your baby needs swinging the most.

When you check out swings in the store, look for a sturdy, stable frame that won't tip. Examine the seat portion carefully to be sure it will be comfortable for your baby and that there are no sharp edges to contact her legs. Seat belts must firmly anchor the child. If you decide to buy a model with a cradle attachment, such as Graco Three-in-One Cradle Swing, inspect its underside to see that it's mounted well.

What's available

The four major baby-product manufacturers who make automatic baby swings are Graco, Evenflo, Fisher-Price, and Cosco, offering a wide range of models and features.

Graco has more than 10 models. Its Classic Wind-Up Swings (Models 1131, 1141; $35, $40) each have a two-position-recline molded seat, several simple toys on the front tray, and a 15-minute windup mechanism. The 2-Speed Swing with Timer (Model 1135, $50) is also a windup, but runs for 30 minutes and has a time indicator. The seat, which offers a four-position recline and two speeds, is more smoothly finished than the Classic Model, and has an easy-open front tray.

For more money, Graco offers battery-operated swings. Model 1602 ($60) features a 4-position recline and a front tray with toys similar to that of Model 1135. The Converta-Cradle Swing (Model 1512, $99 to $109) has both a removable rocker seat and a detachable, mesh-sided bassinet. Both swings will operate for more than 150 hours on four D-cell batteries.

Sleeker, open-topped, battery-operated swings from Graco includes its Battery-Operated 2-Speed Swing (Model 1421, $70). The unit uses the simpler seat of basic windup models (no hinged tray or toys). Next up is Model 1423 ($80), which uses the "easy-entry" seat as above. It has two speeds and no toys. Model 1434 ($95) has three speeds, a four-position recline, an infant head support, and a set of large beads across the front of the tray.

At the top of the line is the Graco Gentle Choice (Model 1464, $99), which runs for 200 hours on a set of batteries and offers music (though it's the tinny computer-chip variety), six speeds, three recline positions, and a lit auto timer.

Messy

Put a plastic or metal high chair under the shower, and let hot water spray over it for a few minutes. Caked-on food wipes off easily.

Evenflo Mobile Swing (Model 4051, $90) and Double Motion Mobile Swing (Model 4052, $100) are compact, open-top for easy access, battery-operated models. Back wheels make them easy to move. The swings offer four speeds and four reclining seat positions. The front tray can be unlatched with one hand, and the foot rest extends. The Double Motion model combines swinging motion with a pushbutton vibration feature. It comes with a removable play tray with a mirror, beads, and several other activities.

Fisher-Price Cradle Swing (Model 79454, $80) and 3-in-1 Cradle Swing (Model 79322, $100) both use a molded cradle seat suspended by a single metal arm, with the swinging mechanism at the top. The swing mechanism can be rotated along with the support arm, so the seat can be rocked in either a side-to-side or head-to-toe direction. The legs of the swing's frame fold together for storage—but you'll need ample space. The seat has two reclining positions, plus a front tray with a crotch bar. The motor offers three speeds and runs on three D alkaline batteries. In

Baby Safe

SWINGS REQUIRE VIGILANCE

Strictly follow the manufacturer's age and weight specifications. They'll tell you when your baby can begin using the swing and when it's no longer safe for your child. There are anecdotal reports of near suffocation when babies fell forward into the front part of the seat and were unable to right themselves. A second type of accident has occurred when a baby who's too large for the swing manages to pull on a frame leg and topple out.

• Watch older siblings, too. They sometimes play with the swing and can get a head or neck caught between the suspension tubing and the swing seat.

• Hold the seat absolutely still when you place your baby in the swing. If the seat moves backward as you "load" baby inside, he could very easily fall out.

• Always fasten the restraining belt that is provided with the swing.

• Limit the amount of time your baby swings to no more than 30 minutes at a stretch—especially at a high or fast setting. More swinging time can make some babies dizzy.

• Stay with the baby constantly during her playtime in the swing.

• With battery-powered swings, start with the lowest setting. High settings may be too rough for your baby.

• Don't use a damaged, broken, or incompletely assembled swing. It could collapse—or entrap baby's fingers, head, or neck.

addition, the 3-in-1 model has a removable seat that can be used as a separate infant carrier.

Cosco's two swings, Quiet Time Elite (Model 08-989, $50) and the Dream Ride Plus (Model 08-980, $19), are both windup models in frames with overhead bars. Both run for 30 minutes per wind. A "Minute Minder" gauge shows remaining running time. An overwind feature protects the mechanism from accidental damage. The swings' steel frames can be folded down for storage and travel. The Quiet Time Elite features a thickly padded, three-position reclining seat with a nylon restraining belt. The front T-bar folds down with a button push to allow the baby to be put inside, then locks back into an upright position. The Dream Ride Plus has L-shaped arms that support a platform for the Cosco Dream Ride car seat, included with the unit. The car/swing seat can be mounted in a reclined (bed) position for swinging side to side, or used in the upright or semirecline position to provide head-to-toe motion.

TRADITIONAL PLAYPENS

Traditional playpens—sometimes called play yards—are mesh-sided pens with raised floors and corner leg supports. More recent travel play yard designs have entirely different folding mechanisms—they can be folded compactly and carried in small cases. You'll find those models discussed in detail on page 141.

The frames and legs of standard playpens are made from steel or aluminum tubing. Playpen legs may be straight, with protective caps on the bottom. Or they can be bent into a hairpin shape with the rounded U part of the leg against the floor.

With a couple of exceptions, standard playpens are square (each side is 36 inches long) or rectangular (approximately 26 inches by 40 inches). The frame's railing, which encircles the top of the pen and is usually covered with padded vinyl, holds up the mesh sides. The floorboard is usually composed of hardboard, such as Masonite, in two half-pieces so that it may fold in the middle. Most pens have a removable vinyl-covered pad on the floor.

All models have shielded hinge covers to protect children's fingers and to help prevent the sides from being lowered accidentally. And all have a rim of plastic around the base of the floorboard, called a "draft guard," which secures the mesh to the floorboard.

To fold the pen, floorboards must be pulled up and the side hinges unlocked. Some models have either one or two dropsides, which allow you to put baby in and take him out more easily. But most are made with sides that lower only when the floorboards are pulled upward as side hinges are released. This construction is safer—if dropsides are accidentally left down, they can pose a risk that baby will fall out and also can create a suffocation pocket between the floorboard and the vinyl draft guard.

As the price goes up, you can expect added padding—on the railings, on the floorboard pad, and on the side tubes of the pen's frame. All top railings should be padded, and the metal tubes on the side of the pen should be padded as well, to protect baby if she falls against the pen, when inside or outside. But not all pens offer that protection.

SHOPPING SAVVY Playpens

Do you really need a playpen? Some experienced parents answer a definite yes, especially when they have extremely active toddlers. A playpen can come in handy when you're, say, cooking or doing housework and want your baby safely out of the way.

But some babies hate being put into a playpen and protest loudly at being confined. And, after the novelty of using the pen wears off, it may end up as a costly, floor-hogging toy chest.

If you decide you need a pen, look for one with firm, thick padding on the top rail as well as padded covering for metal frame components on the sides. Straight legs with protective caps are preferable to hairpin-shaped legs that can mar floors and leave rust spots on the carpet.

Pens with sides that lower only when you fold the entire unit are safest. Because of the potentially fatal suffocation pocket created by the draft guard and lowered side, a number of manufacturers have responded to the suffocation hazard by producing models with sides that lower only during the folding-away process. Look for this feature.

Since babies tend to gnaw on top railings, the vinyl covering should be adequately heavy. You can compare the vinyl on different models by squeezing it between your thumb and forefinger. It should feel thick, not stretchy.

Bolts or rivets that stick out of the outside of the top rails as much as ¼ or ½ inch can catch a pacifier string or clothing and cause strangulation. You'll want smooth outside railings with covered hardware. (For information on playpens with protruding hardware, see Product Recalls.)

Choose a model with well-protected hinges that can't capture your baby's fingers. The floor padding should be firm and stay in place to keep your baby from slipping or from getting at floor bolts or the split where the floorboards join together.

Floorboard thickness is a good sign of playpen quality. Kneel down and

PLAYPENS AND PLAY YARDS

- Keep dropsides up. If you use a playpen with lowering sides, always keep the sides in the upright position to protect your baby from rolling or creeping into a suffocation pocket or pinching fingers on the unlocked hinge mechanism.
- Remove large toys or boxes. Babies may use them as steps for climbing—and then fall out.
- Don't tie anything across the top. If you hang a toy from the side of the pen, the suspended strap should be short enough—never more than seven inches long—so that it won't entangle a baby's neck.
- Inspect frequently for holes. If your baby tries to teethe on the sides of padded railings, he can chew off pieces of vinyl or foam and choke. Inspect the floor pad for loose pieces, too. Do not replace the pad that comes with the playpen with a thicker pad. Though your own pad may seem more comfortable, it can be a suffocation hazard for your baby.
- Watch out for choking hazards and bolts. Inspect staples under the floorboard frequently to make sure they are secure, so there's no danger your baby could pull them out and ingest them. Avoid pens with protruding bolts or rivets.
- Clip loose threads. Babies can get fingers entangled in unraveled stitching and can choke on loose threads. A thread more than seven inches long can also cause strangulation.
- Don't use a broken playpen. Safely discard a mesh pen that has holes in the side. It may trap your baby's fingers or toes or, worse, your baby's head, causing strangulation. Don't use a playpen with a broken floor, missing or loose bars, or malfunctioning hardware.
- Stop using the playpen when your child can climb out. When toddlers start trying to clamber over the side of the playpen, they've outgrown it. Definitely stop using the playpen when your child reaches the recommended maximum height of 34 inches or top weight of 30 pounds.
- Don't leave the playpen outside. Sun and rain can damage the playpen and make it unsafe. If you have to clean it, most manufacturers recommend a mild soap solution.
- Never leave your child unattended in a playpen. You should always have baby in sight and be on the alert for unsafe situations. It may be hard to follow that rule to the letter, but you should be vigilant.

inspect the underside of the pen. If the plastic of the draft guard has been stapled to the bottom, each staple should be securely fastened into the floorboard.

JPMA conducts playpen certification tests to ASTM safety standards. (See Product Recalls for details.) Certified models carry a label that includes a warning never to leave the dropside down or leave a child unattended.

With the advent of travel play yards, you may have a hard time finding a new, full-sized playpen model in the stores. You might want to consider buying (or borrowing) a used playpen, as long as it's in good condition. Look for adequate padding on the railings and frame, completely intact vinyl or mesh, solid floorboards with the draft guards well fastened down on the underside, plastic shields on all the side-lowering hinges, and no protruding bolt heads or rivets on the outer sides of rails.

What's available

Most manufacturers have stopped making traditional playpens in favor of portable, travel yards. Kolcraft, Cosco, and Graco carry a few, although they may lack some desirable features.

A lightweight play yard comes in handy for trips. It folds compactly. Some models come with a carrying case. Buy a new model rather than a used one—millions of older play yards have been recalled for safety reasons.

Kolcraft's four traditional playpens have hairpin legs and protective padding on the railings as well as on side bars. Floorboards have center support bars. Sides can be lowered independently from each other and lock when raised. Each model offers a choice between fabric or vinyl floor padding. The Travel Rest (Model 28245, $60) and Travel Playard (Model 18242, $40) are rectangular, while the Square Playard (Model 18342, $49) is shaped as its name indicates. The Travel Rest also has a removable bassinet that fits onto the bars at the top of the pen.

While the Cosco rectangular-shaped Travel Playard (Model 05-325, $35) and square Padded Playard (Model 05-396, $40) both have padding on top railings and floorboards, they lack protective padding on the side tubes. The Fully Padded Playard (Model 05-388, $44) has the needed bar protection.

The Graco square play yards (Models 2060 and 2360, $40 to $60) have the desirable rail padding along the top.

TRAVEL PLAY YARDS

Portable play yards have now overtaken standard playpens as baby containers. Most are constructed from mesh and metal tubing just as playpens are, but they use lightweight fabric, similar to tent fabric, instead of thick vinyl.

Portables are smaller than standard playpens and are generally rectangular shaped, which allows them to be moved from room to room. And they can be folded down into a compact, golf-bag shape, then slipped into a zippered carrying case for travel or storage.

Folding requires that you first unlatch all sides, then find the handle in a hub on the center of the floorboard, rotate it, and pull upward. The center will then rise and the sides will fold. When you set up the play yard, the side rails have to go up first, so they're standing upright. Then, you press the center hub downward to allow the side rails to snap into a locked position.

Most companies offer a simple, low-end model. Add-ons then raise the prices: wheels; side storage pouches; bassinets; changing areas that attach to the top rails of the play yard; and arched, tent-like canopies that fasten onto the sides of the yard with poles, zippers, or Velcro, and extend over the top to provide shade and insect protection.

SHOPPING SAVVY Play yards

Travel play yards weigh less and aren't as cumbersome as standard playpens. Most are slender enough to be moved through doorways. Their folding capabilities and carrying cases make them handy for vacationing and travel. Diaper leaks and spit-ups are inevitable, but the moisture-resistant, tent-style fabric can be easily wiped clean with a damp cloth.

Most models don't offer cover sheets for the play yard mattress or the bassinet. But you should resist the urge to cover either surface with a pillowcase or sheet or to put in a different mat. Babies get entangled and can strangle in loose sheets or suffocate under ill-fitting mats.

As you'll see in Product Recalls, page 276, play yards have had more than their share of safety problems. Millions of these devices have been recalled, and twelve babies died when side bars didn't lock in place, creating a V-shaped strangulation hazard.

The babies who died were using older models with hinges in the center of each top rail. (Newer models have sturdier side-locking mechanisms.) The top rails appeared to parents to be locked, but the hinges were either not turned inward and down as they were supposed to be, or they somehow rotated during use into the unlocked position.

Loose floorboard fabric also created suffocation pockets. Mushy, nonporous fabric and stretchy sides could continue to pose suffocation dangers in most designs.

Young babies are the most apt to be endangered by cushioned surfaces and potential entrapment sites. And bassinet add-ons are not fail-safe: Babies can catch their necks along mesh sides. Or a bassinet or diaper-changing add-on can accidentally dislodge, particularly if young children fiddle with fastenings or bump the add-on.

Domed canopies that promise to protect from glaring sun, such as at the beach, really aren't safe for babies during hot weather. Rather than deflecting heat, they intensify it while closing off needed cross-ventilation. Heatstroke is life-threatening to babies and young children. In fact, some manufacturers have now included warnings against using yards with domes attached in direct sun. Models that come with a bassinet and a canopy carry strong warnings never to leave the baby in the bassinet with the canopy attached—but parents don't always follow directions.

Some canopies are easily detached by a toddler or a gust of wind. When they come loose, they may expose sharp-ended tubing that could hurt a baby who gnawed on it.

With all these warnings in mind, if you still want a play yard, we suggest purchasing a simple, serviceable model without a canopy, bassinet, or changing table attachment. Wheels are a plus for porting the play yard around, but not a necessity. Use the unit only in the shade, and avoid colorful, flowerlike fabric patterns that attract bees and other insects. Don't use the unit until your baby is old enough to sit unsupported (about six months of age). Finally, don't let your baby sleep in the play yard—especially not facedown. The mushy, "nonbreathing" fabric surface could form a suffocation pocket (see the SIDS warnings on page 53).

Before you purchase the unit, inspect padded sides and all areas where mesh and fabric are sewn together to be sure there are no loose threads that could entangle your baby's fingers or toes. The hard floorboard should fit snugly against the springy mesh sides so baby's head or throat doesn't become captured. Inspect the play yard each time you set it up to make sure the sides are rigidly in place and everything is in working order. And never leave a child unattended in a play yard.

What's available

The most familiar travel yard makers are Graco, Kolcraft, Century, and Baby Trend. The following are easiest to find.

Graco makes Pack 'N Play units. The no-frills Pack 'N Play (Model 9130, $54 to $59) has simple legs and a center floorboard support, patterned fabric floor pad, and padded sides. Model 9135 ($70) has a roll-down flap on one side and an accessory bag. Model 9718 ($90), the Extra Large Size Pack 'N Play, is several inches longer and wider and comes with a removable accessory bag and a pair of lockable wheels on one end.

Graco Model 9260 ($100) is 36 inches square, just like a full-sized play yard, with mesh on all sides and a large alphabet letter in the center of each side. The Canopy Pack 'N Play (Model 9047, $120) has four-sided mesh, one roll-down flap, a detachable accessory bag, and a large, dome-like zippered canopy. It has lockable wheels on one end and center-floor-supporting feet. The manufacturer claims the aluminized fabric in the canopy reduces both UV and infrared rays.

Graco Bassinet Pack 'N Play (Models 9046 and 9046 and additional bassinet models 9346, 9726, and 9716, $100 to $130) have a padded bassinet attachment. Depending on the model, the unit comes with mesh on two sides, swivel wheels on one end, and a removable, washable fabric sheet.

Kolcraft makes triangular-shaped Corner Suite Playards. The advantage of the design is that it fits flush in a corner, a handy space-saver in small quarters.

Protection

Put the Christmas tree inside the playpen to keep it out of a toddler's reach.

Model 18184 ($110) has padding on the three top rails and side legs. The unit has support legs underneath, a clip-on bassinet, zippered storage area, and zippered carrying case.

The Deluxe Playard (Model 10-740, $99) comes with a removable canopy with a zippered side for access to the baby. The Fold 'N Go Care Center Playard (Model 10-751, $99) resembles the other Century models, but comes with two detachable units—a small mesh-sided bassinet and a plastic-topped changing surface with a belt—plus an elasticized pocket for supplies. However, the changer height is so low that all but the shortest parents will have to lean over uncomfortably.

Baby Trend offers six models of its Trend Traveler. Trend Traveler Lites (Models 8010, $59, and 8027, $59) have mesh sides with a toy pouch on one end. Trend Travelers (Model 8110, $69) has a springy "trampoline" floor, mesh on three sides, and an elasticized pocket on the fourth. All come with a nylon carrying case and have a removable, machine-washable mattress cover. Models 8126-WB, 8146-WB ($80), and 8152 ($90) come with wheels on one end and have a bassinet insert that fastens to the sides and covers the entire top.

Chapter 7

BATHING AND DIAPERING

A baby needs less bathing than you think, and more diapers than you ever imagined. Weigh diapering options now.

Keeping baby clean and sweet-smelling can seem like a full-time job. Though bathing takes little time, diaper changes seem endless. Knowing what to expect and planning ahead can make both of those tasks easier.

BATHING YOUR BABY

It's no wonder most parents dread their first time bathing a baby! Baby bathtubs can be large, ungainly containers. A soapy baby is a tiny and slippery creature—and, most likely, very unhappy at that. Young babies, threatened by temperature changes, usually scream in protest when you undress them and lower them into water. And baby skin is so delicate, it can be burned if the bath water is more than mildly warm.

The truth is, small babies don't really need elaborate rubbing and scrubbing. Their skin has a protective covering of oil that helps to ward off skin problems, and too much cleansing removes it. Plus, naturally sweet-smelling babies don't get all that *dirty*. They haven't been outside rolling in the mud (not yet anyway).

For the first year or so, most babies do get tiny bumps and rashes, not necessarily from a lack of cleanliness. Hormonal reactions and viruses have been blamed, but the exact cause is often in doubt. In the diaper area,

Contents

Bathing your baby, page 145

Diapering, page 149

Diaper rash, page 155

Changing tables, page 157

Diaper pails, page 159

Diaper bags, page 161

Shopping savvy, page 161

Toilet training, page 163

they're called "diaper rash" and result from a number of causes. (See our discussion of diaper rash on page 155.)

Practical bathing tips

In the first few weeks after birth, it's all right to forgo a "real" bath. (And don't submerge the cord area until the umbilical cord falls off and the navel heals.) You can simply sponge your baby down from head to toe with a warm, soft washcloth while she's wrapped in a soft cotton blanket. For the diapering area, many baby skin specialists recommend plain water as an adequate cleaner.

Baby's skin can be scalded in water that feels comfortably warm to adults. Your hands are too used to warm water to make good thermostats. Test water temperature with your wrist or elbow.

When baby and you are ready for a real bath, you have several options about where to bathe her. You can use a baby bathtub or the kitchen sink. Or you can use a regular bathtub: Kneel beside the tub on a folded towel and hold baby on top of a slip-resistant bath mat in two inches of water. Or, with someone's help, you can bring the baby into the tub with you, resting him on your bent legs while you bathe him.

If you use the kitchen sink, place a folded bath towel in the bottom of the sink first to help keep baby from slipping. A watering can with a slender,

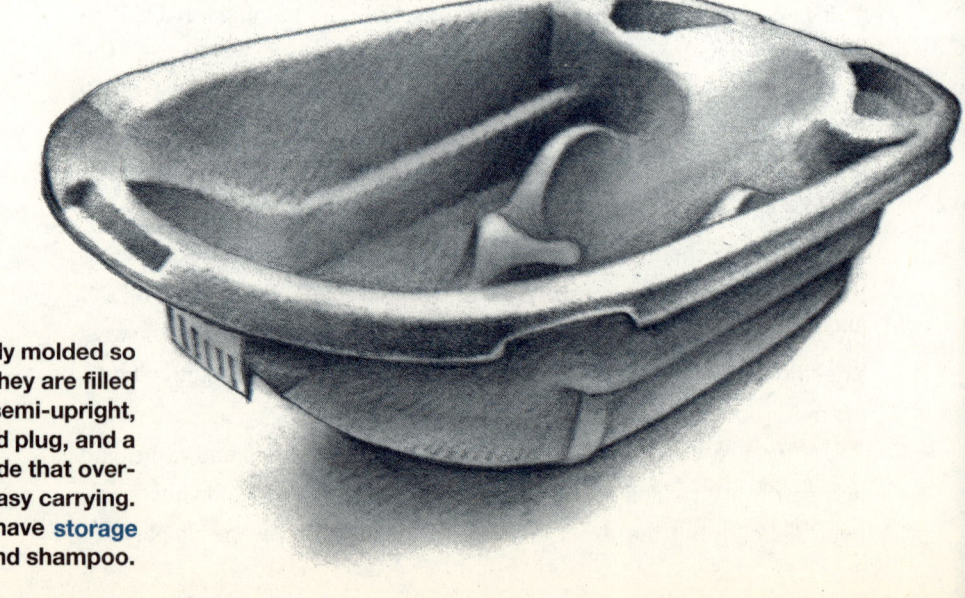

The best tubs are solidly molded so they won't bend when they are filled with water. Look for a semi-upright, nonslip seat, an attached plug, and a smooth rim on the side that overhangs enough for easy carrying. Some models also have storage nooks for soap and shampoo.

long nozzle or a large plastic measuring cup are both handy for rinsing.

Some parents recommend baby-sized foam bath cushions, available in most baby shops for less than $5. You fill a baby bathtub with a few inches of water, then put in the cushion and press down to fill the foam with water. Discard the sponge when it begins to smell musty, or when your baby begins to pick off pieces that could be swallowed.

The bathing process is simple: Get the room comfortably warm. Gather your supplies, including a dry towel, clean clothes, and a diaper. Line the tub or sink with a towel or sponge. Then undress your baby and gently lower him into the tub feet first, supporting his head and buttocks with your hands.

Support him in the tub or sink with one arm around his back, holding the arm opposite you. With your free hand, work your way down from his head to his feet. Once you've finished, wrap him in the towel to keep him covered while you diaper and dress him.

Or borrow a technique from hospital nurseries: Enfold the baby in a lightweight cotton receiving blanket and then lower him into just a few inches of water in the sink or tub while still wrapped. Uncover one part at a time for gentle cleaning.

Bathtub selections

Most major baby product manufacturers, including Graco, Cosco, and Evenflo, make baby bathtubs. Some tubs may have awkward plastic support sections that have to be snapped into place. Others are molded differently at each end—one side for newborns, the other for toddlers. Most tubs have angled seats lined with foam backing to help prevent slipping. Manufacturers warn you to thoroughly squeeze out the foam section after each use and leave the tub out in the open air to prevent the formation of mildew.

A good bathtub is made of plastic firm enough so the tub won't bow from water weight when you pick it up. Look for a plug on the bottom to make emptying easier. The seat should have a nonslip surface, and the seat angle should allow baby to be in a semi-upright position. You'll want a tub that can be used in double sinks, on counters, or in a regular tub.

What's available

You can choose from a variety of baby bathtubs and bath supports.

Early Development's Fisher-Price Deluxe Bath Center (Model 9326, $16) is a deeply angled tub with a foam back support, which can be used in a one- or two-cavity kitchen sink or on a countertop. This seat makes it easier to hold onto baby, with less worry about him slipping down into the tub. There's a drain plug on the base and a rinse pitcher that sprinkles or pours.

First Years Bath Tub/Bath Seat Combo (Model 3129, $20) offers a wide support handle in the back that rotates to allow the seat to recline for a baby or move to a more upright position for a toddler. The dual-position seat is foam-padded. The big handle at the back, plus suction cups on the bottom, are designed to help prevent tip-overs.

Primo EuroBath Infant Seat (Model 320, $17) is designed for babies from birth to six months. This is not a bathtub, but a molded bath support for use in a regular tub or sink—so you don't have to fill a large baby bathtub. It's contoured to conform to a small baby's body in a semireclined position, and offers support between the legs and under the arms. There's a suction-cup base underneath.

Safety 1st Fold-Up Tub (Model No. 164, $13 to $16) is colorful—bright blue with a yellow foam liner. It has a drain plug in the base and folds for storage, especially helpful if you've got limited space.

Skin products

You'll save both money and your baby's skin by avoiding baby lotions, creams, and powders. They contain chemicals that can irritate skin, and

Baby Safe

AVOID SUCTIONED BATH SEATS

Babies and toddlers can drown in only one inch of water. Bath seats do not protect—45 babies died while using them. Most had suction cups to hold them in place.

A typical scenario: A baby is left playing in the seat when someone comes to the front door or the telephone rings. The mother believes the seat will protect her baby. She walks away and is gone for a few minutes. The baby reaches over to retrieve a toy or tries to stand up. The suction on the bottom pops loose. The baby falls forward or slips. The parent finds her baby face down in the tub. But by then, it's too late.

Our advice: Just don't buy one. And never leave a baby or toddler unattended in water, in a regular tub or a baby bathtub, for even a minute. The risks are too great.

some babies even have allergic reactions to cosmetic components, particularly fragrances. (Baby skin-care products are regulated by the Food and Drug Administration. The toll-free number is in the Resource Guide.)

Talcum used in some baby powders can cause a rare form of pneumonia if inhaled in large amounts, such as when a baby is allowed to play with the container and accidentally dumps the powder in his face. Keep the container closed and away from your baby. Rather than sprinkling the powder, put a little in your palm and rub it on. Better yet, don't use powder at all—it serves no useful purpose.

Most baby shampoos touted as "tearless" actually contain anesthetizing chemicals to prevent a stinging sensation, but the shampoo can still irritate a baby's eyes. In the early months, a baby's thin hair doesn't need shampooing, and doing so can lead to scalp dryness and itchiness. Later on, a once-a-week shampoo will be sufficient, except when food gets into his hair. Hold a cloth over your baby's forehead to help protect from shampoo splatters. A stretchable baby visor can also help keep shampoo away from a tot's face.

Soap isn't really necessary in the early months either, and it can irritate baby's skin and delicate genital area. A simple wipe or rinse off with mildly warm water is all that's needed. When you do start to use soap with your baby, look for a cleansing bar that's gentle and unscented, such as fragrance-free Dove, Neutrogena, or Basis. If your baby's skin seems dry, an unscented lotion such as Lubriderm or Eucerin can help.

Baby washcloths, sold in packages of six for about $4, are softer and smaller than regular ones, and seem kinder to a baby's skin than regular terry washcloths. Or you can simply use your own hands to wipe baby down. You may also want to use hooded baby towels to wrap baby and keep his head warm. But roomy, soft terry towels may be even better, and will help keep you dry, too.

Everything that touches baby's skin, including towels and washcloths, should be laundered with a fragrance-free detergent. Avoid liquid or tissue fabric softeners, which add potentially irritating fragrance and can also interfere with fabric absorbency.

DIAPERING

Prepare yourself for a shock. All told, your baby will probably use between 5,000 and 8,000 diapers. It's a good thing babies are so adorable!

Basically, diapers need to be changed whenever they get wet or soiled.

Newborns wet between six and 10 times a day. Stooling is less predictable with younger babies than with older ones, but newborns can use up as many as 100 diapers in a week. Mercifully, diaper demands decrease gradually as the months pass, with ready-to-potty-train toddlers using the fewest number of all.

If a baby's diapers are not changed regularly, the moisture plus the chemical changes of urine and bowel movements start to break down the skin's natural acid balance and oil covering. Skin will become irritated, and that could eventually lead to diaper rash.

It doesn't take too long to determine when a diaper feels damp or heavy, but if you're still learning, you can pinch a small piece of plastic out of the middle of the diaper to help you feel the dampness. In time, you'll become almost intuitive about changing diapers promptly. And each day, let the skin in baby's diaper area have time to air dry. Just let him lie on a waterproof pad or a towel.

Assess your diapering options before baby arrives. You have four basic choices: Disposable diapers made of pulp and fiber are thrown away when they become soiled (we rate disposable diaper performance on page 169). Plain cotton fabric diapers are washed and used again. Washable fabric diapering systems combine thick inner fabric liners and washable outer coverings. Commercial diaper services are available in some areas.

Welcome to the diapering debate

From the moment they're born until that glorious day they become potty trained, you'll have to deal with all those thousands of diapers. What kind should you choose? When it comes to disposables versus washables, parents' opinions usually fall into one camp or the other. Disposable advocates argue that the convenience is worth the $1,500 to $2,100 it costs to use them before a baby becomes a potty expert.

Reusable fans argue that soft cotton diapers are more comfortable for baby. They also express serious environmental concerns about the effects of millions of diapers clogging up landfills and taking nearly a century to degrade.

Parents in favor of disposables praise the convenience of simply taping on a diaper and then tossing it away once it's soiled. And they point to the time and energy resources required to launder cloth diapers.

Cloth diaper advocates counter with the demands of disposables: numerous trips to the store to drag home hefty packages of diapers and late night journeys down the driveway, lugging heavy garbage cans filled with little "stink bombs."

Are disposable diapers worse for the environment than cloth diapers? Except in cases where water or landfill space is in short supply, their impact is about the same. Creating waste in landfills by using disposable diapers is no more environmentally harmful than using up water and energy to wash cloth diapers.

Furthermore, both types can cause problems if they're handled improperly. Before tossing a disposable in the trash or a cloth diaper in the wash, first flush feces down the toilet, where they can be treated by a sewage system.

Cloth diapers are much less expensive than disposables, especially if you launder them yourself. And some parents feel they do a better job of keeping kids dry and free from diaper rash. But most day-care centers prefer disposables over cloth diapers because they help keep germs from spreading.

Really, there's no need to take sides. Instead, you can pick and choose diaper options according to your needs—disposables or cloth or a mix of the two.

For example, if a diaper service is available, you could sign on for a baby's first few months. The service would cover the immense laundering and disposal demands of your newborn. Then, for home use, you might choose to shift to a reusable diapering system that offers thick, highly absorbent flannel pads for the center of lightweight, quick-drying outer pants. And, you could stock up on disposables for the times when you run out of cloth diapers or for any treks away from home. Or, you could choose fabric diapers for daytime and use disposables overnight—whatever option works best for you.

Dry out

Let the baby stay naked or at least bare-bottomed as often as possible—a light case of diaper rash may be air- or sun-cured quickly.

Disposables

If you're among the 95 percent of parents who buy disposable diapers, you may have noticed that features of the leading brands seem to change faster and faster. A few years back, a particular brand might be tweaked every 18 months. Today, because of flat consumer demand and fierce competition in this $3.6 billion industry, it's every six to eight months.

Some changes are marketing ploys. Remember "his" and "her" diapers? There really was no difference, our previous tests showed, and now unisex diapers are back. Biodegradability was also just hype. Other changes appear to be a justification for price hikes. For example, why would Kimberly-Clark add "15 percent more special absorbent material" to top-of-the-line Huggies Supreme—and a 5 percent increase in price—when CONSUMER REPORTS' tests showed that the old Huggies Supreme already absorbed far more liquid than would likely be necessary?

Disposable diapers are found in stores just about everywhere—at full price in most grocery stores and drugstores, and discounted in giant national chains, such as Toys 'R' Us, Babies 'R' Us, Wal-Mart, Kmart, CVS, and Target. They're priced between 15 and 35 cents per diaper and packaged according to size—Newborn, then from Size 1 up to Size 5, used for tots 30 pounds and over. Diaper makers are fully aware that once parents commit to using their product, they'll probably stay with it. Packages of diapers in all sizes from a single company will weigh roughly the same. But as diapers get larger, you get fewer diapers for the price—which translates into paying more per diaper. The difference in price between a Size 1 and Size 5 can be a dime or more per dia-

Tips Save money
BUYING DISPOSABLES FOR LESS

Stores often have disposable diaper sales to induce parents to shop there. Watch the papers for specials and stock up.

• Don't try to skimp on diapers by letting your baby stay wet. It will only lead to painful skin infections and doctor bills that far outweigh the cost of the diapers.

• Plan on your newborn using 100 diapers a week, but don't overstock on the newborn size. Start with one pack of newborn and one pack of size 1. Stock up after you see which size your baby needs. (As a backup to disposables, you can purchase one or two dozen fabric diapers, too, and some small, waterproof pants with side closures. Cloth diapers are handy for burp cloths and milksops.)

• Get your name on new-parent mailing lists by signing up for parenting magazines, contests, registries, and so on. You'll get tons of junk mail, but money-saving coupons, too.

• Try contacting the customer service lines of diaper manufacturers, too, for coupons or special offers. See the Resource Guide for manufacturers' toll-free numbers.

• Experiment with private-label diapers—you may find features you like at a good price. Note: Discount chains may not have all brand options or diaper sizes on any given day, so be prepared to shop elsewhere or have other options in case your own preferred brand is out of stock.

• Don't waste diapers. If your tot is at the stage of peeling off his disposables, try putting the diapers on backwards so he can't reach the tapes.

per. However, older children do use fewer diapers than babies do.

Performance and features. A good disposable fits well without gaps that allow wetness or messies to spill out. The tabs work well; they reclose if you want to check to see if a diaper is wet and stay closed once they're in place. The stuffing absorbs wetness well and doesn't clump. The product doesn't cause rashes or other skin reactions from chemicals or plastics.

After performance, consider a diaper's features. You have three choices: Basic diapers are thicker and bulkier than other types and the least preferred by parents. (We did not include them in the Special Report Ratings.) Ultrathins (or ultratrims), the most popular type, are made with a material that provides the same or better absorbency as other diapers. In fact, the Huggies Ultratrim and the Dri-Bottoms Ultrathin tested did a better job of stopping leaks and had a higher overall score than their premium brandmates. Many ultrathins have a plastic exterior and tape fasteners. Supreme (or premium) diapers are generally more expensive than ultrathins and are more likely to have clothlike covers and Velcro or similar fasteners, which we prefer because they're usually easier to reclose.

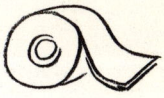

Fix it

Keep a roll of masking tape handy to mend torn tabs on disposables and to mend plastic pants.

Style changes are typically introduced on supreme diapers and are then sometimes picked up by brandmates. As a result, now you'll find many ultrathins with features once available only on premiums. Huggies Ultratrim for Boys and Girls, Drypers, Especially for Baby (Toys 'R' Us) Ultrathins, and Dri-Bottoms Ultrathin come with cloth-like covers. Huggies Ultratrim also has Velcro-like fasteners and a new "waist leak" barrier.

Questionable qualities. Some diaper makers are again touting greater absorbency. That's not a giant leap forward, since the diapers we tested—thanks to gels that trap many times their weight in liquid—already have a capacity that babies with even the busiest bladders would be hard-pressed to challenge. Even Drypers, which had the lowest capacity, still held the equivalent of four or more urinations.

How important is it to buy a diaper with a liner infused with emollients, like the top-rated Pampers Premium, or aloe vera and baking soda, like Drypers? Medical experts we consulted report that although emollients in a diaper may reduce the friction, they won't be transferred to a baby's skin.

Comparison shopping. At any point along the way, it makes sense to experiment with different brands, if the savings warrant it. (See our Ratings, page 169.) Be aware that size can vary from one diaper manufacturer to another, so you may not always get a perfect fit.

It's sometimes worth paying more if another brand offers features you want. For example, superabsorbent "overnight" diapers help tots to sleep through the night without discomfort or leaks.

Reusable cotton diapers

Traditional cotton diapers require a bigger up-front investment than disposables but save money in the long run. They're a viable option if you've got a reliable washing machine and dryer and the time to do laundry.

You will need four to six dozen to begin, plus four to six pairs of waterproof outer pants. Cloth diapers are sold in packs of 6 or 12, and are priced between $1 and $2 apiece in baby stores.

Reusables are made of different types of absorbent fabrics: terry (like toweling, but softer); bird's-eye (similar to old-fashioned tea towels); gauze (thinner, and more lightweight); and flannel (similar to flannel sheets and pajamas, but more dense and thick).

Cotton diapers are sold unfolded (squares of flat fabric to be folded to fit your baby's size), "prefolded" (sewn into a rectangular shape with extra fabric or absorbent layers in the center), and in shaped varieties with a narrow crotch and wide wings to wrap around baby's waist. A few brands come with plastic outer covers sewn onto the diapers, but they don't launder as well or dry as quickly as plain diapers, or as diapers and separate covers.

There's also a new generation of reusables combining highly absorbent

Tips in the wash

DIAPER LAUNDERING

• Wash diapers two dozen at a time. Presoak first, using your washer's highest water level and the hottest water. Launder with a hot wash and cold rinse.

• You don't need to bleach as long as you soak soiled diapers. Bleach cuts down the life of diapers. Use chlorine-free bleach or washing soda instead to remove stains.

• Always use a fragrance-free detergent to spare baby's sensitive skin exposure to irritating chemicals. If your baby is prone to diaper rash, rinse diapers twice, adding three-quarters cup of white vinegar to the second rinse.

• Don't use fabric softener, either the liquid kind or sheets for the dryer. Your baby may react to the fragrance, and it leaves a waxy buildup on the diapers, making them water-repellent instead of absorbent.

cotton diapers with moisture-resistant, quick-drying outer covers that fasten with snap or Velcro closures. The combination of diapers made from heavy flannel plus adjustable, breathable outer pants is far superior to simple pre-folded diapers sold by the dozen in baby stores—and far more expensive, costing as much as $8 per set.

You can't usually find these superabsorbent diaper systems in stores, but you can order them by mail from specialty mail-order houses and a few web stores. Mail-order catalogs carrying diapering systems are available from Babyworks, The Natural Baby Catalog, and Simple Alternatives. (See Resource Guide for contact information.)

An excellent reference book regarding fabric diapers is Theresa Rodriguez Farrisi's "Diaper Changes: The Complete Diapering Book and Resource Guide" (Homekeepers Publishing). The book contains a thorough discussion of diapering options and accessories, lists the addresses and contact numbers for most of the companies selling fabric diapers, and even gives instructions on how to make your own diapers and diaper covers.

If you live in a sizable metropolitan area, you may have access to a diaper service—a more affordable option than you might think. For a monthly fee, the service will deliver two to three dozen fresh diapers (virtually sterilized by high-temperature washing), once or twice a week, and take away the soiled diapers. You'll also be given a diaper pail fitted with a plastic bag. Most companies allot a set of diapers to be solely used by your baby, and guarantee no comingling. And, the good news is the service costs less than using disposables.

DIAPER RASH

Diaper rash, medically called *diaper dermatitis*, is one of the most common problems parents encounter with a baby's skin. The rash usually begins with a few red bumps and spreads around a baby's diaper area in a matter of days. The rash occurs most often on babies between 9 and 12 months of age, when approximately one out of three babies develops it.

Skin wetness is the major cause of diaper rash. Moist skin is more easily irritated, particularly by the friction of a diaper. And the mix of urine and feces also produces substances that can irritate a baby's skin.

Other causes of diaper rash are diarrhea and illnesses. The faster the stool material moves through baby's sensitive digestive tract, the more likely it will carry irritating substances. So it's not uncommon for a baby to have a bottom rash a day or so after an attack of diarrhea. A rough washcloth or

Fresh

Add a handful of baking soda to the next-to-last rinse to keep the diapers soft and fresh smelling. Fabric softener is expensive and may cause skin irritation.

soap can irritate the diaper area even further.

Baby-skin specialists suggest the following strategies for combating a diaper rash outbreak: Change diapers frequently, at least 8 to 10 times a day. If your baby is soiled with urine and stool, rinse the diaper area with plain tap water or sit the baby in a tub or sink containing a few inches of water, then pat the baby dry. Don't use baby wipes; their chemicals degrade the skin's natural protective barrier. A light layer of petroleum jelly can ease any irritating friction—better than talcum.

Choose diapers that keep the baby as dry as possible. Keep urine away from the stool, either by double- or triple-diapering with cloth diapers or by using superabsorbent disposable diapers to bind moisture away from the skin. Until the rash subsides, allow your baby's bottom to go without diapers at least once a day.

If the diaper area becomes damaged, with skin broken or blistered, or if the rash lasts more than four or five days, contact your physician. There are a number of diaper-area infections that may start out as a common diaper rash and develop into something more serious: A fiery-red, bumpy rash, sometimes with scaly edges, may signal a yeast infection. (If you use corn starch as baby powder, discontinue—it encourages yeast and fungus infections.) A brilliant red, swollen ring around a baby's rectum with little tears or fissures that develops quickly, rapidly worsens, and lasts for weeks and results in painful bowel movements may be caused by a strep infection. In either of these cases, prompt medical treatment should be sought to clear up the problem.

If your baby wears disposables, it may help to loosen the elastic bands around the leg to permit air circulation. Make a snip in the elastic on one

List: For the medicine cabinet

A BASIC TOILETRY KIT FOR BABY

- Thermometer.
- Baby nail clippers or small scissors with rounded tips.
- Nasal aspirator (bulb to clear mucus from a baby's nose).
- Zinc-based diaper cream.
- Antiseptic for cord care (ask your doctor).
- Infant's Tylenol, or other acetaminophen.
- Cotton balls.
- Fragrance-free, mild cleansing bar.

diaper leg in the front, and one on the opposite diaper leg at the back. But be prepared for occasional leaks.

CHANGING TABLES

Where will you change your baby's diapers? Some parents elect to use the crib with one side lowered as their changing place. Or you can set up a diapering station in your baby's room, or in the bathroom, if it's large enough. More simply, you can keep pads and diaper supplies in a couple of places in the house, especially practical if your house has several levels.

You may want to purchase a changing table—a baby-length wooden stand surrounded by rails, with a thick, vinyl-covered foam pad on the changing surface and a belt for safety. Most tables also have drawers or shelves underneath to hold diapers and fresh clothing.

Instead of a standard changing table, you do have several other options. You can purchase a chest with a fold-down top containing a padded diapering area at a baby furniture outlet. The top can then be removed when baby's no longer in diapers. Several companies also produce a changing table that doubles as a small baby bed for the early months after birth. More rarely, some tables have alternating drawers that allow the unit to fold, forming a single column for easier storage.

A fold-down wooden adapter for the top of a nursery chest, though convenient, is the least desirable. It does not offer a protective railing in the

Baby Safe

CHANGING-TABLE KNOW-HOW

As with other "baby-holders," including cribs and high chairs, there's the ever-present danger that your baby will fall out in a flash while your back is turned. Falls happen when parents don't anticipate vigorous baby gymnastics—or expect a baby to follow a command to stay still.

• Gather up whatever you need for the changing job, whether it's a damp washcloth or fresh change of clothing, before you lay baby down. Storage shelves can keep basic necessities, (until your toddler starts pulling things down).

• Always fasten the unit's safety belt around baby's waist. For extra safety, keep one hand on the baby, too.

• If someone comes to the door or you need to answer the telephone, take baby with you.

front. And, when a baby's weight is placed on the front edge, the entire chest can topple over.

A changing table may also be available as part of a nursery suite that includes a crib, chest, and armoire. In some cases a changer will be installed on top of a chest or inside an armoire. Coordinating models are typically priced between $100 and $200, but you can find a changing table for much less if you don't insist that baby's furniture be totally matched.

Add a mobile or pictures out of baby's reach but within her sight. You'll also want enough light to see well.

Or you can install a waist-high plywood platform that runs the length of the closet in your baby's room. Screw down a changing pad with a belt, available as a separate unit in most baby stores. Some parents also have taught themselves to change baby in their laps—a skill that comes in handy wherever you are.

What's available

Inspect the table before you purchase it to be sure it's stable and the safety belt works well.

Tall, protective side rails, a firm, wet-proof pad, sturdy safety belt, and easy-to-access storage area are all signs of a good changing table. But you can also change baby right in the crib, with one dropside down.

The Bassett Sugarplum Dressing Table (Model 5068-590, $229), in pine with a variety of finishes, has two useful storage shelves, decorative safety railings on all sides, and a padded baby cushion and safety belt.

Child Craft Encore Dressing Table (Model 1376, $250), in hardwood in a variety of finishes, has two open flat shelves beneath the dressing table. The dressing area is enclosed on all four sides and equipped with a pad and security strap.

Evenflo/Contemporary Changing Table (Model 3651, $90) is a full-size hardwood changing table with two large shelves for storage. There are safety railings on all sides, plus a vinyl changing pad and safety belt.

DIAPER PAILS

The type of diaper pail you'll need depends on whether you are using disposables or cloth diapers. Disposables require that you seal off the diapers until you can get them out of the house and into the garbage can for pickup. Cloth diapers clean better if they're allowed to soak until you're ready to launder them.

Empty as much fecal matter as you can from either type of diaper into the toilet before you roll up the disposable or dump a cloth diaper into a soaking solution. You can also sprinkle soiled cloth diapers with baking soda to help minimize odors.

Pails for disposables

Diaper pails for disposables use plastic trash can bags or specially designed, long plastic sleeves to form an odor-blocking seal around diapers.

The most popular diaper disposing system, the Diaper Genie from Playtex, makes it easy to seal away diapers for maximum odor control. You drop the diaper into a plastic sleeve, turn the twist rim to seal, and close the lid to seal each diaper in its own pocket. When the Genie is ready to be emptied, a built-in device cuts the sleeve, and you pull out the long chain of diapers and throw them away. You might buy several refills ($5 apiece) to avoid return trips to the baby store. The Diaper Genie works only with Diaper Genie refills, which wrap up to 180 newborn diapers each. (Retailers love the Diaper Genie because it keeps parents coming back to the store, where they end up spending money on other stuff, too.) There is also a bigger Diaper Genie designed for larger-size diapers. It holds fewer—but older tots use fewer diapers.

Ready

Keep a thermos of warm water near the changing table at night for quick cleanups. You'll avoid stumbling around in the dark and running the water for what seems hours to get the right temperature.

Odor-free

Use an inch or so of kitty litter or baking soda in the bottom of your baby's diaper pail to absorb the odors of disposable diapers. Change once a week to keep it fresh.

The Diaper Genie does keep odors down and makes diaper disposal a less smelly task. But it's priced higher than most pails, and the cost of refills plus store trips add up. And although the Genie works well for small diapers, larger diapers are more difficult to stuff in, and the unit fills up more quickly. In time, the Genie can start to smell on its own from having absorbed diaper odors.

You have several other options that will save you money over the long haul. A Safety 1st Odor-Less Diaper Pail ($17 to $22), which uses tall kitchen trash bags, also has a lid that twists to seal off diaper odors below. The lid has a large knob underneath that acts like a diaper stuffer, pressing the diaper down into the pail for you. If you purchase trash bags when they go on sale in discount chains, you can save a lot over Genie refills.

Sometimes the simplest answer is also the best and cheapest: Post a large kitchen trash can or even a garbage can with a locking lid nearby. Line it with a garbage bag, either a drawstring or twist-tie type. Seal the bag every time you throw a soiled diaper inside, just as you would "live" garbage. These containers will hold a lot more diapers than small diaper pails, will keep diaper odors down (especially if you spray the inside with disinfectant)—and you'll save money and constant emptying hassles.

Pails for cloth diapers

You'll want a pail strong enough to hold the weight of water but also easy to carry. It should have a comfortable handle and a spout for pouring out the soaking solution. Most importantly, it should have a lid that locks to keep the baby from playing with the diapers, or falling in head first and drowning. (It happens!)

Soak diapers in plain water or water plus a mild detergent or washing soda until you're ready to machine-wash them. A good-sized diaper load is about two dozen diapers. If you buy a diapering system by mail order, ask the customer service department to give you tips on diaper laundering.

Some parents simply use the washing machine to hold soiled diapers until washing time, but that can get in the way of regular laundry. As with other household chores, washing diapers every day or every other day can help to keep the pile of damp diapers manageable (and not so smelly).

Pails such as Safety 1st Diaper Pail (Model 468, $10 to $12) are adequate for the job. The pail has a presser foot to raise the child-resistant lid, a sturdy handle, and is strong enough not to bow from water pressure.

Some diaper pails have an enclosed section in the lid designed to hold deodorizing tablets. Children may try to eat the tablets if they're not safely locked in—we suggest not using them at all. For an extra margin of safety, store the pail inside a cabinet and use a child-resistant latch to keep baby out.

DIAPER BAGS

When even a brief dash to the mall and grocery store demands a pile of baby supplies, a diaper bag becomes your best friend. Prices for diaper bags range from $20 for a low-end fabric or vinyl model to $100 or more for name-brand designer bags found in upscale department stores and boutiques. Baby sections in stores usually carry a variety of models: fanny packs, backpacks, and shoulder totes in conservative black and navy blue or whimsical pastel "baby" patterns.

Although the pastel patterns may be appealing at first, you may tire of those frolicking teddy bears and cutesy prints in the long run. Something more subdued—black and navy and other solids—in a style that both Mom and Dad would feel comfortable carrying can be a better choice. (Advise gift-givers of your preference.)

SHOPPING SAVVY Diaper bags

The sturdiest and most serviceable models aren't to be found on the shelves of retail stores but in the pages of mail-order catalogs such as Lands' End and L.L. Bean, or by ordering directly from small companies whose sole mission in the world is to construct the ultimate diaper tote.

Since the bag might be your constant sidekick for several years, think about size and comfort—as you would with any frequently carried purse or tote. If you're short, buy a bag with shorter handles so the bottom doesn't drag on the floor. If your skin is easily irritated, find a soft, quilted model that won't chafe the underside of your arm.

Now's no time to skimp on quality—cheap vinyl and poorly constructed fabric bags are only going to tear, fray, or get stained and sticky over time. Instead, choose a sturdy bag made from a thick, heavy-duty, moisture-resistant, vinyl-backed fabric like those used in luggage. And look for well-reinforced seams, particularly where handles are sewn onto the bag.

While fanny diaper packs are useful for brief treks, when it comes to serious toting, you'll probably want a roomier bag. Although dark colors, such as navy blue, black, or forest green, aren't as perky and cute as pastel elephants dancing on rainbows, neutrals are less likely to show stains. Plus, you can later convert a large dark bag into a lightweight carry-on or sports bag once the diaper siege has ended.

Look for a generous-sized, washable changing pad that rolls up inside, easy-to-access bottle pockets, comfortable carrying handles, and optional shoulder straps to free your hands for toting baby and other stuff. Moisture-proof storage compartments are essential for porting food, diapers, and other paraphernalia—yours and baby's.

A removable pocket for either soiled diapers or a damp washcloth is a handy plus. But don't go overboard with pockets and separate compartments. The dark recesses inside the bag will only frustrate you when baby's pacifier or your keys get misplaced. Clear plastic or see-through mesh will help you keep tabs on everything. Test out all closures to be sure they'll secure everything inside, since diaper bags get dumped unexpectedly. Zippers are the best bet, lint-collecting Velcro is less dependable, and snap closures the least handy of all. You might want to include separate, sealable plastic bags for on-the-go diaper disposal.

Diaper backpacks with shoulder straps are an emerging design from companies like Baby Bjorn and Evenflo. You can sling the pack over one or both shoulders, or over one arm. Or you can carry it by the handle at the top. Make sure the shoulder straps are well-padded, or wearing the pack won't be comfortable for long, even if it leaves your hands free.

You might consider a standard backpack, a large zippered purse made from heavy-duty fabric, a roomy zippered computer case, or the smallest sized shoulder bag/carry-on in a luggage line. You can sometimes find adaptable bags for a bargain in office supply stores, in store luggage departments, and at factory outlets. Just be sure the bag you choose tucks under your arm conveniently and is roomy enough for a pile of baby things.

What's available

These options represent only a small, select number of diaper bags chosen from the hundreds available. They're roomy, made of sturdy materials, and most have insulated sections for keeping bottles cold. Two are backpacks that make diaper toting easier by freeing up your hands. One listing is for a set of bag adapters.

Baby Bjorn Diaper Backpack ($65) is a backpack with a large zippered rear compartment, spacious pockets for diapers, insulated pockets for bottles, a large changing pad, and wide, well-padded shoulder straps. It's available in navy blue or black.

Dad Gear Niko Bag ($75 to $85) comes with removable changing pad, detachable backpack straps, mesh pockets, insulated bottle pockets on the outside, a key leash, and a diaper storage area. Choose from teal blue, steel gray, red, or bronze.

Lamby Baby Travel Back Pack ($65), in playful multicolored fabric, has a large zippered flap for inside access, plus vertical zippers for side access. The base has a diaper dispenser and spacious changing mat. It features sturdy handles and a variety of pockets: mesh pockets for lotions, one for wipes, and a foil-insulated compartment for bottles and food.

Lands' End Deluxe Diaper Bag (Model 4478-4B14, $50) is constructed of vinyl-backed nylon. There are three expandable zippered compartments inside and an insulated outer pocket with a zippered lid. The bag comes with an extra-large changing pad, padded shoulder straps, and reinforced handles. It's available in hunter green, plum wine (purple), navy blue, and black. Monogramming adds $5.

Weebees World's Best Diaper Bag ($59) is a sturdy, machine-washable pack with lots of compartments inside and side pockets. It comes with a "little tripper" waist pack and two removable shoulder straps. Choose from black, navy, burgundy, and purple.

McKenzie Kids Everything But the Bag ($36) isn't a diaper bag at all—but everything you need to stuff inside your favorite pocketbook, tote bag, or backpack to convert it into a usable diaper bag.

TOILET TRAINING

The age for mastering toilet training is getting later every decade. Forty years ago, the "good mother" had her baby trained by age one. More recently, child psychologists have pointed out that toilet training works better and faster when a child is developmentally able to follow simple directions and link a couple of tasks in sequence, that is, one task after the other. Usually this occurs at age two or later.

With the advent of disposable diapers, babies are delaying learning to use a toilet to age two, three, and beyond. No one knows exactly why disposables have prolonged the diapering stage, but it's thought that greater diaper absorbency makes children less aware they're wet, and that, in turn, has weakened the child's association between urinating or having a bowel movement and needing to use a potty.

Cleanup

Color code washcloths if you use them for cleanup: one color for the bath, one for diapering.

Teaching a child to use the toilet is pretty complicated. Your tot has to sense when he's about to go. He has to have the motor skills to get himself to the bathroom, to pull down his pants, and to back into a potty, or mount the adult toilet, and do it before his immature "holding muscles" let go. For most children, the procedure doesn't come naturally. It takes a commitment from parents to home in on this learned behavior hour by hour until it's mastered. Needless to say, reward—whether praise or treats—works a whole lot better in shaping a tot's behavior than threats and punishment. The latter only raise emotions (and obstinacy) but don't help with the intricate mastery of this often difficult new skill.

Potties and toilet seat adapters

The simplest requirement of a floor potty is that the pot be easy to empty and that the seat holding the pot won't slide away when a child backs into it. For multipiece units, the pot part should lift straight up out of the seat, rather than sliding out from the back or front.

As with other baby products we've discussed throughout this book, potties have become more complicated than they need to be. Simple, one-piece chamber pots, which are actually the easiest to use, have morphed into multi-component contraptions, some without a single part that works smoothly.

The pots inside the seats aren't easily removable, so they jam when you try to take them out, causing spills. *But*, the pots or bases become stepstools when you turn them upside down. *And,* the rings can serve as toilet seat adapters for the regular toilet, *but* only if you've got a standard-sized toilet seat and not an elongated one.

However, even if they can do several things, they can't do them all at once. And most tots haven't got the skills to operate them anyway—to slide out a pot to empty it, to convert a stepstool to a pot, or to retrieve a toilet seat ring and get it back onto the big toilet when it's time to go.

(If you need a stepstool for the bathroom, we suggest purchasing one separately. It should have a nonslip surface on top and bottom. Two examples are First Years Store & Step Stool, Model 3126, for about $12, or Baby Bjorn Safe Step, $15.)

What's available

Here are a few examples of the best designs in toilet training aids.

Nursery Needs Pottysaurus (Model 1553, $20), a low-to-the-floor purple dinosaur molded from plastic, is easy to mount, with the dinosaur's neck serving as a handle and boy's splash guard.

Baby Bjorn Splash Proof Potty ($15), Little Potty ($10), and Potty Chair ($23) are imported from Sweden. The Little Potty has a splash guard and handle in back. The Splash Proof is a similar design but with a higher splash guard (for boys) and a small rim flush against the floor to secure the potty. The Potty Chair is a molded chair base with a high back and arm rest, with a simple-to-remove pot in the center. These pots are well-shaped to conform to a child's bottom, and they're easy to use and clean.

Baby Bjorn's Toilet Trainer ($30), also imported from Sweden, features a curved, comfortable adapter for both standard and elongated toilet seats and a curved splash guard in front. The special adjuster in the rear locks the adapter into the right size for the toilet ring. The apparatus is easily removed with a rear carrying handle.

PU Digital Flip-N-Flush ($13) is a permanently attachable potty seat that fits inside an adult toilet seat. When not needed, the trainer flips up and out of the way. It's available in red, green, blue, and white.

Playskool Magic Reward Li'L Potty (Model 30904, $10) is a simple two-piece pot with a target in the base that changes to a star when the job's well done. The bowl separates from its small stand for cleaning with just a button push.

Playskool Magic Reward Potty Step Stool (Model 31380, $20) has an image at the base of the bowl that changes from a target to a star when wet. The ring lifts off to fit on the regular toilet, and the pot lifts out from the top. The lid can be lowered so the whole unit can be used for a step stool.

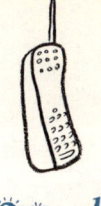

On call

Put an extension phone in your baby's room, or carry a cordless phone with you when you need to change a diaper.

TESTS OF DIAPERS

How Consumer Reports tests diapers

There have been many real improvements in the 37 years since babies were safety-pinned into the first bulky Pampers. Disposables are now more absorbent, they fit better, they have easy-to-use fasteners, and they come in three styles—basic, ultrathin, and supreme (or premium). Indeed, of the 13 types of diapers we tested (CONSUMER REPORTS, August 1998), 8 were judged excellent. There were also winners among the six brands of training pants we tested.

Results for diapers

The most important measure of a diaper's performance is how well it prevents leaks. Over the course of three months, staffers at three day-care centers changed 8,000 diapers on 80 babies and toddlers. The performance results they recorded form the basis of our Ratings chart on page 169.

An excellent diaper must also be able to absorb lots of liquid and keep it away from a child's skin to prevent irritation and diaper rash. It must fit a variety of shapes and sizes well enough to prevent leaks at the waist and legs. Finally, it should be easy and quick to fasten and should stay closed without the fastener losing its grip or tearing the diaper.

All of the top diapers in our Ratings—Pampers Premium, Walgreen's His and Her Dryness Supreme, Pampers Baby-Dry Stretch, American Fare (Kmart) Little Ones Supreme, Huggies Ultratrim for Boys and Girls, Huggies Supreme, and Luvs Ultra Leakguards Stretch—were excellent overall. Compared with other diapers in our test, they leaked less frequently and did a better job keeping children dry. Huggies Overnites were also excellent, but they cost a little more.

Even with top-rated diapers, you may have to experiment a bit to find one that best fits your baby's quickly changing body. In our day-care tests, the three Huggies models and the American Fare (Kmart) Little Ones Supreme fit more than 90 percent of the children well.

Sizes do vary from brand to brand. One brand's "medium" may claim to fit children between 12 and 24 pounds; another brand's "medium" may be for kids 16 to 28 pounds. Although the best performers are relatively expensive, you can save money if you select the smallest diaper your child can comfortably wear; the larger the diaper, the higher the cost. And buy the largest package available.

Overnight diapers

Does a diaper made expressly for overnight use really prevent messy leaks and 3 a.m. changes? We tested Huggies Overnites both in a laboratory and in the real world and found that its claims were true. The Overnites can absorb nearly a full liter of liquid (about the same as top-rated Pampers Premium) but more quickly than the other diapers we tested. The Overnites received an overall score of excellent based on daytime use by our day-care panel, performing slightly better than its two brandmates. A small, separate panel of CONSUMER REPORTS staffers checked them out on their own children at night, comparing them with nighttime use of Huggies Ultratrim. The Overnites leaked much less frequently.

The major drawback to using Overnites in the daytime is the cost—34 cents apiece for large diapers, or a dime more per diaper than Huggies Ultratrim, which was close in daytime performance. Compared with

Premium diapers like those shown at left often have clothlike covers and Velcro closures. **Training pants,** below, are for children who are being toilet trained.

SPECIAL REPORT

Huggies Ultratrim, the Overnites would add about $15 to your monthly diaper bill.

Results for training pants

We performed laboratory-only tests on disposable training pants, which combine underwear design and diaper technology. They're intended for children who are being toilet trained or who may have accidents at night. Children put them on as they would underpants, but the disposables have sides that tear away in case of a messy accident. The medical experts we've consulted consider using them preferable to prematurely forcing toilet training or to putting children who are toilet trained during the day back into diapers at night. Of the six brands we tested for absorption rate and capacity, Drypers Training Pants were the best.

Recommendations

The best performers in our tests included two major-brand supreme (or premium) diapers, a major-brand overnight diaper, three major-brand ultra-thin diapers, and two store-brand supreme diapers. Choose among these for a diaper that fits your baby's body the best. They're typically more expensive than the rest, but their superior performance is worth the difference in cost. Choose features based on what you prefer—from the exterior covering to the fasteners. They'll all work fine, no matter what the ads say.

Among the training pants, Drypers were the best for capacity and quick absorption.

Brands do change, so many of the products we tested may be slightly different from the ones you'll find on store shelves. However, many of the changes appear to be minor, and our Ratings may not be appreciably affected.

RATINGS & RECOMMENDATIONS

DIAPERS

THE TESTS BEHIND THE RATINGS The overall score reflects performance primarily with our day-care panel; results of lab tests were used only to help rate fastener quality. Judgments of leakage and dryness figured much more prominently into the overall score than did the other categories. All regular diapers were tested by 80 children of both sexes, ranging in age from 5 months to nearly 3 years. Day-care testers changed the diapers on a schedule, with additional changes as needed. **Prevents leaks** is as reported by the day-care testers. The best brands leaked roughly 1.5 percent of the time; the worst, about 6 percent. **Keeps baby dry** reflects whether children felt wet to the day-care testers. **Prevents padding shift** reflects shifts in a diaper's absorbent material, which may make a child uncomfortable and can result in leaking. **Fastener quality** incorporates day-care results of fasteners that came undone while a child was wearing the diaper, and results of lab tests in which diapers were opened and closed repeatedly and the force required to pull them open was measured. **Price per diaper** is approximate retail for size 4 (large) diapers in the largest package count available; cost per month assumes 155 diapers used.

RECOMMENDATIONS Spending more buys much better performance. Choose among the top eight performers for a diaper that fits your baby's body the best. Special features such as exterior coverings and fasteners weren't as variable.

RATINGS DIAPERS

OVERALL RATINGS Listed in order of overall score

Legend: E ⊖ VG ⊖ G ○ F ◐ P ●

Brand and type	Price per diaper	Cost per month	Overall score (0–100) P F G VG E	Prevents leaks	Keeps baby dry	Prevents padding shift	Fastener quality
Pampers Premium	29¢	$44.95		⊖	⊖	⊖	⊖
Walgreens His and Her Dryness Supreme	33	51.15		⊖	⊖	⊖	○
Pampers Baby-Dry Stretch	25	38.75		⊖	⊖	⊖	⊖
American Fare (Kmart) Little Ones Supreme	25	38.75		⊖	⊖	○	⊖
Huggies Ultratrim for Boys and Girls	24	37.20		⊖	⊖	⊖	⊖
Huggies Supreme	29	44.95		⊖	⊖	⊖	○
Luvs Ultra Leakguards Stretch	21	32.55		⊖	⊖	⊖	⊖
Drypers	24	37.20		○	⊖	⊖	⊖
Especially for Baby (Toys 'R' Us) Ultrathin	19	29.45		⊖	⊖	⊖	⊖
Dri-Bottoms Ultrathin	18	27.90		○	⊖	⊖	⊖
Fitti	21	32.55		⊖	○	⊖	⊖
Dri-Bottoms Supreme	25	38.75		◐	⊖	⊖	⊖

RATINGS & RECOMMENDATIONS

TRAINING PANTS

THE TESTS BEHIND THE RATINGS **Absorption capacity** is the maximum amount of liquid absorbed. The best pants held 1½ times as much as the worst. **Absorption rate** is how quickly wet training pants could absorb more liquid. **Price per pants** is approximate retail for size 3 (large) training pants in the largest package count available.

RECOMMENDATIONS We found big differences in performance. Of the six models we tested, Dryers were the best in absorption, both in rate and capacity.

OVERALL RATINGS Listed in order of absorption

Key: E VG G F P

Brand and type	Price per pants	Absorption capacity	Absorption rate
Drypers Training Pants	41¢	E	E
Huggies Pull-Ups	42	G	E
Pampers Trainers Ultra	47	VG	E
Luvs Training Pants	43	VG	E
Target Training Pants	35	VG	G
American Fare (Kmart) Little Ones Kid Pants	33	VG	VG

Bathing and Diapering

Chapter

DRESSING YOUR BABY

The top baby "fashion statements" are comfort for your tot and easy care and convenience for you. Look for bargains, and don't overbuy.

Just like your baby, the children's fashion industry is growing by leaps and bounds, and there have never been so many clothing choices.

Out in the stores, you'll find an enormous range of styles: sweet baby pastels and delicately finished laces and bows; bold colors, patterns, and plaids; little-boy sports looks and little-girl dainty dresses; sturdy unisex sweats and coordinated sets. Familiar makers mix with big-name clothing giants, and designers contribute miniature versions of adult chic.

All this fashion is costly, so savvy shopping is essential. Sometimes expensive clothing is just that—expensive. But you may also get denser, softer weaves and quality finishing for your money, meaning that a set of clothes will last through not just one baby but two or three.

PRACTICAL BABY CLOTHES

Fancy frills and rich-looking duds are fine occasionally. But if our babies could talk, they'd probably tell us they wanted to go naked—or at least wear clothes that aren't a hassle to put on and take off and don't hurt their delicate skin.

So most parents opt to dress their babies in very simple, washable clothing that's comfortable for sensitive skin. A basic newborn baby outfit starts with a diaper. Then you can add one of the mainstays: a cotton T-shirt with a

Contents

Practical baby clothes, page 173

Shopping savvy, page 175

Clothes for toddlers, page 179

Footwear, page 181

snap front, a onesie (one-piece shirt that snaps closed over the diaper at the crotch), a gown with an elasticized bottom, and footed sleepwear. You'll find all of them in a variety of colors, patterns, and weaves.

Plan to have six to eight nightgowns or one-piece suits and an equal number of T-shirts on hand. You can always shop for more clothing items after baby comes, when you'll have a clearer idea of needs and size.

Footed stretch suits are popular baby wear, daytime and nighttime. For easier diaper changes, you'll want suits with snap-open flaps in the diaper area. Stretch suits fit well and expand as the baby grows, but poor-quality suits tend to shrink in the dryer and quickly become too tight. Look for a reliable manufacturer and soft, dense fabric.

You may find baby gifts to be especially unrealistic. Gift-givers may choose outfits not made for baby comfort: loosely woven sweater/bootie/hat sets that can trap a baby's tiny fingers, or clothing with scratchy seams, tight elastic, or other uncomfortable touches. Some outfits won't make it beyond one or two washings. Size up any gifts you receive. If you can't use an item every day, exchange it for something more practical.

Selecting a size

Baby clothing sizes vary by manufacturer. And a manufacturer's sizes, such as "six months," often don't actually match a baby of that age, usually running much smaller. So read the pound/length charts found on the back of most baby garment packages. Or open the packaging to judge the size for yourself. Clothing on racks will usually specify weight and length on the back of tags, and most baby clothing stores keep a size chart at the checkout counter.

Most veteran parents advise against buying much in newborn size. Your baby will outgrow these tiny garments very quickly—sometimes in less than

List Couture tips
WARDROBE BASICS

Stock up on basics before your baby arrives:
- Six to eight snap- or tie-front T-shirts (six-month size).
- Three or four items to sleep in (six-month size).
- Three pairs of booties or small socks.
- Two small knit sweaters and a cap (winter).
- Bunting with legs or a hooded jacket (winter).
- Small brimmed hat (summer).

a month—and you can even get away with using a receiving blanket to swaddle the baby in lieu of clothes. Although it's nice to have an outfit or two for the early weeks, it's more practical to stock up on clothing in the next size so baby can grow into it.

If your baby comes early and is really small, you may be able to find preemie sizes of basic shirts in large discount chains, or you can contact Premiewear, a company that makes clothing and caps for tiny babies, sizes three to eight pounds. For information, see the Resource Guide.

SHOPPING SAVVY Baby clothes

Look for comfortable clothing that's easy to put on and take off. Most babies hate having shirts pulled over their heads, so choose front-opening shirts. If you purchase pullover T-shirts, look for overlapped shoulders and extra-wide neck openings.

Inside seams on all clothing should be soft, not scratchy, and lie flat, rather than sticking out. Avoid clothes with tight elastic bands on arms, legs,

A footed sleeper is standard baby gear. Look for soft fabric and seams, a roomy neck, and snap openings for the diaper area. Buy in larger sizes—baby will quickly grow into them.

neck, or waist. Elastic can irritate skin and restrict circulation. Don't use garments that leave red rings anywhere on baby's skin.

Examine fabrics of T-shirts and gowns—you'll want a thick, cushy weave. Avoid thin, semitransparent garments and those that show signs of poor finishing, such as unclipped strings.

Until your toddler is toilet trained, easy access to the diaper area is essential, so opt for snap-open legs or comfortable, elasticized-waist styles. Velcro closures, although they offer both quick release and expansion room, may lose their holding power unless they are laundered in the closed position. Otherwise, they weaken and become filled with loose strings and lint.

Bypass anything scratchy, such as metal zippers and appliqués or snaps with rough backing. Snaps should be painted with enamel, because contact with metal such as nickel can cause a skin reaction. If an appliqué is made of heat-welded plastic, check for jagged pieces of plastic on the back. Tiny

Baby Safe
SLEEPWEAR AND CLOTHING WARNINGS

- For more than 20 years, federal law has required that children's sleepwear be flame-resistant. To comply with this law, manufacturers had to produce clothes made of either 100 percent polyester or certain acrylic fabrics. Since cotton garments couldn't pass flame tests, these had to be treated with flame-retardant chemicals.

- In 1996, the U.S. Consumer Product Safety Commission (CPSC) relaxed its standards, and manufacturers may make sleepwear in sizes under nine months without added flame retardants. The only condition is that the sleepwear be tight-fitting: Tight-fitting sleepwear does not trap the amount of air needed for a fabric to burn. It also reduces the chances of contact with a flame and cuts the amount of time it takes for the wearer to be aware of possible burning. The commission does not recommend that babies and children sleep in loose-fitting, 100-percent-cotton clothing, which could easily catch on fire.

- In 1995, the CPSC also issued guidelines to help prevent strangulation deaths from strings on hoods, waists, mittens, or other parts of children's clothing, which can become entangled on crib posts, playground equipment, doors, and other protrusions. Most major clothing manufacturers have now agreed to remove or sew down and shorten the strings for hooded clothing, including baby clothes. We recommend that parents cut strings on children's clothing or buy clothing without strings.

buttons, hooks, pompons, bows, and appliqués only make dressing baby more time-consuming and difficult. Because your child may be able to pull them off, they can also be a choking hazard. Routinely check clothes and fastenings to be sure there are no loose items your baby could swallow.

As with adult apparel, according to law baby clothing labels must state the fiber content. Most parents we surveyed said they preferred garments made from 100-percent-cotton knits for the soft feel and absorbency. You may find that these knits seem large in the package, but they'll shrink and become thicker with repeated laundering. Poly/cotton blends are less expensive than pure cotton clothing, more wrinkle resistant, and less likely to shrink.

Baby-clothes sources range from catalogs and web sites, to mall stores and major discounters, to upscale boutiques and department stores. Next to or near Gap stores in many malls, you'll find Baby Gap, filled with coordinated outfits and casual fashion for tiny tots—often at big prices. Gymboree, once a baby-exercise franchise, has created a clothing range sold in mall boutiques. Patagonia has launched a line of bantam hats and jackets. Catalog merchandisers like Lands' End offer baby clothes and crib-sized flannel sheets, and L.L. Bean now has L.L. Kids. And many catalogs and web sites cater exclusively to babies. (See the Resource Guide for lists.) In upscale department stores, you'll find Ralph Lauren and Christian Dior in miniature.

To get good quality at reduced prices, watch for sales and specials on brands you like. Buy at bargain prices in your baby's current size, and stock up on larger sizes, too.

Used-clothing bargains

Used baby clothing is a great buy. Scan the classified business section in your local telephone directory under "Clothing, children's," "Clothing, used," or "Clothing, consignment." Sometimes children's resale shops even have new, never-worn clothing at big discounts.

Put the word out among co-workers and other parents of preschoolers and school-age kids. You may get clothes delivered by the boxload to your front door.

Shop at yard sales, too, or buy handed-down clothing from other mothers. For the price of one or two new shirts, you can supply your baby with a dozen bright outfits. And having a wide variety of shirts, sleepers, and other clothing can cut down on how often you have to do laundry.

Hot feet

If footed sleeper pj's are too warm for your child's feet, use a hole puncher to add ventilation holes to the soles.

Dribble

Try a colorful bandanna for a child who's a "bib-resister." The folds may catch some of the spills.

Dressing tips

Newborns have weak necks and little body support for their heads. Young babies normally rest with their arms and legs drawn up in the fetal position. When you dress your baby, try to keep arms and legs in their natural flexed position as much as possible, rather than trying to force them to straighten out. And position the baby to provide head support.

Most babies can't stand to have their faces covered during dressing. Before pulling a shirt over your baby's head, gather the shirt up like a pair of pantyhose and stretch the neck widely. Slip the neck hole over the back of baby's head, then quickly pull it over his face before he has time to get distressed. Pull one hand and arm through a sleeve, then do the other.

Keeping baby warm through the night is a perpetual quandary for parents. Newborns need extra warmth from outside of themselves because of their primitive self-warming systems. But after the first few months, most babies can manage at the same nighttime temperature that's comfortable for adults—usually 68 to 70 degrees F.

Many babies manage to get themselves and their sheets thoroughly wet before morning, even when they're wearing disposables or cloth diapers with waterproof pants. But it won't take long to figure out that it's better to "let a sleeping baby lie" rather than wake him to do a diaper change. If a baby's cold or uncomfortable, he'll let you know.

Some parents have found that sacks—long nightgowns with elasticized bottoms—are great for sleep. They enclose a baby's bare legs like a pillowcase, so they provide warmth, but they also give you access to baby's diaper area for middle-of-the-night changes.

When your baby begins to crawl, overalls or dungarees with shoulder straps and snap-open crotches are easy. Pants with elastic waistbands are often too restricting and ride down as the baby crawls; dresses get in the way during the crawling stage.

If you have the time and patience for sewing, check fabric shops for easy-to-make patterns for baby overalls with adjustable shoulder straps. Cushioned, quilted fabric or padded knee patches offer protection to tender knees.

Right in season

During extremely hot weather, dress your baby in a diaper only and avoid going out during the hottest part of the day. Babies are more vulnerable to heatstroke than children and adults, and the result can be high fever and convulsions. Overdressing can contribute to overheating. Ask your physician about whether to offer your baby water in addition to formula in hot weather.

Even if it's the middle of winter, there's no need to overdress when inside. Give your baby the same number of layers that you would find comfortable. Keep the heat in the bedroom at 68 to 70 degrees F. For babies under six months of age, a one-piece undergarment and pajamas under a cover-up, such as a sack with a drawstring, will work. Outside, a cap is helpful too, since babies, like adults, lose heat through their heads. For babies between six months and a year old, a blanket sleeper with feet will provide plenty of warmth. Steer away from thick, fluffy blankets or quilts that could create a suffocation hazard. But do check to see that baby is warm enough outside. You generate heat as you move—baby is sitting fairly still.

For outdoor wear, consider a zip-up bunting or sack with sleeves and a hood—and legs that won't interfere with the crotch strap in baby's car seat. Baby can wear the sack until she starts to crawl. Don't let her sleep indoors in a sack, though. It will be too hot, and small babies can get captured in hoods or necks.

Any baby clothing with a "dry clean only" label, including a coat, isn't very practical. Babies spit up frequently. Tots get dirty when they climb, fall down, and make mud pies. A garment that can't be washed at home is apt to spend most of the time at the cleaners.

CLOTHES FOR TODDLERS

Toddlers' high energy levels and curiosity keep them actively climbing, touching, and exploring—whatever the cost to their clothes. Fortunately, no one gives fashion ratings for this age group.

Most tots want to choose what they wear. A solution for this "me-do-it" age is to purchase either all patterned tops and solid-colored bottoms, or vice versa. (The first choice is the easiest.) That way, all your tot's outfit selections will go together.

Clothing for this age needs to be durable and stain-repellent. Durability translates into sturdy fabrics; well-sewn seams with overcast stitching to prevent unraveling; and reinforcement, such as additional backstitching at points of stress—especially at the top and bottom of zippers or around buttonholes. Additional knee reinforcement for pants is a plus.

The most practical shirts are colorful T-shirts with snap openings either on one shoulder or down the front. Putting them on and taking them off are painless. Overalls are handy for hiding shirt gaps and bare bellies when growing outdistances a toddler's wardrobe. Soft knits or cotton/polyester blends maintain a relatively wrinkle-free appearance without ironing.

When your baby nears the two-year mark, you will naturally want to shift to pants with elastic waistbands for potty training. They should be loose enough that your tot can pull them up and down without your help. Inside seams should be comfortable—check for scratchy surfaces.

Toddler winter wear

Ideally, snowsuits or other winter outerwear for tots should be water-resistant. There is a real danger of deep chilling if a child gets wet, especially if his diapers are damp too. Purchase a winter garment with a built-in hood, and use it together with a knitted hat for maximum warmth.

Ideally, mittens should have a nonslip surface sewn onto the palm and thumb area to make it easier for your tot to pick up objects or turn doorknobs.

Most toddlers enjoy wearing low-cut rubber or plastic boots on slushy winter days, particularly those boots they can slip on and off themselves. Purchase boots a size larger than your tot's shoes, so they're easy to put on and take off.

Don't buy coats with hood strings or dangling waist strings, or mittens with strings fastening one glove to the other. Children have been injured or strangled when these strings became entangled on outdoor play equipment, especially slides. Or, if you buy such a garment, snip all strings once you get it home.

Underwear

Comfortable fit and ease of putting on and pulling off become more important considerations when your child starts toilet training.

Training pants made from thick, absorbent cotton are supposed to do the job, but most parents find that regular, lightweight cotton underpants give a stronger signal that "things are going to be different." Plus, most training pants shrink considerably during washing, and they tend to bunch and lose their stretchiness quickly.

Disposable training pants are also being sold by major manufacturers of disposables. (See CONSUMER REPORTS Ratings of them on page 171.) The main drawback of disposable trainers is that their absorbency makes them feel the same as diapers. So it's more difficult for your child to perceive wetness and discomfort, and that could delay toilet training.

Once your tot has become toilet trained, look for pants that absorb moisture well to prevent chafing and reduce crotch irritation. Nylon knits—even the cute ones imprinted with colorful animals or superheroes—aren't the best choice. The most comfortable underwear is made of cotton or cotton/polyester blends, and has an absorbent cotton panel in the crotch area.

FOOTWEAR

Booties keep baby's feet warm. Crawlers need foot padding and protection. New walkers are better off without stiff shoes that impede balancing skills.

Booties

Your newborn's hands are usually tightly fisted and seem to be warm. But throughout the first year, a baby's feet will often seem cooler to the touch. (A truer test of baby's temperature is his belly.)

Cold feet probably don't worry babies as much as they do parents and grandparents. But most parents like to keep baby's feet warm, either with booties that tie on or with socks. Each time you slip on baby's footgear, turn each one inside out first to be sure there aren't any looped or loose threads that could capture small toes.

A baby needs enough space in booties or sleepers to freely move toes. Avoid socks that are too tight or sleepers that cause the feet to be "crimped." If a footed sleeper fits well except for tight feet, consider cutting the feet off and hemming the legs.

When baby begins to crawl, toes and knees may get cherry red from chafing against carpets or rough surfaces. Some babies feel so uncomfortable with the rubbing that they develop a crablike stance, with their back ends hiked up in the air. Socks that cover the knees or pants with socks or booties help keep a crawling baby's knees and feet more comfortable.

Shoes for new walkers

A baby learns to stand and balance by adjusting the pressure of the feet and toes on the floor or ground. And that operation is best done without shoes. So-called orthopedic shoes with stiff soles and artificial arches are of no benefit to a normal baby's feet. (Babies don't even have arches for the first two years.) In fact, they may hamper baby's balance.

The main reason for putting shoes on a newly walking baby is to protect

Dry feet

Use your portable hair dryer to dry winter boots quickly.

feet from splinters, cuts, and other foot injuries and to keep them warm. Bare feet or socks with skidproof soles are the best indoor options if baby's in no danger of stepping on anything. That way, she can practice the delicate art of balancing without the frustration of stiff soles.

Crawlers and new walkers do best with shoes that have soft sides and soles, such as flexible, moccasin-like styles. Sneakers are fine, but not models with artificial arches or with crepe soles that could catch on carpeting and cause falls.

Choose shoes that have some wiggle room beyond the big toe—your baby's feet are growing. You should be able to get a pinch of leather or fabric across the widest part of the foot.

The best shoes for experienced walkers have flexible soles with non-slip treads and easy-to-work fasteners such as a single buckle or a Velcro strap. Most kids won't master shoelace tying until they're nearly kindergarten age.

Chapter

FEEDING TIME

For the first six months, breast milk or formula is all baby needs. Begin to introduce solids after the six-month mark.

As parents of a newborn, you'll have a million things to do, but you won't have to plan meals for your baby. Until baby is six months old, breakfast, lunch, and dinner, plus middle-of-the-night feedings, are already taken care of.

BREASTFEEDING

Human milk is the ideal nourishment for babies. The protein in breast milk is particularly suited for a baby's metabolism, and the fat content is more easily absorbed and digested than that of cow's milk. Research also suggests that breastfeeding confers health benefits.

If you decide to breastfeed, however, the latest advice is to express breast milk and bottle feed your baby at least occasionally the first month. This early bottle experience can keep a baby from rejecting a bottle later, if for some reason you cannot continue to breastfeed.

Health benefits of human milk

Research has suggested benefits from breastfeeding.

Allergies. Breast feeding seems to protect from dairy-product and other food allergies and from allergic skin reactions, such as eczema.

Protection from viruses and bacterial infections. Breast

Contents

Breastfeeding, page 183

Nursing bras, page 187

Breast pump, page 188

Bottle feeding, page 194

Juices, page 202

Using bottled water, page 203

Facts on pacifiers, page 204

Solid food, page 206

milk delivers protective antibodies, plus a battery of other infection-fighting agents. Substances in a mother's milk actually ingest and kill harmful bacteria and viruses, and promote the growth of helpful bacteria in the baby's intestinal tract. The milk's hormones also speed up maturation of baby's digestive tract and immune system. Babies receiving human milk have fewer colds and stomach upsets than babies fed formula.

Diarrhea deterrent. Substances in your milk will offer protection from the most life-threatening forms of diarrhea.

Better teeth. Human milk has components that help form strong, cavity-resistant teeth. Suckling leads to better jaw formation than the sucking done on a baby bottle. Better tooth and jaw development may translate to fewer dental problems later.

Reduced chance of anemia. Even though breast milk appears to contain less iron than cow's milk, iron deficiency anemia is rare in young, breastfed babies. That's because breast milk's iron is easily absorbed. Once baby food is introduced, that iron-absorption capacity decreases.

Fewer middle-ear infections. Babies who are fed formula, or breast milk plus formula, are more vulnerable to middle-ear infections. One study of 1,000 babies found that babies who were breastfed during their first four months had 50 percent fewer ear infections than bottle-fed babies. It appears that the antibodies in breast milk help to prevent the infections.

Less obesity. Breastfed babies tend to be leaner than formula-fed babies and have fewer obesity problems as adults. One factor thought to contribute to fat bottle-fed babies is the tendency to coax a baby to "finish the bottle."

Protection against juvenile diabetes. Breastfed babies not fed formula have less risk of insulin-dependent diabetes in childhood.

As to your health, the younger you are when you start breastfeeding and the longer you breastfeed, the lower your risk of breast cancer. By breastfeeding when you're under age 20 for at least six months, you can reduce your chances of getting breast cancer before menopause by as much as 46 percent.

Successful breastfeeding

For breastfeeding to work well, it's best to start nursing within hours of your baby's birth. So it's important to let the health professionals in the hospital or birthing center know your plans. If your baby is fed formula, he may reject nursing, which requires a different sucking motion from that used when a baby is fed with an artificial nipple. You can always gradually wean your baby if you change your mind later, and even a month or two of nursing is better than none at all.

But don't expect to wing it. Study up on how to breastfeed. There are many information sources available at libraries, in bookstores, and on the web. Three excellent books on this topic are "The Womanly Art of Breastfeeding," from La Leche League International, a worldwide support organization for breastfeeding mothers; "Nursing Your Baby," by Karen Pryor and Gale Pryor; and "The Nursing Mother's Companion," by Kathleen Huggins. The books are all available in moderately priced paperback editions in libraries and bookstores, including web stores like Amazon.com.

In addition, La Leche League offers well-informed volunteer leaders nationwide who provide telephone counseling for expectant and new moms, and there are support groups for nursing mothers in nearly every city. To find the nearest group and its meeting times, look up La Leche League in your local telephone directory's white pages or see the Resource Guide for their toll-free number and web site.

In addition to these sources, there are more than 100 sites on the Worldwide Web offering breastfeeding advocacy and information. Web sites change all the time, so we suggest a fresh search using Yahoo!, Excite, or other large search engines, and the words "breastfeeding links." The Resource Guide lists several information sites.

However, be skeptical about any breastfeeding materials produced by formula makers (e.g., Mead Johnson, Ross Laboratories). Although the materials may seem totally objective, they are nearly always slanted to promote bottle feeding to expectant mothers.

Practical help

These basics can get you started with breastfeeding.

Begin to breastfeed as soon as possible. Some babies get "nipple confusion" when fed with an artificial nipple in the first few days because the sucking motion is different from that used in breast feeding. The baby forgets how to nurse and may appear to be refusing to nurse. Get your baby latched onto your breast as quickly after birth as you can (and the baby wants to).

Milk production takes a few days to get started. In the first few days, a woman produces a clear liquid called colostrum, which contains all baby needs. Milk follows on day three or four. You will feel a letdown, which is a full sensation in your breasts. If you become worried about

Burpless

Feed the baby in as upright a position as possible. The bubble at the bottom of the baby's stomach will rise toward the top of the food and be burped easily, preventing the pain of trapped gas.

whether your body's making enough milk (as most new moms do), just count your baby's wet diapers. Six to eight wet cloth diapers or five to six disposables in a 24-hour period signals that everything's going fine. If the diapers don't add up, contact an informed health care professional or a lactation consultant for advice.

Breast milk is supplied on demand. Your body produces milk according to how often and how long your baby nurses. Giving your baby a bottle of formula disrupts an otherwise elegant signal system: It reduces your baby's demand to nurse, which, in turn, may reduce your milk production. So don't let anyone feed your baby formula. But don't try to impose a schedule either. Just let baby nurse whenever she seems to want to. You two will get in sync.

Nursing is not a simple suction process. When a baby is put on the breast, it tongues and mouths until, in a few moments, the breast "lets down" milk—that is, the milk arrives in the larger ducts just behind the nipple. Then the baby rhythmically pulls and tongues to stretch the mother's nipple toward the back of the mouth and suckles in a regular rhythm: suck, release, relax. A moist seal formed by the baby's mouth helps to keep a mother's nipple and areola (the colored portion of the breast) in the mouth.

Don't be surprised at breast milk's appearance. It's cloyingly sweet, more transparent than cow's milk, and a pearly, bluish white color. The initial milk of a nursing session is less fatty, then the main serving has more fat and nutrients. So it's important to keep baby on one breast long enough to get both components. Breast milk is also digested more rapidly than formula, meaning a breastfed baby may demand more frequent feedings—and may delay sleeping through the night.

The milk's color, consistency, and odor may change, depending on diet and exercise. Your baby will let you know. Some babies are turned off by broccoli, for example. Vigorous exercise may raise lactic acid levels in breast milk, giving it a sour taste that some babies may reject.

Eat well. Breastfeeding will make you hungry—and a nutritious diet that supplies your body with a balance of protein, carbohydrates, and fat will help to ensure your milk's quality. Dieting while breastfeeding isn't a good idea. It can affect milk quality by lowering needed protein. You must also get enough fluids—at least eight eight-ounce glasses daily.

Hold your baby in the ideal nursing position. Draw the baby's whole body in toward yours, so that his belly is toward your chest. Your baby should take in as much of your nipple and the areola (the colored tissue that surrounds the nipple) as she is able. To release your baby's suction, slide your pinky finger between your breast and the side of your baby's mouth.

Line up a coach. A La Leche League leader, a well-informed health professional, or a professional lactation consultant can help. The International Lactation Consultant Association (ILCA) maintains a national directory of Board Certified Lactation Consultants from its membership roster who are willing to accept referrals. (For more information, see the Resource Guide.) Breast-pump manufacturers also maintain referral lists of lactation consultants.

Expect some discomfort at first. Nursing may make nipples sore and sensitive. Keep the area dry to help avoid nipple infections. (See "Nursing pads," page 188.) Lansinoh, a mild cream for sore nipples, eases dryness and chafing. It's available from La Leche League (see the Resource Guide).

Comfy

Use a big bed pillow with arms for nursing in bed.

NURSING BRAS

The best time to shop for a nursing bra is between your 28th and 36th weeks of pregnancy, before your rib cage expands, so that the bra will fit comfortably after your baby is born. (A roomy, stretchable regular bra can also be used for nursing.) Generally, you will increase at least one full conventional bra size during pregnancy, say, from a size 32 to a 34 and from a B to a C cup. And some women go up another cup size after birth. After about 10 to 12 weeks you'll most likely return to your prenatal bra size.

Your breast size and rib width will change over time, so look for a stretchable bra with fasteners that allow you to adjust the size. Plus, you'll need room for pads and shields to soak up leaks. Here are some selection guidelines.

Nursing features. The latches that open the cup for nursing should be easy to operate with one hand. Some mothers prefer a center front–latched bra to dealing with separate cup-opening devices.

You will be using the bras over a span of time, so they should be completely machine washable, with no special laundering or care requirements. Elasticized garments like bras hold up better and longer when dried at low in a clothes dryer.

Supply. Three to eight bras should be sufficient, depending on whether you use bra pads. Milk leakage can be a problem during the early months of nursing, day or night. Without pads, you may be changing bras several times a day. You can economize by using your nursing bras during the last months of your pregnancy as well.

Nursing pads. Pads are available in washable fabric-and-foam combinations and in disposable paper versions. Disposable pads are convenient to use, but may contain a layer of vinyl that keeps air from the moist nipple area, making nipple infections more likely. If you use disposables, change them frequently so that your breast stays dry. (Check the LaLeche League web site in the Resource Guide for pads that wick away moisture.) You may also like washable cotton pads.

Other alternatives to nursing pads are cotton handkerchiefs, squares cut from terry cloth, cotton diapers, and folded cotton T-shirt fabric. Toilet paper and facial tissues aren't suitable because they tend to hold in moisture, which irritates the skin.

CHOOSING A BREAST PUMP

You may want a breast pump if you return to work and want to keep breastfeeding, or if the baby's father or other relatives want to feed baby.

Trying to use a pump may feel awkward at first. You'll need to assemble the pump (and disassemble it for cleaning), position it correctly, adjust the suctioning to get the best results—and then convince your breasts to let milk down with no baby around!

The four pump types

Pumps come in four basic models: manual pumps, battery-operated pumps, midweight plug-ins, and hospital-grade pumps. With manual pumps, you produce the suction yourself by squeezing a bulb or a lever, or by manipulating a syringe-style cylinder. Electric pumps range from small, battery-operated units (some with optional plug-in adapters) to midweight plug-ins that work with electric motors to large, hospital-grade pumps that are the most effective for keeping up your milk supply. Prices range between $30 for a simple manual model to more than $500 for a hospital-grade pump.

The best electric or battery-operated pumps don't apply steady vacuum pressure. Instead, they have an intermittent suction action that imitates a baby's suckling. You can judge the quality of a pump by the number of cycles per minute specified on the package and the effectiveness of the suction. A baby's natural sucking rhythm is between 40 and 60 times per minute (one suck per second or a little slower). Hospital-grade pumps have about 50 cycles per minute, and the cycles feel a lot like the rhythm of a baby's suckling.

Motorized pumps without automatic cycling have to be operated by pressing a finger valve or a button to release the suction. But their motors are so weak that it takes a long time for pressure to build back up. So your breasts won't be receiving the amount of stimulation needed to maximize milk production. Plus, your nipple will be held in a vacuum traction for a longer time, producing discomfort. Smaller, non-hospital-grade pumps also provide less suction, collecting milk less efficiently.

Coping with vacuum problems

Most of these breast pumps operate on a vacuum principle that, unfortunately, doesn't duplicate actual nursing. Mothers are often dissatisfied with a breast pump because they mistakenly employ a constant vacuum on their nipple area, which can cause discomfort and even bruising. (Some pumps, such as those produced by Medela, have an autocycling pull-and-release action.)

Take another look at "Nursing is not a simple suction process," page 186. It's no wonder that the unrelenting suction of a pump doesn't seem to be effective or comfortable.

Most manufacturers now supply informational brochures with their pumps. The two critical factors in making a pump work for you are how well the nipple adapter fits your breast contours and whether you operate the suction action correctly.

Manual pumps

The simple bicycle horn–style bulbs found in drugstores should be avoided completely. They aren't effective and can even cause bruising. However, the fairly sophisticated cylinder or piston-style pumps may be worth a try. They're less expensive than electric models, they don't need an electrical source, and they operate silently. Most also allow you to control the amount of pressure exerted—and that can translate into less discomfort.

If you return to work and don't have the privacy you'd like for pumping, an effective manual pump may be your most comfortable (and discreet) alternative—certainly less noticeable than a loud, heavy-duty unit that requires an electrical outlet.

The drawbacks of manual pumps are that they tire your hand and arm and they're not as efficient as large pumps, taking longer to do the job. Models with single-handed holding and operation are easier to use than those that require both hands (one to hold, one to pump).

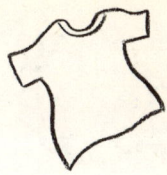

Modest

Unbutton front-buttoning blouses from the bottom for modest nursing. Or wear a cotton T-shirt or pullover to lift up; the baby's head will cover your bare midriff, and the T-shirt will cover your breast.

Enrich

Wear a bright necklace of colored wooden beads or ribbons for your baby to look at while nursing.

What's available

Ameda One-Hand Breastpump (Model 17066, $34) uses a spring-action motion that allows one-handed operation. Its flexible shield is comfortable to use, and the pump is compact enough to fit into a purse. However, it's designed only for occasional pumping needs.

Avent Isis Basic Breast Pump (Model 403, $50) has a horn with a soft silicone shield that flexes in and out to mimic a nursing sensation. This stimulation, coupled with a consistent, reliable vacuum, has helped some mothers to overcome the problem of getting a letdown without baby. The pump uses a molded handle attached to a silicone diaphragm to create an easy, comfortable suction. The set comes with a feeding bottle, a nipple, and a sealing disk. But its pieces can be hard to reassemble after cleaning, and mothers have also reported problems with milk leakage behind the shield, which affects the pump's vacuum.

Evenflo Press & Pump Breast Pump Kit (Model 53138, $40, and Deluxe Model 52137, $46) is a lightweight, portable, semi-automatic breast pump. Fingertip cycle control is created as the user presses the suction control button to stimulate the baby's natural sucking rhythm. The pump comes with a silicone nipple adapter for proper horn fit, a sample pack of four disposable nursing pads, and a four-ounce collection bottle.

Medela SpringExpress Manual Breastpump (Model 67103, $30) uses a cylinder and piston action (like a syringe) that pulls the milk into a standard-sized baby bottle. It has a built-in, automatic vacuum release for each stroke, which creates an action similar to a baby's sucking, and the vacuum pressure is adjustable. The spring action of the pump's cylinder assists with the return motion. The unit comes with a bottle, a sealing ring, a stand, and the pump assembly.

Small electric pumps

Smaller, lightweight pumps are less efficient than the big guys. What a large pump would accomplish in 8 to 12 minutes requires 20 minutes with a small one. With the smallest pumps, which use electric batteries, you'll probably have to manually operate the vacuum with your finger to mimic a natural sucking rhythm, and the suction is slow and tedious. But they can serve during short absences from your baby.

A larger pump that imitates hospital-style units operates much more efficiently. Most offer an automatic cycling feature and adjustable suction, and add-ons such as dual pumping horns (to pump both sides simultaneously), professional-looking carrying cases with insulated storage compartments, and a plug that functions in a car's cigarette lighter.

Look for a comfortable breast shield (funnel) that can be rotated for easier arm positioning; double-pumping action; a vacuum-control knob; easy-to-clean surfaces; and collection bottles that fit regular baby bottles.

The best pumps don't allow milk to come in contact with the gasket that separates the pump from the collection unit. Any parts of the pump that come in contact with your breast and the milk containers should be washed in the dishwasher, or with hot, soapy water, and drained dry before each use.

What's available

Although some general baby product companies, such as Evenflo, First Years, and Gerber, produce small battery/plug-in breast pumps sold in baby

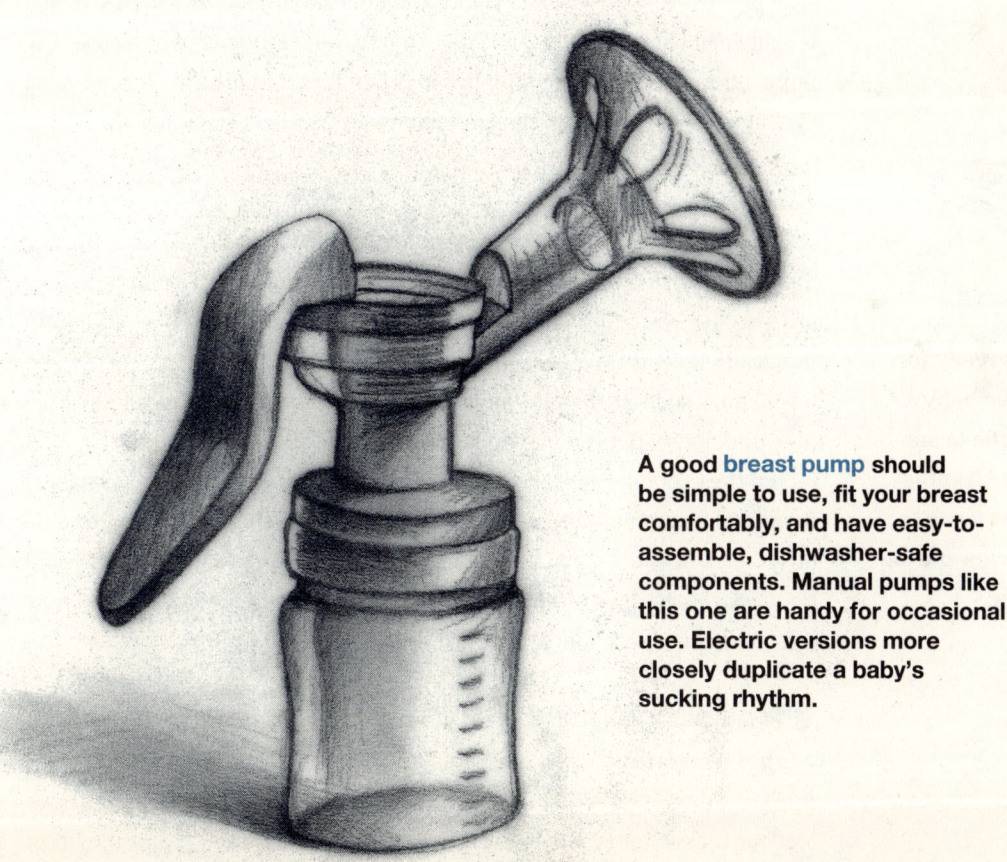

A good breast pump should be simple to use, fit your breast comfortably, and have easy-to-assemble, dishwasher-safe components. Manual pumps like this one are handy for occasional use. Electric versions more closely duplicate a baby's sucking rhythm.

stores and pharmacies, their designs may be flawed and ineffective. The following models are made by companies with years of breast-pump design expertise behind them.

Ameda Purely Yours (Model 17072, $229, with tote; Model 17070, $195, without tote) operates with an AC adapter, a car adapter, or batteries. It allows both single and double pumping; has eight suction settings and four cycle settings; and weighs only one pound. The pump can be used in or out of the black, zippered tote, which features an insulated compartment to keep collected milk cool for up to 10 hours.

Bailey Medical Engineering Nurture III Double Electric Breast Pump (Model 310, $120) is a small, quiet pump that can be used for double or single pumping and has five suction strengths. It uses an AC power cord or an optional car adapter.

Medela Pump In Style ($277) has suctioning abilities similar to hospital-style pumps—including autocycling and adjustable vacuum settings—but it is lightweight and easy to carry. The carrying case resembles a briefcase. The pump allows for double pumping, and has fully automatic suck-release-relax cycling and efficient suctioning. A rechargeable battery pack is optional.

Large pumps

Large, electric, piston-operated pumps, originally designed for hospitals, are the most efficient. They can empty both breasts in 8 to 12 minutes. They are also the best at mimicking the rhythmic sucking action of baby's nursing, using auto-cycling and vacuum pressure. Sensitive controls allow you to regulate suction rhythm, intensity, and pressure. Accessories are available that permit pumping of both breasts at once, which saves time.

But these pumps are heavy (they weigh as much as 11 pounds), making them cumbersome to tote back and forth to work. They're not exactly subtle either, since they have a power cord and make a lot of noise. Both could be embarrassing in an office bathroom. (You might contact your company's medical department to see if you can use a breast pump there.)

What's available

The most well-known hospital-grade pumps are from Medela and Ameda. Pump names include the Ameda SMB, Ameda Lact-e, and Elite, or Medela Classic and Medela Lactina. The pumps are heavy, and they cost $500 and more. But they're readily available for rent in almost every city. Try

Amuse

Have a snack ready for yourself by the baby's nighttime bottle to survive nighttime feedings. And tape your favorite TV shows to view during night feedings.

contacting the International Lactation Consultant Association, a local birthing center, or a La Leche League group to find a local distributor. The Resource Guide, page 292, also lists manufacturers' customer service lines.

Renting one of the pumps temporarily makes sense, so you can use it at home first. Later on, you may decide to purchase a less expensive, more portable model.

Once your baby reaches about six months of age and starts solids, he can go longer periods of time without having to be fed. There may be occasional periods of high demand when an upcoming growth spurt makes baby ravenous. But you may discover that you won't need a heavy-duty breast pump any longer. A simple manual pump may work just as well, or you may be able to keep up a minimum milk supply by simply nursing at bedtime and in the morning.

The key to pumping success

Your body will produce milk more readily if you pump during the times of the day your baby is most likely to nurse. Your milk supply will probably be the most plentiful in the morning.

Stimulating the letdown reflex—an anatomical response that signals the body to release milk into the ducts behind the nipples—is the passport to successful pumping.

Get comfortably seated and relaxed. You can then encourage letdown by applying warm, wet compresses to the breasts; lightly massaging with a circular motion; looking at a picture of your baby; or imagining your baby nursing.

Once the milk lets down, a rhythmical, gentle tugging action that imitates a baby's nursing (i.e., pull, pull, pull, pause) usually works best. If you're using a pump that empties one breast at a time, pump on one side about five minutes, then shift to the second, going back and forth until both breasts are drained.

Storing and preparing breast milk

Human milk is a perishable food that must be stored properly to remain safe for your baby. If you wash your hands well before pumping, your breast milk will be safe for a few hours at room temperature (68 degrees F), but immediate refrigeration is recommended. If you're away from home, milk can be kept for a short time in a cooler with either ice or a frozen cold pack.

Storage. Milk should be gathered in a clean glass or a rigid plastic bottle.

Sterilize the bottles if your baby is less than three months old. Tightly cap the bottle, and label it with the date. (Breast milk and formula should never be mixed in the same bottle, as mixing may affect the potency and protective qualities of the human milk.) Store breast milk in the back section of the refrigerator, which is colder than the front or the door shelves. Use refrigerated bottles of breast milk within 48 hours after pumping; and put any never-frozen, never-used breast milk in the refrigerator or freezer immediately after feeding.

Freezing breast milk is convenient, but recent research has found that freezing for more than a month may affect the breast milk's folate, a vitamin essential for baby's growth. (Freezing up to one month doesn't affect this vitamin.) Breast milk, like most liquids, expands as it freezes, so leave space at the top of the container. Freeze milk in two- to four-ounce portions for quicker thawing and less waste. Date the containers, and use the oldest milk first.

Breast milk should keep well up to one month in a deep freeze (0 degrees F and below) but won't last as long in the freezer section of a refrigerator. If the freezer isn't cold enough or there's a power failure, the frozen milk could thaw and spoil—the best indication being a sour smell.

Thawing. To thaw breast milk, place it in the refrigerator overnight or hold the bottle under cool running water and then shake it to mix the milk. If your baby prefers warm milk, briefly hold the bottle under warm running water. Thaw only as much milk as your baby will drink, and use previously frozen milk immediately after warming or the milk will start to spoil.

Heat and light can alter some of the milk's protective qualities. Don't thaw at room temperature or on a stove. Such thawing methods change the milk's composition. Microwaving is dangerous. Even though the outside of a microwaved bottle may remain cool, the liquid inside may have dangerous hot spots that could burn your baby's mouth.

Thawed breast milk should never be refrozen. Once you've thawed it, you can keep it in the refrigerator for 24 hours. Better yet, use it immediately. Fresh human milk contains living cells that destroy bacteria and viruses in the milk. But freezing kills these protective cells, so the milk is more vulnerable to spoilage. Once the baby has drunk from a previously frozen bottle of milk, discard the remainder.

BOTTLE FEEDING

The baby-bottle market has spawned a $100-million-a-year industry. You'll find bottles made of either plastic or glass. Shapes range from the tra-

Six-pack

Store bottles in the refrigerator in an empty cardboard six-pack bottle holder to keep them together and safe from tipping.

ditional to novelties such as animals or footballs (a frequent shower gift), to easy-to-hold angle-neck bottles. Many parents rely on disposable bottle systems, a combination of nurser and a plastic insert. The major manufacturers include Evenflo, Gerber, Heathflow, and Playtex.

Standard baby bottles

Standard models cost $1 to $3 each, and prices go up for odd-shaped specialty bottles and systems that use their own sized bottles, nipples, and rings, such as those made by Avent. Standard baby bottles offer numerous advantages over disposables. You can go through about five disposables a day. But standard bottles can be used repeatedly, a big savings in the long run. Plus, bottles are easier to fill, and you can gauge formula amounts more accurately. They're also easier to hold, and offer many more nipple options, including the more durable silicone versions. Most breast pumps and all baby-bottle warmers are designed solely for use with standard bottles.

Bottles in odd shapes, such as doughnuts, footballs, or hourglasses, are harder to clean and so can harbor bacteria. Soft, opaque bottles tend to stain from juices. Glass bottles will break if they're dropped.

Clear plastic bottles let you see inside for cleaning and allow you to observe how the milk is flowing when your baby is drinking. And you don't have to worry about breakage, as you would with glass bottles. Unfortunately, we no longer recommend clear plastic baby bottles. See "Plastic Baby Bottle Alert" on page 197.

Nursing bottles generally come in four- and eight-ounce sizes. The four-ounce size is useful with small babies, for storage and freezing of expressed breast milk, and for juice or water later on. Eight-ounce bottles serve older babies. We suggest having four of the four-ounce bottles if you're breastfeeding. Have six of the four-ounce bottles and six of the eight-ounce if you're using formula, with several extra nipples and caps.

Angle-neck bottles

Rather than having straight sides, angled bottles bend at the neck, making them easier to hold. The bent shape causes formula to collect at the nipple end of the bottle, so that baby is less likely to swallow air.

It wasn't until Johnson & Johnson designed and marketed its Healthflow line ($2.50 per bottle) that the concept became popular. Evenflo also offers angled bottles in four- and eight-ounce sizes. The main disadvantage of

Whiter

Remove a formula stain from baby's white clothing by wetting the stain and sprinkling it with scouring powder that contains bleach or baking soda. Brush it out with a toothbrush.

angle-necked bottles is that they're awkward to fill. More recently, First Years offered an angled nipple that collects formula as well but works with a regular bottle (Flowright Angled Nipples, Models 1081-1087, $2).

Disposables

A disposable system consists of a rigid outer holder, called a nurser, that holds a throwaway plastic bag, called a liner. The Playtex Baby Nurser Starter Set (Model 05440, $12) consists of leakproof caps, rings, various nipples, polypropylene holders, disposable polyethylene liners, and an information booklet.

The liner is folded lengthwise and inserted into the nurser, with the top rim of the liner stretched over the nurser's edge. Formula is then poured into the liner. The nurser, nipples, and rings must be thoroughly cleaned after each use. Liner refills cost between six and seven cents apiece. They use a special nipple design, and most have screw-on collars to hold the nipple and secure the liner in place.

The advantage of disposables is that bottles are ready to use and don't have to be cleaned. Manufacturers emphasize that they can be squeezed to prevent the baby from sucking air—but positioning a standard bottle correctly has the same effect.

Occasionally, disposable pouches have flaws, causing tears and ruptures that leak milk. And there have been reports of babies choking on plastic tabs from the sides of the bottle. There may be a remote but potential danger of infant formula becoming contaminated from plastic particles. And if overheated—which could happen if the bottle is put in a microwave oven to warm—the disposable pouch can rupture, spewing scalding liquid on parent or baby.

Disposables are also expensive and, as with disposable diapers, you often seem to run out just when a store trip is most inconvenient. From an environmental perspective, disposable bottles add more poorly decomposing plastic to the nation's landfills.

Nipple selection

Nipples for bottles come in several shapes. The traditional bell-shaped nipple is available with hole sizes ranging from smaller for newborns, to standard, to larger for toddlers or for use with pulpy juices. The "orthodontic" style is elongated on one edge of the top and indented in the center. Disposable nursers use a more flattened nipple that is supposed to resemble a breast.

Latex and silicone nipples. Latex and silicone are the two standard materials.

Amber-colored latex nipples are the most familiar. They are available with a variety of hole sizes to suit the needs of individual babies. But they tend to deteriorate, swell, and crack after two or three months of regular use. They whiten when they're wet for a long time. Saliva, heat, and sunlight can cause them to become sticky and clogged.

Silicone is a clear, odorless, taste-free material that is heat resistant enough to be washed in a dishwasher. It is less porous than latex, making it less apt to harbor bacteria. Although silicone nipples do not rot and become sticky as latex nipples do, they have a tendency to split and tear. There is always a possibility that a teething baby may bite through a nipple, either silicone or latex, or a pacifier, more reason to check them fre-

PLASTIC BABY BOTTLE ALERT

CONSUMER REPORTS recently tested plastic products for infants and young children that might contain potentially harmful chemicals. These included baby bottles made from polycarbonate, a clear and rigid plastic. Studies have shown that bisphenol-A, a substance leached from this type of plastic, can be harmful to lab animals. Among the effects is so-called "endocrine disruption," in which the chemicals interfere with or mimic the action of hormones, possibly upsetting normal development.

We bought six such baby bottles and found that all leached bisphenol-A. Based on our current test results, we calculate that a typical baby who drank formula sterilized from boiling in the bottle would be exposed to a bisphenol-A level of about four percent of an amount previously shown to harm lab animals. Such exposure may sound low. But safety limits for infant exposure can be set as low as 0.1 percent of the level that has adversely affected animals.

- CONSUMER REPORTS urges parents to dispose of polycarbonate baby bottles and replace them with bottles made of glass or made of polyethylene or polypropylene, plastics that do not leach bisphenol-A.

- Although plastic baby bottles do not explicitly identify their materials, there are some ways you can tell. Clear, shiny plastic should be assumed to be polycarbonate, unless the maker tells you it's not. Polyethylene and polypropylene are typically more opaque and less shiny than polycarbonate. If in doubt, call the manufacturer's number, listed on the package.

- Glass bottles are also an option but may be less appealing due to the risk of breakage.

quently for deterioration or damage.

While the majority of nipples and pacifiers made of latex or silicone don't contain phthalates, one pacifier and two models of feeding bottle nipples manufactured by Gerber have been found to contain a chemical related to phthalate. (See page 216 for a discussion of the phthalate issue and Product Recalls for the affected pacifier and nipples.)

Latex nipples can be boiled with a toothpick through the center to enlarge their holes for better flow. The holes in silicone nipples can't be enlarged because silicone is easily ruptured by tears or scratches.

A tear in a nipple can lead to the separation of small pieces, which are a choking hazard. Baby can also inhale a piece into her lungs, which could cause serious injury. If you find that a piece of a nipple is missing and your baby is showing breathing problems, consult a doctor immediately.

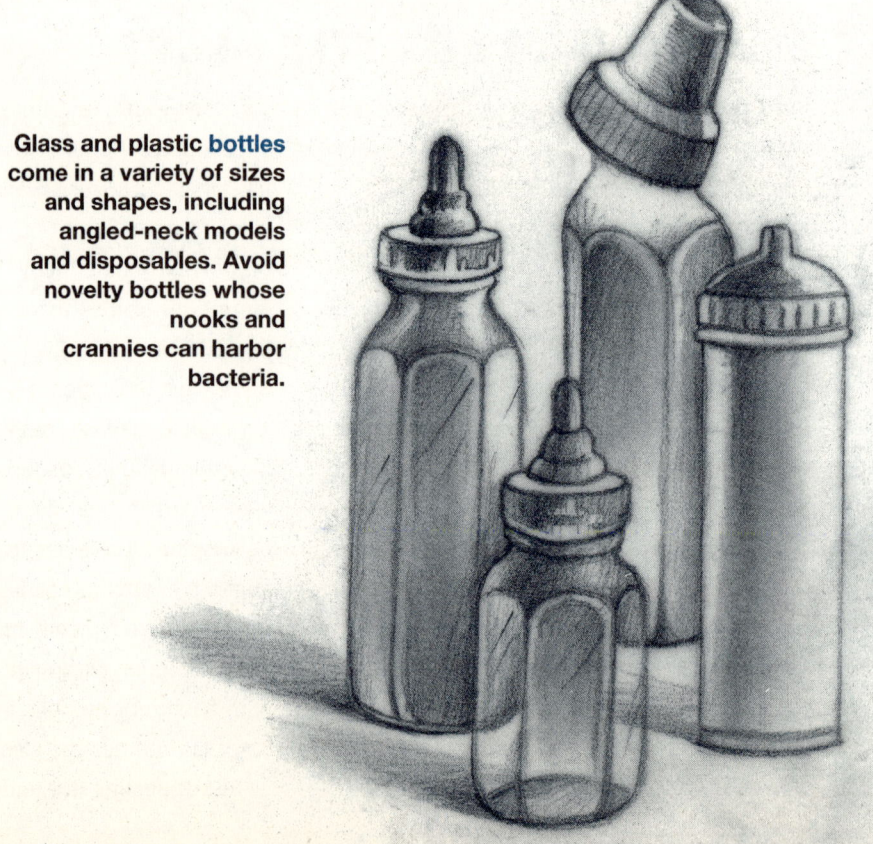

Glass and plastic bottles come in a variety of sizes and shapes, including angled-neck models and disposables. Avoid novelty bottles whose nooks and crannies can harbor bacteria.

Inspect the nipple regularly, particularly when your child develops teeth, and test it by pulling on the bulb portion. Discard it if any tear or crack appears. Replace nipples whenever you detect signs of deterioration. Don't use a nipple as a substitute for a pacifier.

Standard vs. orthodontic nipples. According to manufacturers, orthodontic nipples resemble a mother's nipple when it is elongated in the baby's mouth. Supposedly, such a shape evokes a tonguing action similar to the one used by breastfeeding babies, reducing the tongue-thrusting and bite problems believed to be caused by standard nipples.

Such claims have not been scientifically substantiated, and there is little difference between the performance of orthodontic and traditional nipple shapes. There have also been problems with latex orthodontic nipples quickly deteriorating and becoming sticky, perhaps because the indented center of the nipple makes thorough cleaning more difficult. When an orthodontic nipple weakens, the narrow center often collapses. Plan to replace them frequently.

Nipple flow varies. Not only do bottle nipples vary among brands, but even nipples from the same manufacturer with the same model numbers can differ in the size of the tiny flow hole. You can determine the best

Tips Happy meals

BOTTLE FEEDING KNOW-HOW

Follow the baby's signals for feeding times, and feed promptly when baby is hungry, before she becomes aroused from heavy crying.

- Nestle the baby in the crook of your arm, in a half-sitting position, to prevent choking.
- Hold the bottle so that the neck and nipple are always filled, and don't jiggle the bottle or the baby.
- Be sure the bottle doesn't block the baby's nose, which forces harder breathing and makes feeding uncomfortable.

- Never prop the bottle in a baby's mouth, or leave the baby unattended while feeding. (The baby might choke.)
- Never try to change your baby's feeding schedule by withholding the bottle. Crying will only burn up calories and make baby hungrier.
- Notify your physician if your baby has diarrhea, spits up frequently, is constipated, or shows the following signs of allergies: skin rashes; clear, running mucus from the nose; frequent crying spells; or frequent colds.

nipple flow among different brands by sucking liquid through them yourself. You will discover widely varying resistance to flow. So-called dripless nipples produce such a strong resistance that they may nearly block milk flow, making them more of a hindrance than a help.

A nipple should offer some resistance so that milk won't pour into your baby's throat, causing choking. Too much milk flow during feedings can cause babies to adopt an abnormal tongue thrust from trying to stop the milk. It is thought that this habit may later affect speech patterns. On the other hand, overly-resistant nipples may cause your baby to struggle to get milk and make the nipple collapse. Of the four major brands of silicone nipples—Gerber, Evenflo, PlaySkool, and Pur—only Gerber's nipple has a reinforced neck that gives it a tighter spring-back action, resisting collapse during feeding.

Making a choice. Babies have their own preferences about nipples. We suggest buying a variety of them and experimenting until you find the style that your baby seems to like. You can also increase and decrease flow during feeding by tightening or loosening the neck of the bottle.

Formula feeding tips

There are three types of formula: concentrated liquid that needs some water added; powder that must be reconstituted with water; and ready-to-feed formula in bottles or cans. All formula products should be carefully measured and diluted according to the container directions. If the formula is too concentrated, it can cause a serious overload to the baby's kidneys. Adding too much water can result in malnutrition or overdilution of the baby's bodily fluids.

Your baby's physician is the best source of advice on choosing an appropriate formula. We suggest that you stay with major formula brands and resist the urge to try off-brand formulas from health-food stores or other sources. Babies have had serious malnourishment problems when their parents have experimented with formula—for example, trying to make their own, or substituting soy milk.

In the early weeks after birth, your baby will probably want to be fed six to eight times in 24 hours. Studies show that babies are more apt to be awake at night than in the daytime, so nighttime feedings are normal and should be expected.

A newborn will consume only about two to four ounces of formula during a feeding. As babies grow, they will increase the amount of formula up to about seven to eight ounces by the time he is four to six months of age. A simple rule is to figure on between two and two-and-a-half ounces of formula per day for every pound of weight. Resist the urge to coax your baby to drink more.

Your baby should be fed whenever he seems hungry. Don't try to enforce an arbitrary schedule. At least in the early days, crying is the number-one signal of hunger, and if hunger cries aren't answered, they quickly turn to pain cries. The amount of formula your baby needs can be expected to vary from one day to the next. Growth spurts, activity, and illness can all affect how much and how often she wants to be fed.

Storing and preparing formula

Be sure that your baby is fed the freshest, safest baby formula.

Buying and storage. Check the expiration date on the can before you buy it. Some small grocers may sell formula that has gone beyond safe storage dates. Use formula you have at home before the date printed on the container.

Store unopened liquid and powdered formula in a cool, dry place and out of direct sunlight. Opened cans of powdered formula should be covered; they can be safely stored for up to four weeks in the refrigerator. Opened liquid formula should be covered and refrigerated but should be discarded after 48 hours.

You may prepare all the powdered formula you'll need for a 24-hour period—but no longer. Refrigerate the whole batch, taking out only what you need for each feeding, and discard whatever you don't use within a day. Any unrefrigerated formula, liquid or powder, should be used within four hours.

Milk is an ideal breeding ground for bacteria, so throw away any leftover formula in the baby bottle after feeding, rather than saving it up to be "finished" later. If formula doesn't smell or look right—lumpy, grainy liquid, or clumped powder—discard it.

Sterilizing. Rules about sterilizing baby bottles and formulas, or heating formula before feeding, have become much more relaxed in the last decade. Most physicians now recommend that all baby-bottle equipment be sterilized before being used the first time. After every use, bottles, nipples, caps, and rings should be thoroughly washed in warm, soapy water or washed in the dishwasher.

Very young or vulnerable babies, such as premature babies, may need to have their formulas sterilized initially. (Check with your baby's physician.)

Prepared

Parents of formula-fed babies can make 2 A.M. feedings easier by filling a thermos jug with warm water and keeping it in the baby's room. Mix formula instantly instead of waiting around the stove for 15 minutes.

Formula manufacturers' pamphlets will also give you clear directions on sterilization procedures.

Preparation. Carefully follow the written instructions on the can. Since formula makers change directions periodically, always double-check. Before opening a formula can, shake it to be sure it's well-mixed, and wash the top of the can, then wipe it dry.

Add exactly the right amount of water to powdered mixes, and don't dilute formula to make it last longer. Doing so can cause water intoxication and deprive your baby of needed nutrients.

Infant formula manufacturers give directions for mixing products with water, but they don't usually specify the source of water except that it should be safe to drink. In most situations, it's safe to mix formula with ordinary water from a cold-water tap.

Run the cold water for at least two minutes to flush away impurities, especially if the pipes have not been used for six hours or longer: Standing water may pick up contaminants from the plumbing. Formula should not be prepared with hot water from the tap, because lead is much more soluble in hot water, hot-water pipes, and water heaters. You may also boil the water for one minute, but do not boil longer than one minute, as overboiling can evaporate too much water, increasing the lead content.

Temperature. Most parents prefer to give their newborns warmed formula in the early weeks, but in time they shift, first to room-temperature formula and then to refrigerated formula. Some babies show a clear preference for warmed or cold liquids. Although automatic bottle-heating units are handy at night, you may also warm your baby's bottle in a bowl of warm water or under warm running tap water. But never warm the bottle in a microwave oven—the uneven heating could create hot spots in the formula that will burn your baby's mouth.

JUICES AND SWEETENED BEVERAGES

Adults seldom consume more than one apple or orange at a time, yet fruit juice servings may contain the liquid from as many as four or five pieces of fruit. Although most parents believe that juices are good for babies, that may not always be the case.

When babies drink too much liquid, such as water or juice, this consumption lessens their intake of breast milk or formula, which contains all the nutrients they need. In addition, juices are acidic in nature and may contribute to baby tooth caries, sometimes called baby bottle mouth.

According to the U.S. Department of Agriculture Food and Nutrition Service, some fruit juices, such as apple, pear, cherry, peach, and prune, contain significant amounts of sorbitol, a type of carbohydrate more commonly known as "sugar alcohol." When children consume these juices in excessive amounts, the sugar alcohols, which are poorly digested, may cause diarrhea, abdominal pain, and bloating. These juices should be given to a baby only in moderation. Breast milk or formula is really all a baby needs for the first six months of life.

Citrus juices, such as orange, tangerine, and grapefruit, as well as pineapple and tomato juice, can cause allergic reactions and should not be consumed by babies until they're past the one-year mark.

Even though juices are sold in four- and eight-ounce bottles designed for a nipple, use only a cup to feed them to your baby. It will help reduce the chances of tooth decay, as the baby will not suck continuously and hold the liquid in her mouth. And don't feed your baby sweetened powdered drinks or caffeine-containing beverages such as tea or soda. They can cause your baby's teeth to decay and also deprive your baby of the nutrition provided by breast milk or formula.

Most canned juices made in this country are packed in cans coated with a lining designed to reduce the corrosion rate. Once a can is opened, the exposure to air may increase corrosion, so juices should be poured out of the can and stored in a clean glass or plastic container. Fruit and vegetable juices should never be stored in lead crystal or pottery—the acid in the juice may leach lead from these types of containers. Canned juices from ethnic food stores or those imported from other countries may have lead soldering in the seams and should be avoided.

Never use honey to sweeten baby drinks or food. It may contain bacteria that can cause "infant botulism." (The bacteria are harmless to older children.) The symptoms of botulism are listlessness, irritability, diarrhea, droopy eyelids, and difficulty swallowing and breathing 24 hours after exposure. Severe cases of the poisoning can lead to seizures, brain damage, or rarely, death.

USING BOTTLED WATER

Even though baby food manufacturers are now marketing bottled water for babies, babies should not drink boiled or bottled water as a substitute for breast milk or formula. The U.S. Centers for Disease Control

Bottle Warmer

Slip a lone sock over the bottle to keep little hands warm, if your baby doesn't like holding a cold bottle filled with juice or milk.

warns that bottled water can cause seizures in babies under six months old who are not yet eating solid foods. Bottled water contains little or no sodium, which babies need, and it can dilute the sodium they get from human milk or formula.

Since breast milk and formula contain enough liquid for babies, they should not be given bottled or tap water (boiled or not) or juice without a physician's advice. Breastfed babies seldom have diarrhea, and should continue to nurse if they do. If your bottle-fed baby has diarrhea or vomiting, have your physician recommend a special oral rehydration solution, rather than giving the baby plain water.

Although the Food and Drug Administration (FDA) requires that bottled water products be clean and safe for human consumption, their regulations don't ensure bottled water safety. When manufacturers label their water as intended for infants, the water must meet the same standards established for tap water by the Environmental Protection Agency. The label must also indicate that the bottled water is not sterile. Just as with tap water, it's recommended that you bring the bottled water to a boil and boil it one minute before mixing it with formula.

Bottled water may not always be as safe as it appears. One study of 37 brands of bottled mineral water found that 24 of them contained one or more substances that did not comply with federal drinking-water standards. Fluoride levels also vary among different brands. It's hard to know which products are pure and which aren't.

If you have reason to believe that your water system is contaminated with lead, copper, nitrates, agricultural by-product runoffs, or excessive amounts of naturally occurring fluoride, then you may want to stick to premixed formula or buy bottled water to mix instant formula. Distilled water contains fewer contaminants than bottled, spring, or mineral water. Consult your physician before buying any water product to use with formula or before using well water for your baby.

FACTS ON PACIFIERS

A pacifier is a latex or silicone nipple mounted on a plastic shield for the purpose of allowing a baby to suck and mouth while not actually drinking milk. Some pacifiers have rings on the back, and others have small knobs. Restless and fussy babies may be calmed by sucking a pacifier. Some experts theorize that babies have a built-in need for nonnutritive sucking—

Sparkle

Use denture-cleaner tablets to clean glass baby bottles. Let the bottles soak for a half hour according to directions; swish with a bottle brush and rinse.

that is, sucking that offers no breast milk or formula.

Parents sometimes offer pacifiers in an effort to prevent their babies from establishing a thumb-sucking habit, with some success. Pacifiers may be less likely to interfere with tooth alignment than habitual thumb sucking.

But use pacifiers safely. Don't pin one to clothes or nightgowns. A child may bite or swallow the pin. Never hang a pacifier from a string around the baby's neck or tie it to crib bars, because of the risk of strangulation. Discard a pacifier when the nipple becomes old, sticky, and crumbly, or when your baby begins to chew off pieces of it.

A federal standard requires that all pacifiers be constructed with two ventilation holes in the shields to admit air in case a baby accidentally gets the shield caught in the mouth or throat. Pacifiers must pass a "pull test" after boiling and cooling to ensure that they will not come apart. The size of the shield is regulated to prevent accidental choking. All pacifier packages must carry a warning label advising against use of a string to hang a pacifier around a child's neck because of the strangulation hazard.

Recent research suggests that pacifiers aren't completely harmless. For example, pacifier use has been associated with early weaning from breast-feeding. In addition, a 1995 Finnish study of 845 day-care centers found that children who used pacifiers had significantly more middle ear infections than children who did not use them. In fact, the researchers concluded that

Baby Safe

CHECK PACIFIERS

- Since the pacifier handle can crack, pull to see that it is securely attached to the nipple and shield bracket.
- If the shield cracks, the nipple section will come off, causing choking. The shield should be firm and large enough so babies can't take it into their mouths.
- Ventilation holes, designed to keep babies from suffocating if the pacifier becomes entrapped in their mouths, should be free and unclogged.
- The nipple can tear or pull off from the shield. Make sure it is securely fastened on, has no tears or holes, and hasn't become sticky with age.
- Choose pacifiers without a ring. Otherwise, babysitters and others may suspend it with a ribbon or string from baby's neck.

pacifiers were responsible for one out of four middle ear infections in children under age three.

INTRODUCING SOLID FOOD

For their first six months of life, most babies get all the nutrients they need from breast milk or formula. The digestive system of young infants isn't mature enough to handle anything else. If given food, babies may even push it out with their tongues, a reflex designed to protect them from substances they can't properly swallow or digest. Some studies suggest that introducing solids to infants younger than six months old just adds needless calories, since the baby will still be drinking the same amount of milk.

Around six months of age, your baby's tongue and swallowing movements will have become coordinated enough to eat from a spoon. He'll also begin developing head and neck control and learning to drink from a cup, albeit with spills. Look for these signs that your baby is ready for solids: His good head control enables him to maintain a steady, upright position; he can sit steadily by himself; he can begin to mouth and swallow food without choking. When they're getting ready for solids, most babies will lean forward to watch you eating and may start reaching for your food.

Commercial baby food

Market surveys show that 9 of every 10 babies eat at least some commercial baby food. The average American baby eats hundreds of jars of baby food (including baby-food juices) in his or her first year. Most of those jars bear the Gerber label, with Beech-Nut and Heinz as much smaller players.

Gerber has been making baby food since 1928 and now sells approximately 200 different food products. Recently, the company has introduced a new technology for preparing approximately 40 percent of its fruits and vegetables to better preserve flavor and texture by reducing cooking time. The balance of the line is conventionally processed—that is, heat treated and packaged in jars.

Beech-Nut has been producing baby foods since 1931. Their baby-food line includes about 125 products. Most of their products are conventionally processed and packaged.

Heinz, in business since the 1930s, conventionally produces and packages about 110 baby-food varieties.

All of the big three baby-food makers sell products in three different formulations. Beginner foods are for babies starting solids. The next level is for more experienced eaters anytime during the last half of the first year. And the last step is for children nine months and older.

Beginning foods are usually single-ingredient foods, such as peas, applesauce, or carrots, finely pureed for easy swallowing. Most foods at this level are totally free of added sugars and starches.

Next come multi-ingredient foods, such as dinners and desserts, designed to offer more variety and flavors. Depending on the manufacturer, starches and sugars may be added at this stage to some foods. The texture is smooth, but not as fine as those for beginners.

Foods for older babies offer larger-size portions designed to keep up with baby's appetite. The chunky texture of these foods encourages chewing.

Some companies have added toddler foods to their lines, such as microwavable dinners, fruit and vegetable dices, meat sticks, and snacks, although children at this stage are able to handle table foods that have been cut up for easy chewing.

In comparing baby food prices, Heinz, which does less advertising, is usually priced lower than Beech-Nut or Gerber, which are nearly identical in their pricing. Sales of organic baby food continue to increase, despite the fact that organic food is priced considerably higher.

Earth's Best, owned by Heinz, is an organic line. All Earth's Best products are certified organically grown and processed and are also free from added sugars and starches. Most incorporate whole grains into their formulations. Organic farming used by their suppliers avoids the use of synthetic pesticides or fertilizers, and animals used for meat products are also fed organically grown feed without additives. The line is available in natural food stores nationwide and supermarkets in selected areas. Their web site has a store locator (see the Resource Guide).

The baby-food marketing business

Babies eat baby food—but adults buy it. Baby-food makers have used a lot of gimmicks to try to attract buyers, mainly putting every imaginable food and combination of foods into jars.

At one point sugar and salt were added to make the food more palatable to adult tasters. When criticized for these additions, companies took out the salt, and now most sugar and excess starches have also been removed.

To stay current with changing eating habits, many vegetarian/nonmeat din-

Overboard

Put a plastic tablecloth or an old plastic shower curtain on the floor under the high chair, and wipe up spills easily.

ners are being offered. And, since increased consumption of complex carbohydrates has been recommended for adults, Gerber has a selection of sauces for babies, so they can join the family in a pasta meal. Manufacturers have also added "trendy" foods, such as pasta dishes and yogurt combinations.

Simple dinners—Gerber's Simple Recipe, Beech-Nut's Delicious Duos, and Heinz's Simple & Delicious—combine either a fruit or vegetable with a meat as the sole ingredients (other than water). These products were developed to eliminate the need to open two jars.

The three big baby-food makers—Gerber, Heinz, and Beech-Nut—continue to try to hold on to young eaters, even when they get older. Gerber's Graduates line, introduced in 1992, offers more snacks and diced fruits and vegetables than in the past. Both Gerber and Beech-Nut have extensive lines of microwavable dinners intended to compete with boxed macaroni and cheese, SpaghettiOs, and the like. Heinz recently introduced Toddler Cuisine in microwavable containers intended for toddlers.

Baby-food categories

Most baby food comes in one of seven categories: cereals, juices, fruits, vegetables, meats, dinners, and desserts.

Cereals. Commercial infant cereals are precooked and fortified to supplement the nutrients in breast milk or formula. They usually serve as baby's first solid food, because they are good sources of energy and supply many vitamins and minerals. Pediatricians generally recommend single-grain cereals, such as rice, for infants, so food intolerances can be easily identified. Wheat and mixed-grain cereals, which are more likely to cause allergic reactions, are introduced later.

There are many types of grains used in baby cereals—rice, wheat, oats, barley, corn, rye, millet, mixed. Some cereals have fruits added. Others are available in three forms: dry, jarred, or frozen.

Dry cereals require the addition of breast milk, formula, juice, or water. The nutrition labels do not include the nutrients provided by these added liquids. Most are enriched with iron, as some infants and young children are vulnerable to iron-deficiency anemia.

Juices. Infant juices are one of the most popular baby foods, although baby can drink adult juices diluted with water. Other than the fruit standards, such as apple, pear, and grape, there are many baby fruit-juice combinations, some of which contain yogurt, and also fruit/vegetable varieties. Some have added calcium.

Juices shouldn't substitute for breast milk or formula, because they contribute little nutritionally to a baby's diet. Although they often have extra vitamin C, your baby will probably get enough from other foods.

Fruits. Fruits are usually introduced after cereals, and several baby foods incorporate fruits with cereals. Most manufacturers claim that bananas are the most popular fruit, but you'll find many different fruits and fruit combinations on the shelf. Babies appear to love all of them because they taste sweet. Most fruits will have added vitamin C. Orange-colored fruits such as apricots are also good sources of vitamin A.

Vegetables. Most vegetables are good sources of vitamin A. Peas and legumes contain more protein and B vitamins than most other vegetables. None are important sources of vitamin C, and few are fortified. Certain vegetables aren't suitable for babies: Spinach and beets contain nitrates, and vegetables such as broccoli and Brussels sprouts may give a baby gas.

Meats. Meats provide protein, iron, zinc, and some B vitamins. You'll find about six different kinds of meat in baby foods: beef, chicken, ham, lamb, turkey, and veal. Products made with meat juices may be labeled "with broth"; those with added starches will carry the words "with gravy."

One meat product should be strictly avoided: toddler meat sticks shaped like small hot dogs. Their conical shape and flexible texture can form a perfect plug to a baby's throat, leading to suffocation.

Reading the labels

The best way to make decisions about commercial baby food is to read the ingredients list and nutritional values which appear on the label. The Nutrition Labeling and Education Act (NLEA) requires baby foods to carry complete nutritional labels.

There's one significant way that baby-food labeling differs from that of foods intended for adults. While dietary guidelines recommend that adults restrict fat intake to no more than 30 percent of their total calorie intake, that rule doesn't apply to young children.

Fat plays a critical role in the growth and development of babies and young children, so fat shouldn't be restricted. Therefore, federal regulations forbid both the fatty-acid profile and cholesterol labeling you see on adult items on foods intended for children under the age of two.

In addition, labels of foods for children under age two cannot carry the

Grown-up

When young children no longer want to drink from a baby cup or "tippy cup," give them commuter cups to use. They hold more and spill less. And they make a child feel grown-up.

FDA-approved health claims about the relationship between a nutrient or food and a health problem (for example, vitamins A or C and cancer) or claims about the foods being "low-fat" or "low-cholesterol." Only a few claims are allowed, such as the percentage of the daily value (DV) that a vitamin or mineral in the food provides, and the terms unsweetened and unsalted.

Daily values for fat, cholesterol, sodium, and dietary fiber have not been established for children under age four. The FDA has only set DVs for young children for protein and certain vitamins and minerals.

You'll find that beginner foods offer the purest ingredients. Sweet potatoes are sweet potatoes, peas are peas, without the addition of sauces or flavoring.

Certain foods can be bought much less expensively in other parts of the supermarket. Canned pumpkin, for example, is just that, and well-pureed.

Baby Safe

BABY FOOD ADVICE

Baby food is regulated by the U.S. Food and Drug Administration (FDA) with the exception of meats, which are the domain of the U.S. Department of Agriculture (USDA). To help ensure that products you feed your baby are fresh, wholesome, and free of glass or any other foreign particles, the FDA offers the following advice:

- Don't buy a sticky or stained jar of baby food. It's either cracked or has been in a case with other broken jars.

- All baby-food jars have a depressed area, or "button," in the center of the lid. A popped-out button indicates the product has been opened, or the seal broken. Reject any jars with the button popped out.

- Listen carefully when you open a glass jar. You should hear a characteristic "whoosh" or "pop" when you break the vacuum seal. A grating sound may indicate the presence of glass particles stuck under the lid.

- If the jar is hard to open, don't tap it with a utensil or bang it against a hard surface. Instead, run it under warm water for a few minutes to loosen the lid's seal.

- Always examine the food when you transfer it to a feeding dish. And always use a dish—a spoon put in the baby's mouth will in turn contaminate the jar of food.

- If you suspect something is wrong with a jar of baby food, call it to the attention of the manager at the store where you bought the food, or contact the manufacturer. (See the Resource Guide for toll-free numbers.)

Applesauces, too, are usually quite smooth. Fresh bananas, or canned peaches and pears, which can easily be mashed, are much less expensive than the same fruit in a baby food jar.

How to introduce solids

It's best to introduce the various solid foods one at a time, at intervals of a week or so. You'll find it much easier to identify any food intolerances, which might show up as loose bowel movements, rashes, or other allergic reactions. Pediatricians usually recommend starting with infant cereals, which are fortified with vitamins and minerals—particularly iron—that complement baby's diet of breast milk or formula.

Start with a teaspoon or so of the new food. Use a small spoon that fits baby's mouth well. It's likely your baby will push the first spoon-fed foods out of his mouth with his tongue. It will take him a while to get used to the feel of the spoon and how to swallow.

If you wish, you can mix the new food with breast milk or formula to make the foods easier for baby to mouth and swallow. But don't try to feed your baby solids from a bottle with a widened nipple—even solids combined with formula. The solid food may cause choking and clog the nipple.

Feeding time should be relaxed and pleasurable. Keep in mind that each new food presents a new taste and texture. Offer food in small amounts, and don't worry if you're getting more on the baby than in the baby. (A good plastic bib with a trough at the base will help.)

Don't feed the baby straight from the jar. Bacteria from the baby's mouth will be transferred from the spoon to the jar, where they will continue to grow.

Put only as much as you need into a bowl, cover the rest in the jar, and store it in the refrigerator. The majority of baby food manufacturers claim that meats, vegetables, and dinners may be kept refrigerated for 48 hours. Fruits and single-serving juices have a refrigerator shelf life of 72 hours. If you don't use the food within the allotted time, throw it out and start with a fresh jar. As teeth begin to erupt between the seventh and ninth months, soft, chewable foods can be introduced. Finger foods will help develop fine hand movements. Between 10 and 12 months, your growing child can chew many table foods, will use fingers for most of the meal, and can begin using utensils.

By the time babies are around a year old, their digestive processes should be functioning at nearly adult proficiency, so most of their foods can then come from the family table rather than from a jar.

Solid

Mix yogurt or applesauce instead of milk with dry cereal for a manageable solid when a child hasn't yet mastered handling a spoon.

Mouth Wash

Use your hand, dipped in water, to wash the face of a reluctant child. Most children don't seem to fight as much as if you use a cloth, and you'll do just as good a job.

Making your own baby food

Pulling out a jar of commercial baby food makes sense when your family's having pizza, but it seems silly to feed your baby a mixed dinner in a jar while the rest of you are chowing down on a fresh version of the same thing—baked chicken and steamed vegetables, for example.

Homemade food can be cheaper than commercial baby food, and it's often very simple to prepare. Plus, carefully prepared home-cooked foods retain some trace nutrients destroyed by the high temperatures of commercial processing. When you do your own mashing and chopping, you can make sure you've got control over the variety and texture your baby's receiving.

Pesticides in the foods you feed your baby are also a concern. See "Pesticides in produce," below, for fruits and vegetables with both high and low pesticide residues and how to lessen your child's pesticide exposure.

You don't need exotic equipment for making baby food—a fork for mash-

Baby Safe

PESTICIDES IN PRODUCE

In a first-of-its-kind study of Department of Agriculture data, CONSUMER REPORTS analyzed the results of USDA testing done between 1994 and 1997 on 27 food categories, covering some 27,000 samples (a sample is about five pounds of produce). We analyzed not only the amounts of pesticides on produce but also how toxic those pesticides are and gave each food a toxicity score.

Of the 27 foods the USDA tested, seven—apples, grapes, green beans, peaches, pears, spinach, and winter squash—stand out as having toxicity scores up to hundreds of times higher than the rest. This is because these crops are treated with more, or more-toxic, pesticides, and because the foods are often eaten unpeeled. (Peeling can remove some pesticide residue.) A high toxicity score doesn't automatically mean a food is unsafe. Personal risk depends on age, susceptibility to the effects of a compound, how often you eat a particular food, and how much you eat relative to your body size.

Other fruits and vegetables had very low scores, including apple juice, bananas, broccoli, canned peaches, orange juice, and canned or frozen peas and sweet corn.

The pesticides on virtually all tested produce are within legal limits. But many of those limits are at odds with what the government now deems safe for young children. And children eat far more produce per pound of body weight

ing the food, or a baby food grinder, food processor, or blender will do nicely. Wash your hands and all utensils with soap and hot water, and always wash surfaces that have had raw meat or fish on them using warm, soapy water. Cook everything but ripe, mushy fruits. Foods with hulls, such as peas and corn, should be well pureed. And go slowly with gas-producing foods, such as broccoli, cauliflower, and kidney beans or other types of beans. Don't add butter, oil, or salt.

Mash, grind, or puree the food, adding cooking water, breast milk, or formula to make the texture smooth, then place food in a small serving bowl for feeding. You can prepare food in quantity, then freeze it either in ice cube trays or like cookies on a cookie sheet. Once the food has hardened, transfer it into sealable plastic freezer bags for warming up later.

Fresh and frozen vegetables make good baby food: carrots, winter squash, sweet potatoes, sweet peas (well pureed), green beans, and potatoes. Steam

than adults and are more sensitive to some effects of pesticides because their nervous systems are changing and developing so rapidly.

The Food Quality Protection Act, passed unanimously by Congress in 1996, requires the Environmental Protection Agency (EPA) to review pesticides and tighten exposure limits to make food safer for young children. But any transition and implementation will take time.

In the meantime, you can minimize your child's exposure to pesticides. One thing you should not do is stop serving fresh produce, which provides a host of vital nutrients. Instead, consider taking these steps:

• You can still use baby food. Pesticide levels in unpeeled, unwashed, non-organic produce are higher than those found in baby foods.

• You can chose to prepare your own baby food. Clean and peel all fruits and vegetables, remove seeds, and cook whatever you can.

• Avoid giving children large amounts of the foods with the highest toxicity scores.

• Peel those foods with a high toxicity score, such as apples, peaches, and pears. That usually removes much of the toxic residue. Washing unpeeled fruit with very diluted dishwashing detergent also helps.

• Consider buying organically grown produce, which is increasingly available. When CONSUMER REPORTS tested organic fruits and vegetables, we found that they had few or no toxic persticide residues.

Berry happy

Arrange berries or pieces of fruit in a design on cooked cereal so your child will eat it.

them in a pot with a steamer basket, or boil them, covered, with a little water.

Fresh fruits can be mashed if they're soft or cooked if they're crunchy. Bananas, apples, pears, peaches, apricots, melons, mangoes, and plums all make fine baby dishes. (Apples and bananas may darken with freezing.) Don't use honey as a thickener or sweetener, due to the risk of potentially fatal infant botulism.

At about eight months of age, your baby will be ready for protein foods. The fresh-meat list includes cooked lean beef, chicken, fish, turkey, and egg yolks, water-packed chicken and tuna, and cottage cheese and cheese chunks. All should be mashed or ground.

Most bookstores and libraries have baby-food cookbooks for more suggestions about what to fix for your baby. You can also ask your pediatrician.

Choking dangers

Babies and young children can choke to death on a variety of foods. Sometimes the food gets stuck in their throats, sometimes it goes down the wrong pipe and blocks their air passages, and sometimes the choking happens when they vomit.

Statistics reported in the *Journal of the American Medical Association* pointed to hot dogs as a very hazardous food for babies. Of the 100 choking deaths of children under age four that were studied, 17 were caused by hot dogs. Nuts were next most dangerous, causing eight deaths. Seven deaths were caused by candy and grapes, seven by cookies and biscuits, six by carrots, five by apples, and four each by beans, bread, popcorn, and meat. Other foods on the list include macaroni and noodles, peanut butter, cheese, chewing gum, and shrimp.

The message is clear: Babies can choke on almost anything, so feeding time should be closely supervised. Many baby-food labels don't warn parents about this. Parents should use common sense about which foods to give their baby, and stay close by while baby is eating. Hot dogs, a particular problem, should be sliced lengthwise into thin strips before serving.

Chapter

PLAYTIME GEAR

Look for toys that are safe, age-appropriate, and engaging to your child. But remember, your baby's favorite activity is being with you.

Each year, parents and gift-givers shell out more than $564 million for baby play things. Plush animals, mobiles, teethers, rattles, balls, activity centers, play gyms, wheeled trucks, and toys that spin or can be pulled or pushed are touted as musts for child happiness and development. Toy companies spend millions of dollars on ads showing small children hugging stiff plastic dolls while exclaiming "I love you!" or screaming with delight at the performance of huge toy trucks or ungainly play monsters.

But you soon discover that your child doesn't find toys as lovable or delightful as the ads promise. You may picture your baby or tot so overjoyed with the toy you've brought home that she'll play with it contentedly for hours. In reality, babies have very short attention spans. They may be more attracted to the brightly colored wrapping paper and flashy ribbons on the outside of the box than to what's inside. Before you start spending, learn about toy safety hazards—and discover the types of toys your child might really enjoy.

Contents

Baby toys, page 215

Playtime options, page 222

Walkers, page 228

Entertainers, page 232

Jumpers, page 235

BABY TOYS

Playing with parents, siblings, grandparents, and other caregivers is really how babies learn about the world—not through the toys themselves. Warm human interaction teaches babies and young children that the world is a trustworthy place. Without that nurturing contact, the lesson may be that the world is a lonely place—in spite of lots of toys.

Newborns and young babies have very limited body skills. They enjoy observing the world around them, with all its shapes, lights, and colors. But their hands aren't unfolded enough to grasp and play with objects. Their needs are simple: They want to be held, rocked, and fed on time. And they respond to being talked to and to hearing novel sounds. However, they may enjoy looking at toys, even if they don't really play with them.

Baby Safe

THE PHTHALATE (PVC) ISSUE

In 1998, the U.S. Consumer Product Safety Commission (CPSC) requested that toy manufacturers remove a chemical called diisononyl phthalate (DINP) from soft polyvinyl chloride (PVC) baby toys—especially teethers—that babies and children are apt to chew. DINP is used as a softener in PVC toys and children's products.

By late 1998, nearly 90 percent of U.S. toy manufacturers agreed to remove DINP from soft rattles and teethers. According to the CPSC, companies cooperating in removal were Chicco, Little Tikes, Disney, Mattel (includes Fisher-Price, Arcotoys, Tyco Preschool), Evenflo, Safety 1st, The First Years, Sassy, Gerber, Shelcore Toys, Hasbro (includes Playskool), and Warner Brothers Studio Stores.

While awaiting the reformulated toys, major toy stores, including Toys 'R' Us, Wal-Mart, Sears, Target, and Kmart, have removed phthalate-containing teethers and rattles from store shelves.

The scientific community doesn't agree on whether the chemicals—which, when administered to lab animals at high doses, have been shown to cause cancer and damage the liver, kidneys, and other organs—pose any risks to babies. And it's still not clear how much DINP is released from children's products when they're mouthed and chewed by babies. CPSC scientists tested 31 different children's products, including toys, containing DINP and found that the amounts released from products when mouthed varied widely and deemed the amounts generally well below levels that could cause harmful effects. Still more studies are needed, CPSC says, and it has formed a scientific panel to assess the results.

Meanwhile, the CPSC has issued a caution to parents to dispose of soft plastic teethers, rattles, or toys that their babies have mouthed for long periods of time. The chemical has been banned in toys in a number of other countries.

Once a baby starts creeping and crawling, then cruising from one piece of furniture to another, play becomes an insatiable urge to explore the unknown. At that stage, your baby will hungrily move around the house, trying to find some new feat to master, some tiny intricacy to finger, or a new object to stick in his mouth. You'll soon discover that baby toys aren't really a top priority on your baby's list of "things to do." Instead, there are the VCR buttons to push, the dirt in the potted plants to taste and scatter, the hole in the couch upholstery to examine, and the pots and pans to clank. Bright colors, interesting patterns, and a variety of textures can engage baby's attention.

Everyday household objects are very intriguing items to a tot. Batting an inflated paper bag may keep your two-month-old's attention, jangling a set of measuring spoons might appeal to a six-month-old, or pushing an upside-down plastic laundry basket around the living room may engage a new walker. Bath toys and other household gadgets are likely to appeal to one- to two-year-olds—plastic containers (some with holes in the bottom), a washcloth, unbreakable cups of different sizes, or a ladle.

SHOPPING SAVVY Toys

The ideal toys adapt to more than one stage of a child's interests and abilities. At best, there should be a fit between a baby's specific developing skills and her inner drives to explore. But deluging a baby with dozens of toys is counterproductive—they only cause confusion and litter the baby's room and the rest of the house.

The most familiar baby-toy brands are Fisher-Price, First Years, and Playskool. Toy-only companies, such as Arcotoys, Brio, Discovery Toys, Lego, the Manhattan Group, and Shelcore, also offer toys for babies, preschoolers, and school-aged children.

Baby toys are sold in toy stores, such as Toys 'R' Us; in the baby departments of retail stores, such as Sears, JC Penney, and Montgomery Ward; in the toy sections of giant baby-only stores, including Babies 'R' Us, Baby Superstore, and Baby Depot; and in small, virtual toy stores on the web, including eToys. The best toy bargains can be found during seasonal sales, such as those around Christmas, when competition heats up.

Used toys, if they're in perfect condition, are a great buy. Thrift stores, consignment shops, and yard and garage sales are good places for discovering sturdy hand-me-downs, such as solid, molded-plastic items.

Examine every toy carefully before you buy to ensure that it's age-

Safe

Play "Peek-a-boo" frequently to help a little one understand that you can disappear and still return.

appropriate for your child (check the box for the age range).

Poorly constructed items—the kind often sold in grocery stores, drugstores, service stations, airports, and dollar-buys-all stores—are no bargain. Flimsy plastic toys often have small parts that can break off easily, or sharp edges that can be dangerous to both babies and young children.

A good rule: Buy one intriguing, quality toy rather than five cheap toys that can break or be potentially dangerous.

Baby Safe

SUPERVISE TOYS

Thousands of times each year, all across the country, parents rush their babies to doctor's offices and emergency rooms as the result of toy-related accidents. Babies have a natural urge to mouth toys, and they can easily get a small object, toy, or toy part caught in the throat (or nose or ear). The consequences range from gagging to suffocation.

• Most reputable U.S. toy manufacturers conform to voluntary industry standards, and all toys made in this country must meet federal standards. (See Product Recalls for specifics.) But you'll want to supervise toys and play.

• A simple size test for a toy is to try slipping it through the center tube of a roll of toilet paper. If it passes through, it's too little for baby to play with. Also, be aware that small toys and small parts of toys intended for older kids—marbles, Lego pieces, wheels that pull off trucks, small pieces from monsters and doll sets, and dolls with sewn-on metal or plastic eyes that could be chewed off—could get into baby's hands.

• Don't buy little toys, such as miniature stuffed animals or animal/rattle combinations, if they've got ears, arms, legs, or snouts that could be bitten off or partially swallowed. Rattles sewn inside soft toys should be large enough so that they can't be swallowed if your baby gnaws a hole in the toy.

• Toys made of soft, chewable plastic should not be made of PVC or DINP. (See "The phthalate issue," page 216.) The CPSC has assured parents that "few, if any, children are at risk" because the amount of DINP they ingest is well below the level believed harmful. Still, until more is known about the chemicals' effects, it makes sense to limit exposure to them. As a precaution, CPSC says parents may wish to discard all teethers, rattles, or toys made of soft plastic unless you're sure they're made from plastics other than PVC. Most toy makers have indicated they'll voluntarily switch to less controversial materials, including polyethylene or EVA plastic, which contains no plasticizers.

• Stuffed animals or any toys made of fabric should be washable and bite-proof. Fur should not come off in clumps in baby's mouth. Dyes should be colorfast. And there should be no

Baby play stages

Babies move through a series of distinct developmental stages as they mature. The best (and safest) toys match both a baby's level of interest and his basic, evolving body skills. The stages below describe the average child's development progress.

From birth to three months. Baby is alert for only brief periods of time. His chief desire, beyond food, is to be held and rocked. He can lift his

loose strings or ribbons or other sewn-on parts, such as eyes, buttons, or wheels, which could be chewed off and choked on.

• Any baby toy should be unbreakable, with no sharp edges or hinges; pinching parts; small wires that could poke through; strings, cords, or necklaces that can strangle. Porcelain dolls and cheap plastic toys are in the breakable category.

• Blocks are dangerous if a wobbly baby falls onto them. Activity centers with small hinged doors and dump trucks with hinged backs can pinch small, inept fingers.

• A crib should be a place to sleep, not to play (especially unsupervised), so keep all toys out of the crib. Soft toys and decorative pillows can suffocate a small baby. Toddlers get hurt when they jump around in the crib and fall on hard toys. They may also use larger toys as stepping stones for climbing up and over the railings, risking a fall.

Even if you're careful to buy safe toys, it's important to mind the way that your baby uses them. Here are our safe-use suggestions:

• Discard colorful wrapping paper (the ink may contain lead) and plastic wrappers, which may pose a suffocation hazard.

• If you buy a ride-on toy, make sure there are no stairs to fall down, or hard surfaces that could hurt the baby in case of a fall. Outdoors, beware of curbs, sloping driveways, open pools, ponds, or other dangers that could cause harm in a fall.

• Supervise your baby closely when she is playing with any toy. Frequently examine all toys and discard any that are damaged or broken, with cracks, tears, loose parts, or sharp edges.

• Balloons are very hazardous to babies. Small pieces of latex balloons get caught in a baby's throat, causing asphyxiation. Never let your baby have a balloon to play with. And never tie a balloon on the side of the crib or anywhere in the baby's room.

• Never allow a toddler to run with a toy in her mouth. Tragedies have occurred when a fall pushed a rattle into the throat of a child with such force that parents couldn't remove the rattle in time to prevent suffocation.

head briefly to gaze at faces, lights, and contrasting patterns but can't reach out for them. His hearing is fully mature. He brings his fists into range of his eyes and mouth, and thrusts his arms and legs. By the third month, he briefly raises his head and chest by pushing with his arms when placed face-down. He watches faces, can follow moving objects, and smiles at family members and toys. Baby will cycle arms and legs, open and close his hands, swipe at objects, and begin to grasp them.

Baby can play with toys with high-contrast patterns, such as simple black-and-white pictures, bull's-eyes, checkered patterns, and simple faces; musical crib mobiles with toys or bright patterns that face toward baby; toys with mirrors for reflecting light; rattles that make intriguing noises; and hanging toys they can bat with arms and legs. For safe mouthing, toys should be smooth-edged, with nothing sharp.

From four to eight months. She rolls from front to back and back to front and sits briefly, first with support, then alone. Baby can now reach with one hand and grasp objects, move things from one hand to another, pat and stroke textures, and play with her feet. She'll search for sources of sounds.

She'll enjoy floor gyms; textured soft toys that can be safely mouthed; soft balls with sounds inside; musical toys and rattles; chewable vinyl or cloth baby books; and toys with flaps or lids that can be opened and closed.

Baby Safe
CRIB-MOBILE SAFETY TIPS

Mobiles are intriguing to young babies but must be used with caution. Although mobiles are fun to look at, they're not to be touched or played with. The small toys can be a choking hazard, and strings and suspension hardware can pose a strangulation risk.

Follow these safe use tips:

• Don't put the mobile directly over your baby—hang it completely out of reach.

• Fasteners, including strings, straps, and clamps, should be attached tightly to the crib and checked frequently.

• Do not add any additional strings or straps that could pose a safety hazard.

• Remove the mobile from the crib and put it away when a baby is able to push up on hands and knees and grab for toys, usually at about five to six months of age.

From eight to 23 months. Baby first sits alone, then propels forward on his belly, then learns to balance on hands and knees, and finally crawls on all fours. He'll next pull up to a stand, and cruise by holding on to furniture. Finally, he'll stand, then walk, beginning with a few steps without support. He'll develop a pincer grasp. He plays by shaking, banging, throwing, and dropping toys; searching for hidden objects; taking objects out of containers; poking into holes with his index finger. At the young end, he'll enjoy baby games such as "Peek-a-boo," "Where's Baby?", and waving "bye-bye."

Your baby would now like stacking and building toys with rounded edges, bath toys, squeeze toys, soft dolls, puppets, cars, lightweight balls, baby books, musical toys, push-pull toys, and toy telephones.

By two years. She walks unaided and pulls toys behind her while walking; stands on tiptoe; learns to run and kicks a ball; and climbs stairs and scrambles onto and off furniture. Your toddler can build block towers, likes playing with large balls, turns pages of books, uses sorting toys, piles blocks—and then knocks them down. She's interested in toys that can be taken apart and put back together again, likes to imitate, and plays simple make-believe with toy animals and dolls.

Consider cardboard books, blocks, nesting toys, simple sorting toys, buckets and shovels, dolls, balls, child-size trucks, cars, and trains; bath toys; swings; toy telephones; and child keyboards.

By three years. He climbs, kicks balls, pedals a tricycle, and can draw with crayons, build with blocks, and turn handles. He'll play make-believe with toy figures, animals, and people; sort objects by shape and color; and solve simple puzzles.

Look for building blocks; puzzles with knobs; clay, crayons, and paper; outdoor play equipment; props for make-believe play; and dolls and stuffed animals.

"Age range" is a safety warning. When you're toy shopping, look for the very important manufacturer's recommended age guideline on the front of the toy package, such as "six month to two years." Take this guideline seriously.

Much more than a friendly hint, this information is a powerful safety warning of danger to a child younger than the specified age. The real message should read: "This toy could hurt your baby," or, more realistically, "This toy has hurt babies in the past."

Read

Schedule a daily reading time, whether it's during or after a meal, before a nap, or at bedtime. Make it a relaxed and fun time—not a chore.

Never buy or allow babies to play with a toy that's not in their correct age range. Besides following the manufacturer's guidelines, test and inspect the toy yourself. For how-to's, see "Baby safe: supervise toys," page 218.

PLAYTIME OPTIONS

The toys shown here are a sampling of what's available. They demonstrate positive, baby-intriguing features—bright colors and engaging sounds and actions. Age recommendations are those of the manufacturers. Retail prices vary widely, so don't be surprised if the price in this book and the price you find in the store are different.

▲ **Infantino Remote Control Mobile (Model 184-520, $50, birth to five months).** This musical crib mobile features four suspended small bears holding colored swatches. Parents can spin the bears by using a separate, battery-operated remote control unit. Do not hang mobile directly above baby.

▼ **Chicco USA, Inc. Spin and Turn Shape Sorter (Model 66101, $15, one to four years).** Six brightly colored, differently shaped blocks fit into holes in a bright blue container. When shapes are in their proper holes, knobs on each side rotate to release the shapes into the container below. Blocks are easily removed from the lower chamber through a small door.

▶ **International Playthings Early E. Bird (Model E00102, $12, birth and up).** A variety of bright patterns and textures with attached chewing rings.

▲ **Kids II Bright Starts Activity Flower (Model 816-4, $11, birth to three years).** The big, puffy, fabric flower has a smiling face and five petals providing visual contrasts, rattles, teething opportunities, or other small playthings. (But note we do not recommend putting any toy in a baby's crib.)

Step 2 Push-About Fire Truck (Model 7781, $23, two years and up). Truck has a reversible handle so kids can choose whether to push or pull. Two chunky firefighter figures fit onto the lift-and-swivel ladder, and the truck is great for loading and unloading. ◀

Playtime Gear

▼ **Learning Curve Lamaze Infant Development System First Mirror** (Model 97105, $20, birth and up). This fabric-covered foam wedge has a removable, unbreakable mirror on one side. The mirror portion can also be attached to the side of the crib, but we suggest not putting any toys in the crib.

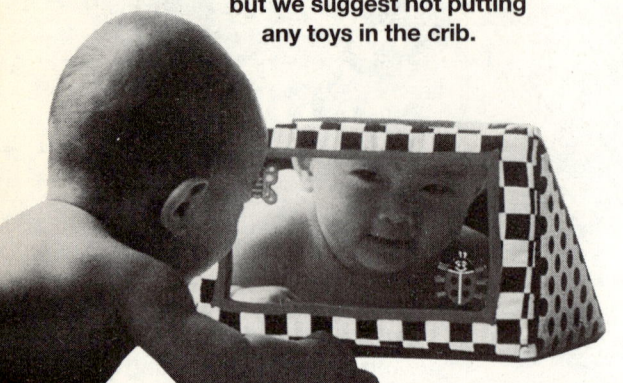

▲ **Little Tikes Nesting Pots 'N Pans** (Model 1535, $10, 6 to 36 months). The seven-piece set includes a fry pan with a mirror on the inside, different size pots with lids, a colander for water play, and one little green pea with a squeaker inside.

▶ **Maya Group Tiny Love Gymini 3-D Activity Gym** (Model 00401, $45, birth to 10 months). The cushy, padded "gym" is made with a quilt and foam-filled arches that hold colorful, soft, suspended toys.

▸ Today's Kids Play 'N Fold Clubhouse (Model 370, $60, nine months to three and a half years). Four folding sides form an open-air playhouse for crawlers and tots. One panel has a small door with mail slot and doorbell; another has a small window with a picture frame inside; the third has a big green circle to climb through; and the fourth, a small sliding board. All parts fold flat for storage.

▸ Gerber Push-N-Pop Rattle (Model 78240, $4, six months and up). When baby presses the base of this handheld toy, colorful balls pop wildly around inside a plastic dome. Or the rattle can just be wiggled around for noises.

▴ Sassy Circle Rattle (Model 846, $5, three months and up). Bright patterns, vivid colors, and a variety of textures capture baby's imagination.

▸ Maya Group Tiny Love 1-2-3 Discovery Lane (Model 00470, $50, 3 to 18 months). The thick fabric circle provides activities for belly lying babies, crawlers, and tots. Inserted into the play circle are a mirror, crinkling squeeze toys, a water mat with fish inside, geometric shapes, and toys that make animal sounds when squeezed. The circle opens into a curving pathway for a crawler and shapes into a small teepee for older tots.

Playtime Gear

▶ **Sassy Pogo Rattle (Model 822, $7, three months and up).** A hard plastic rattle features concentric oval rings in a variety of patterns and textures.

▼ **Discovery Toys Measure Up! Cups (Model 1640, $10).** A dozen round plastic cups in bright green, yellow, red, and blue, with patterns stamped on the underside, are great for teaching sizes, playing in the tub or the wading pool, or for carrying snacks.

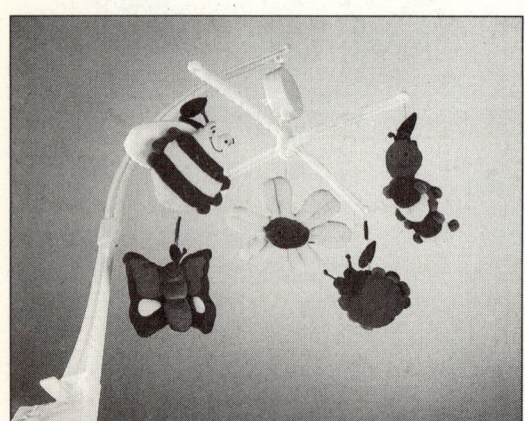

▶ **Manhattan Baby Enchanted Garden Musical Mobile (Model EG589, $40, birth until baby can pull up on all fours—about five to six months).** The mobile fastens to the side of the crib and features five stuffed creatures made from soft fabric—a pudgy bee, caterpillar, daisy, ladybug, and butterfly. A windup music box plays Brahms' Lullaby as the creatures turn slowly.

▶ **Playskool Spin Around Bear Rattle (Model 33165, $4, 6 months and up).** When this bright yellow rattle with an easy-to-hold, U-shaped handle is shaken, the colorful balls inside roll and rattle.

▼ **Lego Walker** (Model 2010, $25, 6 to 24 months). The four-wheeled cart with a high back and toddler-sized handle contains giant Lego blocks for stacking and building.

▼ **Discovery Toys Stacks of Fun Soft Shapes** (Model 1351, $20, one year and up). The four soft shapes that stack on a foam rod and base are each covered in textured, patterned cloth and offer squeaks, rattles, or crinkles.

◀ **Playskool Roll N' Rattle Shaker** (Model 35220, $4, three months and up). Colored beads make a dry rattling sound whenever the clear rattle is flipped, turned, or rolled across the floor.

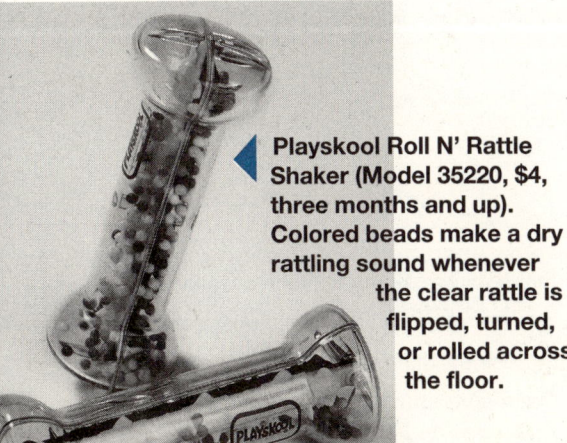

▲ **Fisher-Price Activity Center** (Model 71175, $15, three months and up). The panel contains 11 activities, including a dial, a spinning wheel, a rattling spinner ball, a squeaker, and other noisemakers that baby can operate. There's also an unbreakable mirror in the center and a handle. Although the activity center can be fastened to the center of a crib with a supplied strap, for safety's sake we recommend using it outside the crib only.

Playtime Gear

WALKERS

A walker is a baby seat with wheels on the base. Walkers come in different shapes—circular, rectangular, or square—and most have four to eight wheels on the bottom. Walker heights can be raised or lowered, using either a locking mechanism located under the front tray, slots in the base of the walker, or adjusters on the inside of the seat. Walker seats vary by the height of the seat back and the amount of padding. Some models offer a bouncing feature, and most have rimmed trays. There may be toys attached to the tray, or removable, U-shaped frames that dangle toys in front of the baby.

Walkers are designed to be used by babies who can sit up unassisted. The typical age range is from 5 to 6 months to whenever a baby becomes a steady walker, usually from 12 to 15 months. A baby uses a walker to propel herself around, using her feet and toes. It's been estimated that as many as 3.6 million walkers are sold every year in the U.S. and as many as half of all babies use them at one time or another.

Walkers don't enhance walking skills

Despite the name walker, the device won't actually speed up your baby's inborn walking timetable. A walker actually calls for an entirely different set of leg and back actions than those required for crawling or balancing on two feet. Plus, posturing your baby in an upright position for long periods of time, rather than allowing vigorous crawling, may interfere with the normal

Baby Safe

WALKERS MOVE FAST

- Never use a walker near stairs, steps, or thresholds, whether they're gated or not—any type of gate can loosen.
- Always keep your child in full view.
- Make sure there are no hot surfaces, such as fireplaces, woodstoves, oven doors, space heaters, or containers with hot liquids inside, that baby can reach while in a walker.
- Beware of dangling appliance cords and tablecloths that can be pulled over.
- Make sure your baby can't get near toilets, swimming pools, or other sources of water and that all doors to the basement, garage, and yard are securely closed.

unfolding of physical skills. Creeping and crawling strengthen back and thigh muscles critical to later walking and coordination.

In fact, a walker may actually slow down the development of real walking. One study compared babies who spent time in a walker with twin siblings who weren't put in a walker. The babies who used walkers walked with stiff legs and shortened steps, and they leaned forward more than their siblings who were given the freedom to simply crawl on the floor. The ill effects did not appear to be lasting, though.

Walker dangers

Parents may buy a walker because they believe it will help to keep a baby quiet and happy, that it will help the baby learn to walk, and that it provides exercise. Some parents use one to hold a baby during feeding. One out of three walker owners also thinks that it will keep a baby safe. But accident reports show that walkers aren't safe at all. In fact, walkers are responsible for causing the most injuries of any baby product.

Because walkers are on wheels, they give babies quick access to harmful situations. Babies in walkers travel up to four feet per second, which means they can get into trouble very quickly. They can plummet down stairways or steps between levels; turn over when wheels get snagged by cords, door thresholds, and carpet edges; roll themselves against hot stoves and heaters; and, when outdoors, fall over concrete curbs and tumble into swimming pools. Typically, accidents occur in only a minute or two, while a mother or father has a back turned or when a sibling opens the basement door or back door, allowing the tot to wheel out.

The CPSC estimates that, in 1997, walkers were involved in 14,300 hospital-emergency-room-treated injuries to children younger than 15 months. Walkers also have been involved in 34 deaths since 1973. Most children sustained injuries when their walker fell down stairs.

One medical survey found that walkers accounted for 45 percent of falls down stairs causing head injuries. In some cases, the falls occurred in spite of safety gates. Another study confirmed that one third of the walker/stair accidents happened when gates were in place. Either the gates were closed incorrectly or they didn't hold up to the impact of the walker. (We discuss gates and their hazards on pages 253 to 258.)

The serious injuries in walker-related accidents include concussions and broken bones. And, amazingly, even after their babies had been injured by

Clean

Shake unwashable stuffed toys in a bag with generous amounts of cornmeal. Brush out the cornmeal, and the dirt will come with it.

walkers, one out of three parents put their babies right back in a walker again or used walkers for other children.

The new walker standard

To make walkers safer, the CPSC worked with the baby-products industry to create a new standard. Walkers that meet the 1997 standard, developed by the American Society for Testing and Materials (ASTM) and certified by the Juvenile Products Manufacturers Association (JPMA), are required either to be too wide to fit through a standard 36-inch doorway or to have features, such as a friction strip, to stop the walker at the edge of a step.

The CPSC has stated that it expects that with the new standard, baby walker–related injuries demanding emergency room treatment will decrease to less than 10,000 per year by 2002.

Walkers that conform to the newer standard carry one of the following statements on the shipping carton: "Meets new ASTM safety standards for steps and stairs," "Meets new Walker ASTM stair standard," or simply "Meets new safety standards."

The certification standard addresses stability issues, the finger pinching or cutting potential of X-joints, springs that could hurt small fingers, and the sturdiness of stitching on fabric parts. It also requires that there be no caps, sleeves, or plugs (which could be choking hazards) and calls for protection from sharp edges, points, or entrapment of fingers or toes.

Still, it's up to the consumer to heed warnings on the walker, including never to use it near stairs, steps, or thresholds; never to leave a child in it unattended or out of sight; and never to carry the walker with a child inside. Consumers are advised to check that surfaces where the walker will be used are flat and free of objects that may cause tipping over, and that both feet of the child in the walker touch the floor or ground. They're also warned to keep the child away from ranges, radiators, space heaters, fireplaces, and other sources of heat.

SHOPPING SAVVY Walkers

After reading about the accidents associated with walkers, you may decide that the very real risks of putting your baby on wheels outweigh the walker's possible merits. If so, take a look at the stationary entertainers in the next section. They offer equal or greater play value than a walker, while still letting you keep baby under control.

If you decide you want a walker for your baby, the type you purchase will depend on the layout of your home. Choose a model with an extra-wide base if you're concerned about containing your baby in a room with standard, 36-inch-wide doorways. These models take up a great deal of floor space, though they fold for storage.

If you've got any staircases in your house, even those protected by doors, you'll want a walker with a friction strip (made of rubberized material) underneath. This strip, which touches the floor when the wheels fall away, makes it very difficult for a baby to push the walker forward. So this type will at least give you a head start on grabbing your baby before he can work his way over the top stair.

Note that models that meet the new standard can still get into trouble, say, through the interaction of another child. Remember, too, that the safety standard is voluntary, not mandatory. Manufacturers can continue to sell traditional, uncertified walkers that can easily endanger your baby. (We review certified walkers below.)

Avoid old X-frame walkers. They've long since been discontinued in stores, but you may encounter one in a garage sale or thrift store. Basically, they have hammock-like seats suspended between two tubular frames, like folding TV tables, with no protection to guard against pinching and shearing. The design has been responsible for many injuries, including finger amputations when a baby's hand gets caught in the closing X-joint of the frame. They should be discarded.

Talk

Get your child a toy phone to talk on while you're on your phone.

What's available

CONSUMER REPORTS tested walkers from the six companies that make models conforming to the new voluntary safety standard—Cosco, Delta Enterprise (Delta Luv), Graco, J. Mason, Kolcraft, and Safety 1st. All the models tested have adjustable seats and trays, and fold for storage.

Four of these have friction strips underneath. They look like conventional walkers, but the strips can stop the walker at the edge of the first step. If you choose one of these, make sure you keep the strip clean and in good shape.

Cosco SureStep (Model 04-251, $40) has a deep front tray, adjustable seat, raised back support, and a bumper on the base to help protect furniture. The walker comes with a removable set of spinning toys, a mirror, and a squeaker. Our tests showed that the friction strip should be affixed more securely.

Delta Luv Jet (Model 277-70, $50) has a tray with a small steering wheel, lights, rattles, rollers, and other noisemakers. It performed well in the stair test. Its two rear wheels prevent the walker from moving backward.

Graco Tot Wheels Entertainer (Model 665EX, $45) has a high-back, covered seat. The rear wheel acts as a brake at fast speeds and can be locked completely, which allows a child only to swivel. This walker can also be made completely stationary by lowering its parking stand.

Safety 1st Mobile "4 Wheelin" Walker (Model 45701, $50) resembles a tot-sized car. It has a plastic steering wheel, rear view "mirrors," and a small roll bar in the back. The rear wheel can lock. Assembly instructions say nothing about tools, but we needed them.

The two other walkers tested have a circular bumper guard that makes them too wide to fit through a normal door. The bumper also helps keep kids away from electrical outlets and dangers otherwise within reach. But these bumpers are not meant to keep a child from falling down the stairs.

J. Mason Safe Surround (Model 1800 series, $40) is 38 inches wide. It comes with a detachable toy bar holding suspended rings and rattles. This model was fairly easy to assemble.

Kolcraft Room Rover (Model 14203L, $50) has a high back. The assembly instructions don't call for tools, but we needed pliers to do the job.

All manufacturers would do well to make sure consumers can easily assemble these walkers. If parents have trouble attaching a seat or other part, they may do it incompletely, which can compromise a child's safety.

Even with the new walkers, you should always keep an eye on your child—and never use a walker near stairs. The safeguards are not foolproof.

STATIONARY ENTERTAINERS

Entertainers are relatively new inventions; they have evolved in response to concerns over walker dangers and injuries. Basically, entertainers are all-in-one baby play stations that resemble walkers, but without the wheels. Babies can use them as soon as they can sit up independently (about 6 months) until they're sturdy walkers (12 to 15 months). You'll get the most use out of one during the three-month period right in the middle of this timetable.

Most entertainers have built-in baby recreation features. Their seats can swivel 360 degrees (a full circle), allowing baby to see all around. Surrounding the seat is a tray with attached interactive toys that make sounds or actions when baby plays with them. The units' legs have built-in springs that bounce when baby moves. And a few models have rocker

Absorbing

Make changing time easier as your child becomes more active by having a special toy that comes out only at changing time. Give it to the baby the moment he or she is lying down.

bases so that the whole unit rocks.

Seat heights are adjustable to three or four levels. More expensive models have thicker seat padding and more toys. Units usually come unassembled in a carton, but assembling isn't very difficult.

Entertainers can be found where baby toys are sold.

What's available

Models with freestanding legs can "walk." We suggest getting an entertainer with a solid, flat base so the unit doesn't move around when you're not looking. If an entertainer has a rocking base, check for a locking mechanism. Avoid models that cannot be anchored in a stationary position. Also, examine attached toys for size (large enough not to fit through the center of a toilet paper roll) and for small parts that might break off.

Evenflo, the originator of what it calls "the walker alternative," sells the majority of stationary entertainers. In fact, "exersaucer," a name coined by Evenflo, is commonly used to describe the whole category.

Evenflo Exersaucer Plus (Model 605994, $40) has a rocker base and six toys that click, squeak, move, and flip built into the tray. The seat in the center of the tray rotates 360 degrees, offers three height adjustments, and has a removable, washable pad. Pop-out feet lock the rocker base. The Exersaucer Deluxe Plus (Model 605912, $60) has additional toys on the tray, including electronic toys, a soft elephant toy, and a spinner ball. The Supersaucer Exercise and Entertainment Center (Model 6081A7, $80) rocks, bounces, and has a rotating seat. It features a new line of large interactive toys, including a mirror, clackers, and rings.

Baby Trend Play-in-Place Exercisers (Models 3617, $49; 3643, $49; 3666, $49; 3727, $44) all have a frame with a rotating metal arm that allows a baby to move in several directions—left to right, forward and backward, diagonally, or in a circle. Both the seat and the tray swivel. The seat offers three height positions. Some models have a detachable keyboard/soundmaker. The unit folds flat for storage.

Baby Trend Bouncer & Entertainment Tables (Models 3843, $29, and 3866, $29) have four bouncing legs that can be locked to hold the entertainer stationary, a center seat that swivels, and two toys mounted on the table corners. With the center seat removed and a cover (included) placed over the seat hole, the bouncer converts to a children's table.

Graco Bouncing Entertainer (Model 4118, $70) has a floor for baby's feet, three legs with springs, high and low leg-height adjustments, and a swiveling seat. Tray toys include a flexible teether, squeak button, bottle holder, turn-and-click wheel, and floating duck. (Some models made in mid-1998 have been recalled for a loose toy screw. The flaw has been corrected.)

Graco Model 4622 ($60) has a rocking base with a stabilizer foot, plus a rotating fabric seat. Toys include a removable musical play tray with a telephone, steering wheel, horn that beeps, spinner, mirror, and musical buttons, in addition to a turn knob, an arch with beads, and a teether. Model 4627 ($50) has the same toys but no musical tray.

Cosco Bungee Bouncer (Model 04-466, $30) is different from other stationary entertainers: The seat is suspended from the frame by four bungee-like cords. It can be adjusted to four heights.

Safety 1st Bouncing Buggy (Model 45608, $50 to $55) is molded to look like a small car. The "chassis" bounces, and the unit can rock forward and backward. It has three height adjustments. The swivel seat has a removable, machine-washable lining. Toys are mounted on back and front. (Note: Earlier versions of this model have been recalled—see Product Recalls, page 283.)

Baby Safe

OVERSEE AN ENTERTAINER

- Although most babies love being in an entertainer, some hate it. If you can, borrow a unit from a friend so your baby can try it out before you buy one.

- Remember that just like walkers, entertainers force your baby to maintain an erect posture at a time when his body is more comfortable on all fours and make him use his feet when they aren't fully strengthened and prepared to support his body weight. Making your baby sit up for prolonged periods, rather than encouraging a strong crawling career, may train him to use his back, leg, and foot muscles in ways they're not designed to be used yet.

- As an alternative for keeping your baby occupied for a longer period of time, we suggest blocking off a room and letting your baby do his exploring on hands and knees. In the entertainer or out, your own constant supervision of baby is always needed.

- Use caution with entertainers that have rounded, saucer-like bases that allow the device to rock. If you've got other kids in the house, the base could cause a pretty serious bruise to the toes or fingers of a child standing or playing near the unit while baby rocks.

JUMPERS

Jumpers are baby seats that can be suspended by springs and belts from the top of a door frame. They use clamps that look like ice hooks and have nonslip tips. Each jumper manufacturer has very specific requirements for the door frame measurements that will allow the product to be safely used.

While some babies from five to eight months old really enjoy being in a jumper, others dislike them or even get "seasick" from the motion.

Jumper dangers arise when straps or the clamp break, allowing the hardware and baby to fall; and when babies run into the sharp sides of the doorway, either because they're jumping vigorously or because a sibling tries to swing the baby in the jumper.

What's available

Cosco Bungee Baby Jumper (Model 04-461, $25) fastens to almost any standard doorway and has a foam bumper to help protect woodwork. It adjusts to the height of the child and has a tray to hold toys or snacks. Cosco packages its Bungee Combo Exerciser/Jumper (Model 04-468, $50) as a combo pack that allows the seat from the Bungee Bouncer to be converted into a jumper.

Graco Doorway Jumpers (Model 8750, $35 and 8740, $30) have a foam bumper guard; removable, washable pad; and handle grips.

Evenflo Johnny Jump Up Baby Exerciser (Model 60411, $20) is a doorway jumper for babies four months to walking age (24 pounds maximum). The deep pocket seat is washable and has support bars in front and back.

Baby Safe

JUMPER CONCERNS

- Don't use a jumper unless the door frame meets the maker's specifications.
- Always inspect the jumper before you put baby inside to be sure the straps are securely fastened and the clamp will hold.
- Never let baby out of your sight. Limit jumping times to 15 minutes at a stretch, so baby doesn't become dizzy or get back strain.
- Do not allow siblings to play nearby or to push baby in the jumper.

Chapter 11

KEEPING BABY SAFE

Babies and toddlers can get into trouble in an instant. Remove every hazard you can, and consider safety devices.

Babies and toddlers are both physically vulnerable and unaware of the hazards all around them. Baby-proofing your house, plus some child-protective devices, can help you safeguard your tot. But there's truly no substitute for your own vigilance.

BABY-PROOFING YOUR HOUSE

Don't wait until your baby starts crawling to plan for a safe home. As you go through each room, use a critical eye—and even get down on your knees for a toddler's point of view. Here's a room-by-room rundown on what to look for when you do your home-safety scan of your home.

Kitchen

Sharp knives, glass bottles and dishes, household chemicals under the sink, burning-hot cooking surfaces, electric appliances a tot can pull to the floor—your kitchen contains all kinds of accidents just waiting to happen. For maximum safety, keep baby out of the kitchen entirely when you cook. Use a gate at the door or passageway, or put baby in a play yard or a high chair, out of harm's way, but always in view.

Dishwasher. Dishwasher detergent can cause severe, disfiguring chemical burns to a child's mouth. Lock the cupboard where you keep it,

Contents

Baby-proofing, page 237

Baby monitors, page 248

Gates, page 253

and don't put detergent in the dishwasher when baby is around.

Small appliances. Babies are injured when they tug on cords and pull coffeemakers, food processors, toaster ovens, and other appliances down on top of themselves. Wrap up and fasten cords out of reach with twist ties or rubber bands. Or tape cords to the wall with duct tape. Unplug appliances when they're not in use: Coffeemakers and microwave ovens have caused fires even when turned off.

Refrigerator. Every year children die needlessly in refrigerator-suffocation accidents. Typically, parents move an old, unused refrigerator outside for pickup. Children playing hide-and-seek decide to climb inside and close the door, and they suffocate before they can be rescued. Always remove the doors from an old refrigerator and store the unit facedown.

In addition, keep small refrigerator magnets out of baby's reach. They can cause choking. You might pack them away until baby is older.

Range and ovens. A baby's skin burns a lot easier than yours. If your oven door has a front window that gets really hot, or if you have an older model with poor insulation, consider replacing it with a newer model. Prince Lionheart's Stove Guard (Model 0089, $20 to $24), molded of heat-resistant polycarbonate, adjusts to act as a shield for the front of stoves from 24 inches to 36 inches wide. It can be removed for easy cleaning.

You could use a microwave oven placed high and out of baby's reach for some family meals. Don't use microwaves for heating baby-food jars or milk bottles. Microwave heating can create severe hot spots in the food or milk that can burn a baby's mouth and throat. It may also cause jars or bottles to explode.

If your range has front knobs, pull them off and store them out of reach until you need to cook. Tot-proof knob covers are also available. Turn all pot handles toward the back of the cooktop when you're cooking so baby can't pull on them and you won't knock them over. When possible, cook on the back burners.

Cabinets and drawers. Remove all detergents and household chemicals from under the sink and put them in a locking cabinet. Keep knives, scissors, and other sharp objects in drawers equipped with child-resistant safety latches installed from the inside. Lock liquor away—it's dangerous for babies. Pad sharp corners of countertops, and keep stools and chairs out of reach so your baby won't use them for climbing.

Safety 1st Cabinet Latch & Drawer Latches (Model 116, 4/$1.59) latch-

and-catch systems screw-mount inside a drawer or cabinet door. The latch keeps the drawer from opening more than a few inches, but an adult can open the cupboard by pressing down the latch.

First Years' Cabinet Safety Lock (Model 3232, $1.79) consists of a plastic U-shaped piece that fits over knobs or through cabinet handles and is then held together with a plastic strap. This style of closure has some drawbacks. It won't work on cabinets without handles or knobs or those that have very small ones. Nor will it work if the knobs are too far apart (more than 7¾ inches), and it can allow the upper of two drawers to be accessed if both drawers are pulled out.

Plastic bags. Plastic bags—garbage bags, laundry bags, and food-storage or grocery bags—can suffocate children who play with them. Lock them up, and tie them in knots when you throw them out. Plastic food-wrapping can also suffocate a child if he puts it over his face. Also put away any food-wrap packaging with serrated edges.

Living room

Prevent shock hazards from electrical outlets and extension cords, burns from heat sources such as fireplaces and woodstoves, and cuts and bruises from sharp furniture edges.

Coffee table. Coffee tables send thousands of babies and young children to emergency rooms every year when they fall against sharp corners and edges. Use stick-on safety padding for table edges—or completely remove the coffee table and store it during baby's first three years.

Fireplace or woodstove. Babies are drawn to fire, not realizing that heat sources are dangerous. Reinforce the words "Hot! Don't Touch!" so your child comes to respect your warning. Keep matches and lighters safely out of children's reach. Consider installing a fireproof safety railing around the fireplace, always use a fireplace screen, and put fireproof padding around sharp brick edges on raised hearths.

Lamps. Babies may tug on a lamp cord and pull down the lamp. Wrap up cords with a cord shortener, or use twist ties or rubber bands at the base of the lamp so there's no slack. Position lamp cords to the back.

Safety 1st Cord Holders (Model 218, 3/$1.49), small plastic cases that attach to the wall with double-sided tape, help keep loose telephone cords and electric cords out of reach. An adult can easily open these two-part holders to release a cord. Safety 1st Cord Shortener (Model 10114, $3) helps

Study

Keep a notepad in a convenient place in your home to make running notes of questions you want to ask at the baby's check-ups. Note your baby's "history," including sleeping, crying, and eating patterns, elimination habits, and such.

keep excess electrical cord from becoming a tripping hazard. Insert the cord into a slot in the spool and turn the knob.

Electrical outlets. Typically, an accident with electricity involves a baby sticking a key, diaper pin, or hairpin into an open socket, causing a sudden and severe shock. Use safety outlet covers to prevent contact with a live outlet. Check that all outlets have ground fault interrupters; if any are missing, install them. Safety 1st Auto-Swivel Outlet Cover (Model 10401, $2) is a plastic electrical-outlet cover plate with a spring-loaded outlet guard. It

Baby Safe

HOW BABIES GET HURT

Babies are injured in the same ways again and again. Know the dangers and how to guard against them.

Falls. Any surface that elevates an active, squirming baby—cribs, changing tables, backpacks, high chairs, and even infant safety seats—has injury potential. **Safety measures:** Always fasten safety belts. Check frequently for broken parts or malfunctioning hardware. Do not leave your baby unattended, even when fastened in. Since babies often fall against edges and corners, pad any sharp protrusions in baby's vicinity.

Choking. Small parts that are broken or chewed off can cause choking—toy and furniture parts, including nuts and bolts; pieces of vinyl covering; seat and rail padding; even bits of nipples and pacifiers. Chunks of food also pose perils, as do nonfood items like coins. **Safety measures:** Keep small objects out of baby's reach—check toys, pick up clutter, stash an older sibling's small-parts toys, like Legos, in that child's room. Stay with baby at feeding time and avoid foods with choking potential (see page 214).

Strangulation. Young babies have soft, easily compressed throats. Any pressure applied to the outside of a baby's neck can cut off the air supply. **Safety measures:** Remove neckline ties or strings and be sure that necklines or pacifier ribbons cannot snag on crib posts or other protrusions. Put any string, ribbon, or cord—such as those on crib bumpers, wall hangings, and window blinds—safely out of baby's reach. Once baby can pull up, remove crib mobiles and do not string any other item across the crib. Watch for anything that could trap a baby's neck, such as spaces between a playpen side and floor (see page 139), or areas at the side of an adult bed (see page 54). Beware of gaps where a baby can get stuck if he slips through: stroller leg openings, the openings between the seat and tray of a high chair, or

screws over an electrical outlet in place of a regular outlet plate, and the cover blocks access to the empty socket.

Extension cords. When a baby mouths or bites on an extension cord, saliva sets up a pathway for electricity, which can cause severe shock and mouth burns. Purchase new, safety-oriented cords equipped with locking plug holes. If you've got an old house that's overloaded with extension cords, consider getting the house rewired—for everybody's safety.

between crib, cradle, or gate bars.

Suffocation. Babies have a limited ability to lift their heads, at least until six months or so, when neck muscles strengthen. If placed facedown, they can get mouth and nose buried in a suffocation pocket created by cushioned surfaces or materials that adhere to their faces, such as plastic. Pieces of plastic or latex balloons that get caught in the throat can also suffocate. **Safety measures:** Always put baby into the crib or stroller faceup, unless otherwise instructed by your physician. Buy the firmest crib mattress you can find. Do not add any cushioning to the crib or stroller, such as pillows, sheepskins, or blankets. Inspect bassinets and play yards to be sure no loose fabric or mesh can form a suffocation pocket. Keep plastic away from baby—all plastic bags, as well as balloons.

Finger entrapment. Hinges can crush and even amputate a baby's fingers, and fingers can be cut by sharp edges and metal hardware. **Safety measures:** Thoroughly check toys, strollers, high chairs, play yards, and gates for sharp edges and potentially-dangerous hinges. Be sure safety locks can prevent hinge collapse. Keep baby safely clear whenever you fold a stroller, gate, or play yard.

Burns. Babies get heat burns from scalding water, metal hot water taps, vaporizer steam, and overheated bottles. Chemical burns are caused by caustic household cleaners, such as dishwasher detergent. Biting extension cords, wires, and electrical outlets produces not only shocks but electrical burns. **Safety measures:** Turn the water heater down to 120 degrees F, and test water with your wrist before bathing baby. Protect baby from faucets—consider a spout cover for the tub (see page 242). Keep any humidifier far from the crib. Bottles need only slight heating (see page 202). Keep household chemicals and electrical wires out of baby's reach (see page 244).

Keeping Baby Safe

Area rugs. To prevent slips, secure all area rugs in place with foam carpet backing or double-sided tape.

Bathroom

Typically, babies die in bathroom accidents in one of four ways: drowning, poisoning, scalding, or electrical shock. Keep your baby out of the bathroom by using a gate or by latching the outside of the door. Toilet and diaper pail lids with safety locks will help keep baby out of trouble. You may also want to cover the inside door lock with duct tape to keep baby from locking you out.

Medicine cabinet. Toddlers can be very inventive about climbing on sinks to get into the medicine cabinet. Inspect your cabinet and flush all outdated medications down the toilet. Install a locking medicine cabinet. Put medications on a high shelf, on a top closet shelf, or in a childproof locking box. Choose child-resistant packaging for prescription and over-the-counter medications and supplements. Put supplements out of reach, too. Iron pills are a leading child poisoner. Keep activated charcoal and syrup of ipecac, available from pharmarcies in case your child is poisoned. Post the number of the local poison-control center near the medicine cabinet and next to your kitchen telephone. Always call the poison-control center before you administer any poison remedy.

Bathtub. A baby can drown in as little as one inch of water. Typically, a parent goes to answer the telephone or the door, and comes back to discover an unconscious baby facedown in water. Always stay close when giving your baby a bath. That means keeping one hand on the baby at all times and never leaving the baby alone, even for a minute.

Suctioned and other types of bath seats are extremely hazardous (see page 148). Don't buy or use one. Install a rubber mat in the tub so that you and the baby won't slip. Infants can also be bathed in a small tub that fits in the sink or in a kitchen sink.

The bathtub spout can also be a danger spot. Safety 1st Sof' Spout Cover (Model 103, $3) is an inflatable cover that is force-fitted over a bathtub spout to help protect kids from falling onto the spout or getting burned by it. The cover is hard to blow up or deflate, but once inflated, it's easy to fit on the spout and to remove.

Toilet and diaper pail. Babies also drown in toilets and diaper pails. Invest in a diaper pail with a tamper-proof lid equipped with a solid locking device. Toilet-locking devices are also available.

Gerber Toilet Lid Lock (Model 76597, $3.93), a spring-loaded lever, mounts on the toilet lid with double-sided tape. When the toilet lid is shut, the lever automatically snaps into place. First Years All-purpose Safety Latch (Model 3350, 2/$3.79), a strap with a buckle, sticks onto a toilet bowl, medicine cabinet, or refrigerator to keep it closed. (For a look at diaper pails with locking lids, go to page 160.)

Electrical devices. Handheld hair dryers and other appliances, such as radios, fans, and heaters, can cause fatal electrical shock when they fall into water. In addition, curling irons (and irons for clothes) cause deep burns. Don't store or use these appliances in your bathroom or near baby. Install ground-fault interrupters for electrical outlets.

Bedroom

The bedroom may seem like a safe place, but adult-sized furniture and open windows are perilous for infants.

Adult beds, waterbeds, and beanbag chairs. According to the U.S. Consumer Product Safety Commission (CPSC), over 200 babies have suffocated or been strangled in adult beds since 1985. In most cases, babies became wedged between the mattress (or the bed frame) and the wall. In some cases, adults have rolled onto a baby while the baby was in an adult bed. When a baby is positioned facedown on a waterbed or beanbag chair, a suffocation pocket is created that can cause death. Use a crib for all of baby's napping and sleeping.

Unshielded windows. About 70 babies and children die in falls from windows every year. Don't depend on screens to keep your child from falling—they can give way. Avoid placing furniture near windows that your child could use to climb up to the sill. Open double-hung windows from the top instead of the bottom. Or put a removable nail on each side of the sash to stop windows from opening farther than a few inches. You can also install locks that prevent sliding windows from opening more than five inches. If local fire codes permit, install window guards. Burglar bars should be easily removable in case of fire.

Basement and garage

Basements have staircases and appliances that can pose dangers. A garage is simply not a safe place for children. Install a lock on the door leading to the garage, or consider installing a self-locking "Dutch door" that

Hot

Run the cold water last so that if the baby touches the faucet it won't be hot and burn him or her.

Keeping Baby Safe   243

allows you to pass groceries into the kitchen without letting your toddler out.

Basement stairs and other staircases. To prevent falls down basement stairs, install a lock as high as you can reach on the basement door, and keep the door closed and locked at all times. Make sure stairs are well lit, and keep all clutter and toys off steps. If railings on staircases and balconies are spaced more than three inches apart, install Plexiglas to prevent your child from falling through.

Water heater. Turn the water heater thermostat to 120 degrees F to prevent painful scalding of a baby's sensitive skin.

Chemicals. Store gasoline, insecticides, antifreeze, and other dangerous chemicals behind locking cabinet doors. In the basement, put detergent, bleach, and other cleaners in a locking cupboard. Keep all chemicals in their original containers; never transfer them to soda bottles or other beverage containers. Don't use bug spray in the house without cleaning up the pesticide residue.

Buckets. Over 200 toddlers and young children have drowned in five-gallon buckets since 1984. Typically, a baby finds a bucket with water, throws a toy in, and then leans over to retrieve it. Toppling in headfirst and unable to get back out again, the baby drowns. Never leave a bucket of water or other liquid unattended when small children are around.

Lawn mowers. Mowers throw rocks and can mangle small hands and feet. Keep your tot indoors until you've finished mowing, and never joyride your child on the mower. Pour gasoline into the mower while outdoors, not in the garage or basement, where spills can be ignited by the pilot lights of water heaters or furnaces.

Power tools. Keep children away from your workbench while you work. Don't expose your child to risk by assigning tasks he or she doesn't have the hand skills to do safely. Store power tools and sharp objects out of reach. Install plug guards on unused outlets.

Your car. The biggest danger in your garage is your car. Babies can be run over when drivers don't see them. Be especially cautious when backing out of your garage—take your time and make sure your kids aren't in the path of your car. Never leave children unattended in a parked car.

Garage doors. Each year children die or suffer brain damage when crushed under automatic electric garage doors not sensitive enough to reverse when they encounter a small child's body. To test a garage door's sensitivity, place a two-inch-high block of wood on the floor in the path of the garage door. If the door does not stop and reverse when it touches the wood, operate the door manually. Or replace it with a door equipped with optical sensors that keep the door from closing if somebody is in the way. Caution your toddlers about garage and garage-door dangers. Store tricycles and ride-on toys in a safer place.

Decks and porches

Falls from outdoor decks and porches can cause serious injuries; outdoor furniture and grills also pose hazards.

Falling hazards. Spaces between porch or deck railings should be no more than three inches. If they are wider, keep your baby away from them to prevent him from falling through, and consider installing a railing guard (see page 247). Furniture near railings or benches attached to railings can entice children to climb up. If possible, move furniture away from railings. Keep doors to the deck closed and secured so baby can't go out when you're not watching. Put decals on glass patio doors so that no one crashes into the doors on the mistaken perception that they're open.

Barbecue grills. Remove propane gas tanks and store in a place where children can't reach them. Never allow or leave a child near a hot grill while you're barbecuing.

Backyard

Sometimes tots slip out when least expected. Many parents have told tales of finding their naked two-year-old running down the street or of discovering their baby poised on the edge of a neighbor's pool.

Outdoors, babies require constant adult vigilance. (Other children, such as siblings, should not be relied on to watch babies.) To help make sure your youngster doesn't go AWOL, install a latch high on the backyard door and firmly lock and secure patio doors with a bar. You may even want to purchase an alarm that sounds if baby strays away.

Baby-size wading pools and swimming pools. Unprotected pools with as little as one inch of water can cause drowning accidents. That's because a baby's head is heavy and babies lack the strength to right themselves if they fall facefirst. Make sure that all outdoor containers of water, including buckets and wading pools, are emptied and stored upside down, or in the garage. If you have a backyard pool or live near water, keep a life jacket on your tot outdoors. Surround your pool with a fence

Open

Fasten an old sock over the doorknob with a rubber band. Adult hands can squeeze hard enough to turn the knob; small hands can't.

(required by most building codes) and a locking gate, and cover it during the off-season. Swimming pool alarms for in-ground pools provide some measure of protection—they sound an alarm if a child falls in—but they tend to sound many false alarms.

Ride-on toys. Tricycles and other ride-on toys can be hazardous for young children, who can fall easily, although the lower the toy is to the ground, the less the falling distance. Don't purchase a wheeled toy until you're certain your child is mature enough to use it safely. A four-year-old can manage a tricycle fairly well, but a two-year-old can't. Don't try to rush your little one into balancing large-wheeled, imitation bicycles—they're dangerous. Be sure your home area has a safety zone that allows your child to ride toys away from traffic and steep hills or driveways; otherwise, don't buy ride-on toys for use outside. Equip your child with a bicycle helmet every time he or she uses a ride-on toy outside.

Swing sets. Securely anchor the swing set in concrete so it won't tip. Fill the entire play area with at least six inches of mulch or sand or other fall-absorbing material. Buy units with soft seats and safety belts. Swings should have smooth edges and surfaces, with no ragged seams or corners and no nooks and crannies that could trap a baby's fingers. Follow safety instructions provided by the manufacturer.

Don't put your child in a swing until she is able to sit up unassisted. If her muscles do not yet provide adequate head and neck support, she may fall forward against the front of the swing and be unable to sit up again.

Grabby

Don't use tablecloths until your child in the high chair is past the grabbing stage.

A young child should never be left alone in or near a swing without adult supervision. Children may let go of swing chains or ropes or decide to jump out when the swing is moving. Babies and toddlers don't understand the pendulum motion of swings or the possibility of side-to-side movement, and are often hit while crossing in front of or running between swings.

Additional safety products

Baby-proofing aids like these are found in baby stores, baby departments of stores and discount chains, and baby sections of larger grocery stores and pharmacies.

Blind-cord protectors. Babies get entangled in blind cords, especially if they're placed next to cribs. The Safety 1st Blind Cord Wind-Up (Model 222, 2/$2) is an enclosed spool that winds up excess cord. It doesn't require tools, but you'll have to reposition it a few times to figure out where to place it on the cord, and readjust the cord length each time you raise and lower the blind. To remove the whole unit, pop off the cover.

Door locks and knob covers. If your tot can open a door, he can get into trouble with appliances, chemicals, and other unsafe products. And once he can walk, he can get out the door and wander the neighborhood. You can keep doors locked. And some companies also offer door-knob covers that can only be squeezed open only by an adult.

Slamming doors can also pinch and crush kids' fingers. Stops are available to keep doors from closing. Or you can fold a towel several times and hang it over the door near the hinge. Hooking a thick, plastic coat hanger over the top hinge between the door and the jamb also works.

Corner and edge guards. The corners of tables, low shelves, and fireplaces can hurt babies who fall into them. Stick-on pads and corner guards act like bumpers to protect children during falls. They also help shield older children who are roughhousing.

Railing guards. Railings on stairs, porches, and balconies are often so wide apart that a child can get his head caught in between, or actually fall through to the level below. Railing guards, made of mesh or clear plastic, can be laced onto railings to enclose the gaps.

How safe are safety products?

The effectiveness of any baby-proofing device depends a lot on your toddler's age and body skills, with protective abilities of products lessening as children get older and more skilled. If a tot watches how "the trick" is done, he may master it a lot more quickly. Plus, most safety products don't actually prevent a child from getting into trouble; they just slow him down a bit.

Researchers at Temple University in Philadelphia showed two-year-olds and four-year-olds how to remove three different kinds of electrical outlet covers. The experiment was conducted with typical small, plastic plugs with flexible prongs sold in baby stores. It took four-year-olds only 30 seconds to pull the plug out, and one out of three two-year-olds could do it just as quickly when given a chance to watch someone else do it.

The best devices call for actions that are hard for a child to perform but relatively easy for parents. In the past, child-resistant caps for aspirin and other medications have made packaging too hard for older people to open. A new standard requires that child-resistant packaging should take most children more than 10 minutes to open, but adults must be able to open the packages within five minutes.

When a product fails, it's sometimes because parents haven't taken the time to read the directions carefully, or they forget to put the protective device back in place—for example, leaving hinged electrical outlet covers open, or forgetting to rewind cord shorteners.

BABY MONITORS

"What if my baby wakes up, and I don't hear her crying?" That's a familiar worry, especially if you've got a newborn in the house. Now, thanks to the wonderful world of technology, you can turn on a baby monitor and listen to or watch your baby—even if you're downstairs in the kitchen or out in the yard. And a baby monitor could alert you to abnormal sounds or sights like choking, which require quick action.

Audio monitors

Audio monitors have two components—a larger transmitter designed to sit on a flat surface in baby's room, and a smaller receiver for parents to tote around. A tiny microphone inside the baby's unit picks up sounds that are then transmitted by a selected radio frequency to the parent's receiver.

Most monitors offer AC adapter cords for plugging both the baby's transmitter and the parent's receiver into electrical outlets, and most also offer a battery option. Baby monitors quickly use up batteries—a set can be depleted in only a matter of days of continual use. So plugging in a unit whenever you can will save you time and money. Even though most units have low-battery indicator lights, this signal can be easily overlooked. (Shopping tip: Stock up on batteries when they go on sale—for example, during the holidays. Store packets in the refrigerator; they keep longer that way.)

Some transmitters have built-in, soft night-lights that can be turned on or off and may also turn on automatically when baby makes noises. Other units play lullaby music for a few minutes, but don't expect the soothing sounds of a symphony. You're more likely to hear annoying tinkling sounds produced by a computer chip.

The parent's unit is designed for portability and resembles an overgrown beeper. Most come with a clip on the back that fastens the unit to your waistband or pocket. Antennas, usually flexible and covered with a cushioned sleeve, are fragile. They shouldn't be gripped when carrying a receiver, even though some U-shaped antennas resemble carry handles.

Most monitoring systems have a switch enabling you to choose one of two separate frequencies. If choice A is filled with static, you simply switch over to B. Unfortunately, in densely populated areas such as apartment buildings, where other people may be using monitors, finding a clear channel can be a problem. You may have to move the receiver in different directions just to fight the static. And some brands have more static than others. Gerry monitors are noted by parents as having static problems; Fisher-Price models have a better performance record.

All models have an on/off switch, and some also offer a volume-control knob, an option that lets you decide whether you want to hear baby's every breath or only baby's cries. The volume control on some units causes a loud squealing sound if accidentally turned up too high.

Manufacturers are now introducing high-powered audio monitors that operate at 900 MHz—a frequency similar to that used by cellular telephones. These monitors allow for clearer transmission at farther distances

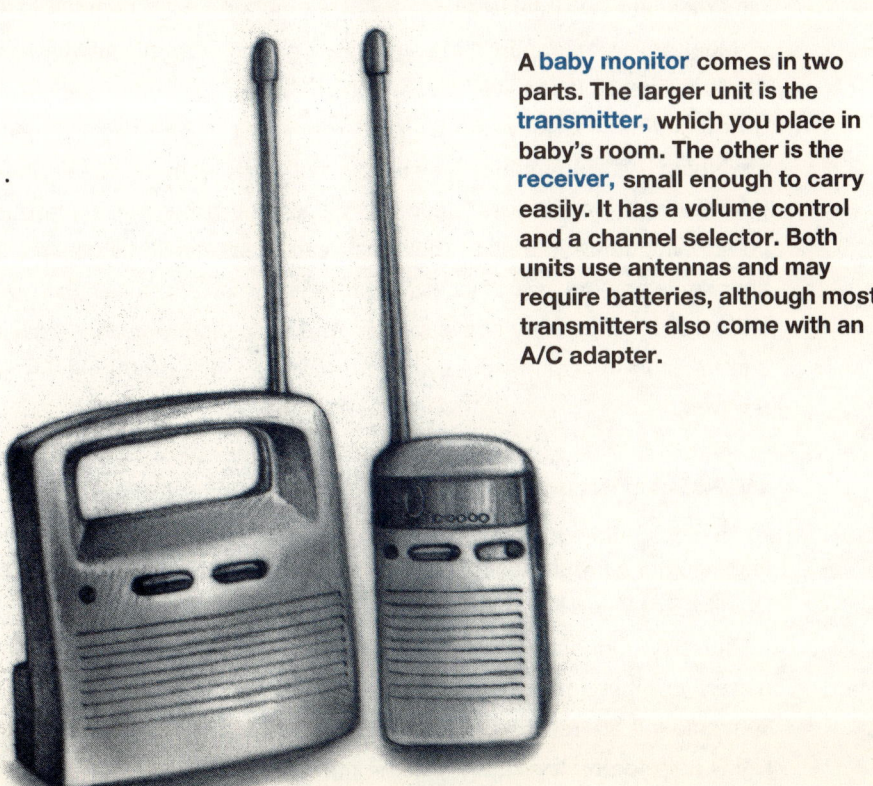

A **baby monitor** comes in two parts. The larger unit is the **transmitter,** which you place in baby's room. The other is the **receiver,** small enough to carry easily. It has a volume control and a channel selector. Both units use antennas and may require batteries, although most transmitters also come with an A/C adapter.

Keeping Baby Safe ■ **249**

than weaker, more basic models. You can expect to pay for that advantage, though. Systems can cost $50 to $60. The new frequency may also interfere with any cordless phones you have in your home.

SHOPPING SAVVY Baby monitors

The more compact a parent's receiver, the more portable it is—but that increases the odds of misplacing the parents unit under a couch cushion or in another room, so you might want a clip or caddy if you're moving around. Occasionally, a unit will get lost, chewed on, or dropped into the toilet by an inquisitive tot. Basic monitors have their drawbacks. Distance or barriers like concrete walls can alter your reception.

Worthwhile monitor features include a low-battery light and a light to alert you when your baby is making sounds, helpful in the event that you're not paying attention. One design even places multiple lights on the top of the unit so you can "see" how loudly or softly your baby is crying. Some models have special signal lights to tell you when you've moved out of range, a feature we think is a real plus.

Monitor owners report that sometimes you may end up hearing more than you expect. If you live in an apartment building where neighbors also own monitors, you may find yourself responding to cries from someone else's baby. Or, your monitor may pick up cellular telephone conversations. Conversely, baby-monitor broadcasts can also be picked up on cordless phones, including your own. The signals can even be read by police scanners a mile or more away. Since your privacy is at stake, you'll want to carefully watch your nursery conversations. And keep the product's packaging and the store receipt, in the event your compatibility problems can't be resolved.

What's available

Monitors are manufactured primarily by six companies, as part of their lines of other baby products. The best-known manufacturers are Baby Trend, Evenflo, First Years, Fisher-Price, Graco, and Safety 1st.

Nursery monitors are becoming more sophisticated every year. The newest crop uses cellular-phone technology to deliver clearer sound. Some models are rechargeable so you're not stuck feeding them batteries. Lights help to emphasize the volume of baby sounds. Other extras are a nightlight, alarm clock, and walkie-talkie capabilities that allow you to talk to your baby. The following descriptions give you an idea of price ranges and options in today's baby monitors.

Graco Ultraclear Monitor (Model 2700, $29.99) uses advanced phone technology to cut through static and radio-wave interference. Lights allow you to "see" as well as hear baby's sounds. The small parents' unit has a clip on the back to fasten to a belt or pocket. Graco also offers the monitor with two receivers, so both parents can listen (Model 2750, $40).

Fisher-Price Cordless Nursery Monitor (Model 71562, $50) operates like a cordless phone. Parents can use the receiver during the day without cords and without having to replace batteries. Then the parent's unit is placed on a base overnight to recharge it—while still monitoring the baby. A low-power indicator shows when the monitor needs recharging, and there's also a charging light. The rechargeable battery is included. The unit features a volume control plus two channels to minimize interference.

Fisher-Price Sound 'N Lights Monitor (Model 71565, $30) offers a variable light display to let parents "see" and hear baby's sound level, and it's sensitive enough to pick up quiet sounds as baby sleeps. The baby's unit requires an electrical outlet. The parent's portable unit can work with an AC adapter or on a battery. The monitor offers volume control, two channels to minimize interference, and indicators for out-of-range and low batteries.

Fisher-Price Infant-to-Toddler Monitor (Model 71577, $50) is both a monitor and a toddler safety guard. Its strong, 900-MHz technology provides more clarity and a wider range than models that use older technology. It offers two channel selections to minimize interference, and is water resistant for outdoor use. Its parent's unit can be used with an AC adapter and automatically converts to battery power when removed from the base. Both the baby's and parent's unit have power/low battery indicator lights. Sound lights let parents hear and "see" their child's sounds. Later, a part of the transmitter can also be attached to a toddler's clothing with a child-resistant clip. It will sound an alarm on the parent's unit if the link between parent and child is severed.

Fisher-Price Direct Link Privacy monitor (Model 71566, $40) signals with an alarm and light when you lose connection with your baby's unit. A coded scrambler blocks outside listeners. The parents' unit has "sound" lights, two channels, and a volume-control knob. Two AC adapters are included.

Evenflo Monitor & Intercom (Model 613, $59) is a traditional audio monitor

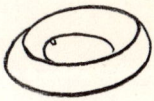

Tippy

Place an inflated small pool tube around the waist of a baby just learning to sit to cushion any sideways falls.

with a two-way intercom communication feature. The monitor has sound lights. The unit allows parents to respond vocally to their babies and other household members, and this two-way feature can be used as children get older.

Evenflo/Gerry Ultra-Sensitive Nursery Monitor (Model 611, $23) has two channels for clear reception. Sound lights allow parents to see as well as hear baby's noises. The portable parent's unit uses an adapter (included) or a battery. The Evenflo Static-Free Rechargeable Monitor (Model 614, $40) features rechargeable batteries. The portable parent's unit has low or high sensitivity choices for static-free reception, sound lights, and it comes with an out-of-range indicator.

First Years Crisp & Clear Plus 900 MHz Rechargeable Monitor (Model 3813, $60) uses phone technology for extra-clear transmission and reception up to 400 feet. It comes with a sound-activated light bar. Both units are portable and use a rechargeable battery system.

Baby Safe

MONITORS AREN'T BABY-MINDERS

Nothing can monitor your baby better than you can. Use a monitor only as an extra baby safety precaution.

- Keep any monitor out of baby's reach. Some tots have managed to wrap the electrical cord around their necks, nearly strangling themselves. Others have gotten the adapter loose from the monitor and chewed on the live end.

- Most transmitters operate best at a distance of less than 10 feet. Position the baby's unit close enough to pick up sound while keeping the cord away from small hands.

- Like all electrical devices, monitors can be a shock hazard. They shouldn't be used near bathtubs, sinks, pools, or in wet basements.

- Propping the unit on a bed, sofa, or other soft surface may cause overheating when air vents are blocked. Position it on a firm surface, such as a dresser or table.

- Handle your monitor carefully. They're delicate devices and can be damaged when they're dropped. Monitors are also sensitive to sunlight, dust, moisture, and excessive heat.

- Monitors may give you a false sense of security. The monitor isn't watching baby. Only a responsible human being can do that.

- If your baby has a spiking fever or is being suffocated by soft bedding, the silence you'll hear is much more noteworthy than all those snorts, sighs, and whimpers.

Video monitors

In addition to audio monitors, you'll also find state-of-the-art video systems for baby-gazing. A scanner can be positioned in the nursery on a tall chest or mounted on the wall to peer into the crib from another room. You get to witness your baby's every move on a lightweight, small-screened, black-and-white television monitor. One model has a VCR plug to allow you to record your baby's movements. Units like these can cost over $200—a hefty sum for zeroing in on your sleeping baby.

Several years ago, CONSUMER REPORTS assessed three video monitor systems. All three used light-emitting diodes on either side of the camera's lens to provide enough illumination to monitor a baby even in a totally dark room.

The best pictures weren't large enough or clear enough to reliably determine if a baby's eyes were open or if the child was breathing. All you could tell was whether the baby had turned over or covered its face. And most staffers who tried one out at home felt an audio monitor was enough; they didn't need to watch the baby on TV to feel reassured. So you may discover that a video monitor is an unnecessary expense.

GATES

Adjustable gates that fit into doorways are often used as barricades to wandering toddlers. Sometimes manufacturers call them "security" gates or "safety" gates. But past CONSUMER REPORTS' gate tests showed them to be unreliable. Think of them only as a supplemental safety measure.

Types of gates

There are basically two types of gates on the market: hardware-mounted gates that are secured to door jambs with plates and screws, and pressure-mounted gates that rely on rubber bumpers pressing against the wall to hold them in place.

Hardware-mounted gates, if installed properly, are not as likely to come loose as pressure gates. They do leave holes behind when they're finally removed, but these can be filled in.

Pressure gates are usually constructed with two sliding panels that adjust to fit the gate to the door opening. A pressure bar or other locking mechanism then wedges the gate in place.

Pressure gates are really easy to install. But it doesn't take much of a push to dislodge them. They're particularly unsafe at the top of a stairway. Even

Quadruped

Put socks or booties on your crawling baby's hands to allow mobility while making it impossible to pick up and eat forbidden things.

Keeping Baby Safe 253

very stable pressure-mounted gates will eventually work their way loose. At best, pressure gates are useful where falling is not a major concern, such as in a doorway separating two areas or at the bottom of a stairway to discourage a child from venturing up the stairs. Still, you'll need to stay on guard in case you have to rush to the rescue of an adventurous tot.

Gates are not an effective deterrent once your tot reaches age two. A gate should stand at a minimum of three quarters of your child's height. When a child reaches a height of over 36 inches or weighs more than 30 pounds (both at about 24 months), stop using gates. They won't work anymore.

SHOPPING SAVVY Gates

A voluntary standard for gates was developed by the American Society for Testing and Materials (ASTM) in cooperation with the Juvenile Products Manufacturers Association (JPMA). The standard (ASTM F1004) addresses the size of openings, the height of the gate, the strength of top rails and framing components (including a vertical dislodgement test), bottom spacing, and the configuration of the uppermost edge.

Certified gates must provide a permanent label warning consumers to install the gate according to manufacturer's instructions; advising that the gate is designed for use with children from 6 months to 24 months of age; and stating that it won't necessarily prevent all accidents.

Users are warned to install the gate with the locking mechanism on the side away from the child. (This warning specifically applies to pressure-mounted gates with locks on other points besides the top.) Locks on top must have a dual-action mechanism, requiring two actions to release. Consumers are also warned to never leave a child unattended.

Companies with certified gate models include: Evenflo, Fisher-Price, Gates for Tots, Gerry Wood Products, Kidco, North States Industries, Regalo, Safety 1st, and Seymour Housewares.

What's available

The following gate descriptions can give you knowledge of features to help you as you shop. The first four models use hardware, the next four are pressure-mounted; the last three offer both options.

Evenflo/Gerry Extra-Wide Expansion Gate (Model 160, $30) is a hardware-mounted gate with wood slats, similar to old-fashioned accordion-style models. The top of the gate is covered with a rigid plastic rim. The lock

Bon mots

Keep notebooks of your children's great sayings to read from when they're a little older and to give them when they're grown up.

squeezes to open, allowing the gate to be compressed and swung outward—but try it. You may find the lock uncomfortable to use. The gate can be quickly removed by unclasping the hinges. The gate is for doorways from 24 inches to 60 inches wide.

Evenflo/Gerry Walk-Through Stair Gate (Model 1050, $35) uses metal hardware, and can also be removed from the hardware for times when you want the doorway free. With optional, additional hardware, you can move the gate to various other places in the house as needed. The gate expands in length from 27 to 42 inches

KidCo Safeway Gate (Model G20, $60) is an expandable metal gate constructed of heavy tubular steel and coated in a nontoxic white plastic finish. The mounting equipment also includes a hinge template to eliminate measuring tools. The gate can swing open in either direction according to how you install it. It takes only one adult hand to unlatch it. Its width expands from 24¾ inches to 43½ inches.

Safety 1st Top of the Stairs Gate (Model 41801, $34 to $37) is a hardware-mounted wooden model, constructed with vertical slats and top and bottom rails. When installed correctly, the gate will only swing open away from the stairs for maximum safety. The gate opens with a lift-up handle

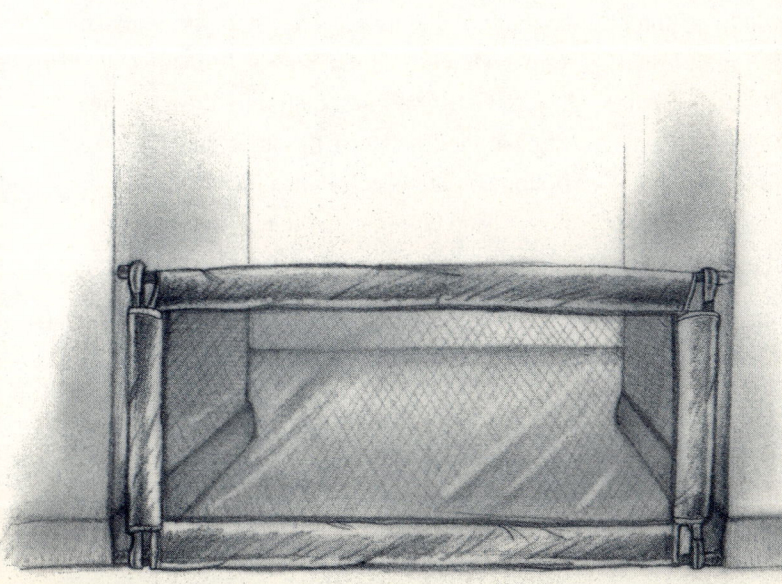

Safety gates This mesh, pressure-mounted gate will work to separate areas on the same level only, not stairwells, as it can tumble over when pushed by a child or bumped by a walker. Safer models use hardware that screws directly into the wall. Also, avoid old-style accordion gates or a gate with any type of protrusion.

on one side. It fits doorways measuring between 27 and 42 inches.

Evenflo/Gerry Extra-Wide Soft Gate (Model 526, $30) is a pressure-mounted gate constructed of metal poles supporting soft fabric mesh.

Evenflo/Gerry's 4 Sure Gate (Model 525, $18) is a pressure-mounted gate with molded plastic mesh panels. Spring-loaded steel tubes hold the gate in place. To open the gate you pull back the telescoping poles at top and bottom and lift the gate out of the opening. The gate expands from 27 to 42 inches wide and is designed to work with uneven openings and baseboards.

Evenflo/Gerry Quick-Release Plastic Mesh Gate (Model 222, $20) is a

Baby Safe
GATES AREN'T FOOLPROOF

- Don't use a pressure-mounted gate to block steps and stairs. CONSUMER REPORTS' tests have shown that pressure-mounted gates can dislodge under child-level forces. They are recommended for separating same-level rooms only.

- Check for an even finish and sturdy construction. Inspect hardware for sharp edges. Be sure wooden surfaces are smooth, splinter-free, and fashioned with rounded rather than sharply squared edges. Vertical slats or bars should be no more than 2⅜ inches apart.

- Beware of climbing hazards. Don't purchase a gate that could give your child a foothold, such as a wide-holed mesh gate.

- Have measurements of the width of the doorway opening with you when shopping. Gates cannot safely extend beyond their specified width. Pass up any model too narrow to fit the space you want to block.

- Follow the manufacturer's safety and installation instructions carefully. Be sure to check the hardware frequently. It can loosen from the gate or break with use. Also inspect where hardware attaches to the wall.

- Never use either a pressure-mounted or hardware-mounted gate that swings out over the top of the stairs.

- Gates with a pressure bar should be set up so that the child cannot tamper with it. Make sure the bar is on the side away from the child.

- Never leave more than one to two inches of clearance between the floor and the gate bottom. A large gap can allow the child to push or slip underneath the gate.

- Keep large toys—stuffed animals or riding toys—away from the gate. They can be used by the child as step stools to climb over.

- Avoid buying or using gates with openings or protrusions at the top edge. Clothing, necklaces, strings around the neck, or sweatshirt drawstrings can get snared and cause strangulation.

pressure-mounted gate with two wood-framed, patterned-plastic or wire mesh panels that slide past each other. To open, you pull up a plastic center handle while lifting the gate. The gate's width is 27 to 42 inches wide.

KidCo Gateway (Model G-10, $70) is a walk-through gate that uses pressure screws with rubber tips to tightly mount the gate to the wall. A simple, one-hand release allows the gate to be opened in either direction. It's designed for openings from 28 to 34 inches wide. Optional extensions are available.

North States Supergate III (Model 8615, $20 to $30), made of two molded plastic sliding panels, offers both hardware and pressure-mounting options. Door and rail sockets are included for more security in pressure-mounted operation and for use with wrought-iron railings. Hardware is also included if you want to hinge mount your gate; a pressure handle on the side releases the gate to swing it open. It fits openings 26 to 42 inches wide.

North States Supergate V (Model 8648, $40 to $50) fits openings from 22 to 62 inches. It is made of four plastic sliding panels with a molded mesh design. With an easy one-handed operation, the gate opens with a locking lever and by lifting up on the gate. The Supergate V slides together and swings out of the way when not in use.

Safety 1st Swing 'N Lock Gate (Model 41780, $30 to $35) offers both pressure and hinge-mounted options and can be adapted to wrought-iron railings. The gate opens with a lift-handle that slides two plastic mesh panels past each other. Locking knobs help secure the gate to uneven surfaces. It's designed for doorways measuring between 26 and 42 inches.

Sizing up gates

Gates may have flaws that could harm your child. Be on the lookout for design problems in any gate you are currently using or planning to buy.

Accordion-style gates. Old-fashioned, accordion-style wooden gates that open to form diamond-shaped spaces with wide Vs at the top have trapped children's heads and necks, causing death by strangulation. New accordion-style gates have smaller and much less dangerous openings, but some models have wooden tabs or protrusions at the top that could ensnare a child's clothing or pacifier string.

Following an agreement with the CPSC in January 1985, the manufacturers of child safety gates permanently halted production of old-fashioned accordion gates, but that agreement did not include a recall of the 10 to 15 million accordion gates still in use, or even of the smaller number that were still available in many retail outlets. If you have such a gate, destroy it and replace it with one of the models free of entrapments or entanglements.

Additional hazards. Active toddlers can climb over some gates, especially models with widely spaced mesh or other toehold providers. Fingers, toes, arms, or legs get caught in the mesh or in between the sliding panels of some models. Several gates have hinged joints that can pinch fingers, and sharp hardware that can result in cuts.

Small parts, such as screws and mounting heads, can break off or loosen. Babies love to put small things into their mouths. If they ingest, inhale, or choke on these parts, they can suffocate—an all-too-common tragedy. So regularly check the gate to be sure all small parts are secure.

Gate alternatives

As an alternative to a gate, you might consider installing an actual door, a screen door, or a half-door with a latch that is out of your child's reach. At the entrance to your toddler's bedroom, installing an additional screen door with an outside latch at your height would allow you and your child to be in continual visual contact while providing assurance that the child is safely contained. This door may also prevent your tot from roaming the house in the early morning while you're sleeping.

If you do install such a door, experts suggest adding a strong self-closing mechanism, particularly if there is a potential for injury in the area to be blocked off, such as a stairway leading to a basement. Unfortunately, a baby's fingers can be injured if a door with a self-closing mechanism slams too quickly. As a safeguard, install a pneumatic or hydraulic door-closer that comes with a pressure adjustment to slow the door down in the last few seconds prior to closing—and keep an eye on your child.

Chapter

PRODUCT RECALLS

Important safety recalls of baby products from 1996 through February 1999.

The majority of baby products are regulated by two federal agencies: The National Highway Traffic Safety Administration oversees child car-seat safety, and the Consumer Product Safety Commission administers mandatory federal standards for cribs, seats, pacifiers, rattles, and toys. Federal regulations also apply to most products, in regard to small parts that a baby could ingest, sharp edges and sharp points that can cut, and lead in paint. Also, manufacturers of baby products are required to report consumer complaints about injuries or deaths.

The agencies monitor consumer complaints and injuries, issuing a recall when there's a safety problem. And sometimes manufacturers will recall products voluntarily. However, you may never hear about a recall unless you stay informed.

Mail in all product-registration cards for car seats so the manufacturer can contact you. (If you lose your car-seat registration card, call the NHTSA hotline at 888 424-9393 for a new one.) And check product safety information sources yourself.

A selection of the most far-reaching recalls appears monthly in CONSUMER REPORTS and on its on-line service at *www.ConsumerReports.org*. If you have questions about a car-seat model, you can call the NHTSA hot line, or check their web site (*www.nhtsa.dot.gov*) for recalls. To report an unsafe product

Contents

Certification, page 260

Cribs, page 262

Furniture, page 264

Nursery equipment, page 266

Car seats, page 266

Strollers, page 270

Baby carriers, page 270

Baby seats, page 272

High chairs, page 272

Infant swings, page 273

Playpens, page 274

Portable play yards, page 276

Clothing, page 277

Pacifiers, page 278

Toys, page 279

Entertainers, page 282

Baby monitors, page 283

Gates, page 284

Product recalls ■ **259**

or get recall information, call the CPSC hotline, 800 638-7272. Consult their web site (*www.cpsc.gov*) for up-to-date recall data. If a product has been recalled, follow the remedial action advice.

Should your child have a mishap that's clearly a product's fault, such as hardware that fails or parts that cause harm or entrap, report the problem in writing to the manufacturer, giving the model number and all the details you can supply about the model (usually on a manufacturer's sticker or label somewhere on the product). However, realize that if you have a serious complaint, some companies may try to convince you the product's failure is your own fault. By law, manufacturers must report injury data to the CPSC or face being sued and fined. A few may try to evade responsibility. Don't hesitate to contact federal agencies to help get satisfaction from the manufacturer, and, by alerting government regulators to the problem, to help protect other babies from danger.

Are certified products safer?

The Juvenile Products Manufacturers Association (JPMA) sponsors and administers a voluntary certification program for juvenile products. Programs are currently in effect for full-size cribs, high chairs, portable hook-on chairs, playpens, strollers, gates, and walkers.

The JPMA retains an independent laboratory to periodically perform or witness tests of sample units. Products are certified if they meet the minimum safety performance standards developed by the American Society for Testing and Materials (ASTM). They may then carry a sticker reading "CERTIFIED: This model tested by an independent laboratory for compliance with ASTM safety standard." But certification isn't fail-safe, so don't view the sticker as a safety guarantee. Voluntary standards cover only major hazards and require only minimum safe-performance levels. Standards vary in strictness from one product category to another. Plus, tests are conducted on brand new products, not those that have sustained the daily wear and tear of baby use.

Nor do stickers list the hazards that are addressed by the standards tested. (For specifics on test standards, see the separate product categories throughout the book and in the following recalls.)

In the crib category, specific models aren't certified, just the companies that make or market them. The manufacturer must certify that all its models are in compliance. Cribs from certified manufacturers have been recalled in the past when bars worked loose from rails. This is much less likely in the newest models because cribs are now subjected to much stricter durability tests.

In the other categories—high chairs, portable hook-on chairs, playpens, strollers, gates, and walkers—the individual models are certified. That means a company can sell certified models alongside uncertified models. Certification, of course, doesn't guarantee certainty. For example, although a particular gate is certified, it may not always hold up to daily use or to a determined tot.

Still, our advice is to look for the certification sticker—but also look over any product yourself.

You can obtain the most recent directory of certified products by contacting the Juvenile Products Manufacturers Association. See the Resource Guide.

PRODUCT RECALLS

Cribs

Typical problems: Bars separate from railings; hardware on dropsides breaks or malfunctions.

Safety standards: The JPMA/ASTM certification sticker on the crib's frame pertains to the manufacturer, not the individual model. Tests evaluate overall construction; corner post protrusions (a strangulation hazard if posts catch clothing or strings worn around the neck); interior dimensions and spacing of components such as bars; and sturdiness of mattress-support attachments, latching mechanisms, and teething rails. Cribs must also carry a safety-warning label advising frequent inspection for missing or broken parts; placement away from windows and drapery cords; and regular latch checks. The label also warns buyers and others about mattress dimensions and age limits on use.

Safety advice: Very hot, humid, or cold storage conditions cause wood to swell or split and glues to deteriorate. Disassembling and reassembling cribs shreds screw holes, weakening crib's frame. If screws are changed or any crib parts altered, the manufacturer is no longer responsible for safety or performance.

Coaster Company of America (COA) full-size metal cribs
A design defect poses entrapment and choking hazards.
Products: 900 Model 2368, sold from 1/93 through 12/96, and 900 Model 2364, sold from 6/96 through 4/97.
What to do: Return the crib to the store for a refund or replacement. For more information, call 800 221-9699, Ext. 157.

Okla Homer Smith cribs and strollers
Side slats separate from side rails, creating a suffocation hazard.
Products: About 278,000 cribs manufactured between 4/92 and 12/93. Models 30562, 80005, 80007, 80010, 80012, 80023, 80029, 80035, 80038, 80054, 80056, 80057, 80068, 80090.
What to do: Check the dropside rail slats to make sure the slats are secure. If the rail slats are missing or feel loose, contact the company to arrange for a free dropside rail replacement or retrofit kit. Do not use a crib with missing slats. For more information call 800 261-3440.

Baby's Dream Cribs
The front drop gate poses a finger-entrapment hazard.

Product: 13,000 Generation oak cribs with identifying numbers 194 through 1897, sold 12/94 through 6/97.
What to do: Lock the drop gate in the closed position and call 888 866-4217 for free repair kit.

Cosco metal cribs
Mattress platform may have been installed as die rail with wide-spaced slats that could trap a child's head.
Products: 390,000 full-size tubular metal cribs on wheels made since 1/95 and sold for $90 to $150, including the following models: 10T01 (red, white, or blue); 10T04 (red or white); 10T05 (red or white); 10T06 (multiple colors); 10T08 (white and brass); 10T14 (white); 10T84 (multiple colors); 10T85 (white); 10T94 (white); 10T95 (white and brass); 10M06 (multiple colors); 10M84 (multiple colors); 10M85 (white); 10M94 (white). Affected models bear date code of 0195 (Jan. 1995) or newer, which appears on sticker on bottom of an end panel. Hazard exists because slats are spaced more than 2⅜ inches apart, a violation of Federal Safety Standard. Such spacing could allow an infant's head, but not the body, to slip through, leading to strangulation.
What to do: Inspect crib for misassembly by trying to pass a soda can through slats on side rail. If can passes through, stop using crib immediately and call Cosco at 800 221-6736 to arrange for free in-home repair. Alternatively, Cosco will provide instructions for proper do-it-yourself reassembly. Company is offering owners gift to encourage repair.

Cosco cribs
Slats could come out of side rails and entrap child's head or allow child to fall out.
Products: 190,000 full-sized cribs made of welded red, white, blue, or multicolored tubular metal. One side rail is fixed; other one can be raised or lowered. Most cribs were sold 1/91 to 4/94 for $95 to $150. Affected cribs include Models 10T01, 10T04, 10T05, 10T06, 10T09, 10T11, and 10T14. Manufacturer's identification, which includes model number, is at bottom of either side rail.
What to do: Call 800 314-9327 for free repair kit.

Cosco Cribs
Mattress on tubular metal crib could collapse, trapping child and causing subsequent injury or suffocation.
Products: About 62,000 mattresses sold with tubular metal cribs. When a baby stands up in the crib, the mattress can compress and be pushed between the bars on the crib's platform. The baby can slip between the bars on the crib's platform and become entrapped. Cosco has received 12 complaints of mattresses compressing and entrapping babies. An 11-month-old baby boy died after becoming entrapped. Cosco is offering consumers a $25 check to purchase a new mattress on their own. The mattresses were sold for Cosco model "M" tubular metal cribs, manufactured from 7/94 through 9/97.
What to do: Stop using crib or place a board about 27 inches wide and 51 inches long between the mattress and crib platform.

Francisca full-sized wooden cribs sold through JC Penney catalog
Spindles could come off side rails, creating spaces large enough to trap child's head and cause strangulation, or to allow child to slip through and fall out.
Products: 6,000 cribs, models 343-3935 and 343-4065, sold 8/96 to 4/97 for $200. Crib came in hardwood or cherry finish. Model number is on bottom of mattress support.
What to do: Return crib to nearest JC Penney store for refund or replacement.

Gerry cribs
Mattress and underlying support could collapse if side rails are assembled improperly.
Products: 17,043 cribs, models 8200, 8300, and 8500, sold 5/94 to 8/94 for $90. Unassembled cribs came in various shades of natural wood and were packaged in brown cardboard box labeled, in part: "Gerry Fold-Away Crib. Compact crib that folds in seconds . . ." Fully assembled, crib is 39½ inches long, 25½ inches wide, and 38 inches high. Hazard exists when side rails are put on backwards, contrary to manufacturer's instructions.
What to do: Check manufacturer's date code on label attached to hinged mattress support; if crib is affected, call 800 525-2472; company will send supplemental instructions to help you determine whether crib was assembled properly.

Furniture
Typical problems: Unstable construction can cause tipping; poor workmanship can cause parts to break or fall off; excess lead found in paint.

Safety standards: Furniture is governed by federal standards concerning lead in paint.

Safety advice: Look for solid construction and stability. Furniture should not wobble or easily tip, even if drawers are open or filled. Finish should be smooth and even, with no bubbling, streaking, rough spots, or glue splatters.

Cosco Youth Options furniture
May tip over and injure anyone nearby if several drawers are opened at once or if heavy objects are placed in top drawers.
Products: 550,000 chifforobes (wardrobe/chest of drawers combinations) and 309,000 four-drawer dressers sold since '91. White laminated furniture was sold unassembled. Affected chifforobes, models 80813 and 88813, consist of closet on left side and two shelves and three drawers on right side; they measure 51 inches high, 46 inches wide, and 16 inches deep, and sold for $89 to $109. Dressers, models 89413 and 88413, measure 38 inches high, 30 inches wide, and 16 inches deep; they sold for $79 to $89. Both items came with round, black-plastic feet that can be attached to bottom of furniture; Cosco says feet make furniture tip easily.
What to do: Remove feet so furniture sits flat on floor.

Children's furniture sold at Target stores
Paint contains excess lead, which is toxic if ingested.
Products: 8,300 pieces of furniture, decorated in circus or princess theme, sold 4/98 to 7/98 for about $15 to $80. Pieces include: Seal Wall Mirror (purple seal with yellow-framed mirror balanced on nose); Circus Rover (purple box/cart on yellow wheels with circus pictures on side); Circus Table and Chair Set (yellow table with red legs and two yellow and red chairs); Clown Coat Hook (wall coat rack with clown face and red hooks); Circus Wall Shelf (with large red and yellow clown face); Clown Stepping Stool (aqua two-step stool with clown on top step and arms and clown body on sides); Clown Tot Stool (with red top, yellow sides, and circus pictures); Banana Coat Tree (with yellow star at top, pictures of monkey, and banana-shaped coat hooks); Rocking Elephant (red, with yellow seat and aqua rockers); Princess Step Stool (two-step stool with pictures of castle on sides and rose on top step); Princess Rocker (pink with "PRINCESS" printed on back); Crown Wall Hooks (pink crown-shaped rack with red clothes pegs); Princess Table and Chair Set (with picture of crown on each corner of tabletop and on each chair back); Crown Mirror (rectangular; pink, white, and yellow-green); Crown Wall Shelf (white, with picture of pink crown on back); Crown Tot Stool (white, with pink top and picture of crown on each end); and Crown Coat Tree (pink, with picture of crown on top).
What to do: Return furniture to any Target store for refund or call 800 935-5060.

Iris clear plastic toy storage chests with red or blue lid
Could entrap and suffocate child.
Products: 100,000 chests sold since 1/96 in various sizes for about $25. Model WT-80 is about 19¼ x 21¾ x 18¾ inches; model WT-120, about 19¼ x 30¾ x 18¾ inches; model WT-175, about 19¼ x 30¾ x 28¼ inches. Model number is on instruction sheet and on label on front of chest. Label also shows chest being used for toy storage and includes warning: "CAUTION: Do Not Sit On Lid. Do Not Climb in Trunk." Lid lacks support device. Also, chest lacks adequate ventilation when lid is closed, and it has latches that can hold lid shut. (Current chests have label that reads "WARNING: SUFFOCATION HAZARD. NOT FOR USE BY CHILDREN." Label also shows items other than toys in chest.)
What to do: Return chest to store for refund.

Fabric-covered foam chairs sold at Ames Department Stores
Child could unzip fabric cover, ingest thin plastic liner, and choke on it.
Products: 20,000 chairs, 11 inches high, 11 inches wide, and 15½ inches deep, sold 1/94 to 6/96 for $50. Fabric cover features pictures of animals and childlike drawings. Zipper is on bottom of chair, as is white label that reads, in part: "NOW PRODUCTS INC." Chairs were sold with matching ottomans and sofas.
What to do: Discontinue use and call Now Products at 800 535-3218, ext. 33, for free repair kit.

Nursery equipment
Halcyon WaterSpring Dex Wipe Warmer electric heating pad for baby wipes
Device could overheat, melt, and catch fire.
Products: 536,000 warmers sold 1/94 to 12/96 for about $10 to $15. Warmer, 27 inches long and 3½ inches wide, wraps around disposable plastic container. It has white cloth cover with pink, blue, yellow, and green handprints, and Velcro fasteners. Tan or off-white plastic warmer unit beneath cloth has white sticker with model number WW-01. Warmer came in mostly purple box labeled "Dex Products Wipe Warmer. A must for every nursery!" in white print. Warmers sold after 12/96 with red bar across top of white label on warmer unit are not subject to recall.
What to do: Call 888 735-5585 toll-free for refund or free replacement.

Car seats
Typical problems: Harnesses and buckles fail; integrated seats installed incorrectly; seat has inadequate restraints.

Safety standards: All car seats sold in the U.S. must pass a simulated front-end crash test. Tests do not assess effect of rear-enders or side crashes, or how varying types of adult belts affect performance. Car seat should have a sticker indicating it meets "Federal Motor Vehicle Safety Standard (FMVSS) No. 213." In 1999 the federal government announced new standards that require an anchoring system that doesn't rely on safety belts, but on a tether system. Tether anchors will be required in most new vehicles beginning in September 1999 for passenger cars and September 2000 for light trucks (including sport-utility vehicles and minivans).

Safety advice: Be sure seat is correctly anchored so it does not move either side to side or front to back. Check harnesses and buckles to be sure child is well secured. Use seat every time.

Individual car seats (sold as separate units)
Britax child safety seat
Belt buckle can be opened by a child.
Product: Freeway Model 101, made from 6/96 through 4/97.
What to do: Call 800 683-2045 for a newly designed replacement buckle and installation instructions.

Century child safety seats and car seat/stroller systems
Buckle could release on impact, resulting in increased risk of injury in crash.
Products: 376,000 infant seats (models 4525, 4535, 4560, 4565, 4575, 4590) 4-in-1 infant car seat/stroller systems (models 11-570, 11-597, 11-600, and 11-650) made 9/95 through 5/96. Date of manufacture and model number appear on side of seat.

What to do: Call Century Products at 800 837-4044 for free replacement buckle kit and installation instructions. Seat owners may also obtain buckle by writing to company at 9600 Valley View Rd., Macedonia, Ohio 44056.

Century SmartMove safety seat
In forward-facing mode, seat may not provide adequate protection in a crash.
Products: 11,000 seats, model 4750, made 12/95 to 2/96. Model number (first four numbers) and date of manufacture (last six numbers) appear on label on side of seat base. Affected seats also have white label attached to black Y-shaped adjuster strap on back of seat that bears one of the following codes: WO#-136716-01; WO#-136716-02; WO#-136716-03; WO#-138442-0.
What to do: Call 800 583-4093 for replacement latch assembly.

Cosco car seats
The shell may not hold up to a crash in the forward-facing recline position.
Products: Touriva 5-point and Touriva Overhead Shield, made in 8/97.
What to do: Call 800 221-6736 for inspection instructions and a repair kit.

Downunder booster seat
Unclear instructions for use of Velcro shoulder belt positioners, or missing Velcro shoulder belt positioner.
Products: Kangaroo booster seats built prior to 1/97.
What to do: Call 800 459-5209 for revised shoulder belt placement instructions, or for a Velcro shoulder belt positioner for booster model #3.

Evenflo Two-In-One booster car seats
Seatback could separate from base in crash, increasing likelihood of injury to child.
Products: 32,000 child seats with cloth pad, designed for children weighing 22 to 65 pounds. Recalled seats were made 1/98 to 3/98 and have six-digit model number starting with 636 and 637. Date of manufacture and model number are on label on back rest. Seats are plastic with cloth pad.
What to do: Call 800 985-7328 for free replacement seat.

Evenflo On My Way infant car seats/carriers
When used as carrier, seat could flip foward and toss infant to the ground.
Products: 800,000 seats made 12/95 to 7/97 and sold since 1/96. Model 492 "Travel System" includes stroller; model 207 doesn't. Model number and date of manufacture are on bottom of seat.
What to do: Call 800 203-2138 for free repair kit, which includes redesigned latch buttons. Until seat is repaired, continue using it in car, but don't lift it with the carrying handle.

Evenflo Sidekick booster seats
May not adequately restrain child in crash.
Products: 35,856 booster seats, with model numbers beginning with 244, made 4/23/96

to 5/20/97. Model number and date of manufacture appear on label on seat shell. Hazard exists only when seat is used with its shield. Shield is necessary if booster is secured with lap belt. Evenflo advises owners to use Sidekick without shield in seat equipped with lap-and-shoulder belt. Safety note: Don't use safety seat in car's front seat.
What to do: Evenflo will give partial refund if you can use booster seat in seating position with lap-and-shoulder belt, and full refund if you can use booster seat in seating position equipped only with lap belt. Call 800 233-5921 for refund.

Evenflo Champion, Trooper, and Scout child safety seats
In the front-facing position, child's head could swing too far in crash, increasing risk of injury.
Models: 150,000 safety seats, with model numbers beginning with 219, 224, 225, or 229, made 10/96 to 2/97. Model number and date of manufacture appear on label on seat's shell.
What to do: Call 800 233-5291 for replacement harness-adjuster assembly.

Evenflo Champion and Scout child safety seats
In most upright front-facing position, seat may not provide adequate protection in crash.
Products: 1,122,000 Champion safety seats, whose model number begins with digits 224, made 6/93 to 11/96. Also 118,000 Scout seats, with model numbers beginning with digits 229, made 6/93 to 12/96. Model number and date of manufacture are on label on seat shelf.
What to do: Call 800 490-7497 for replacement recline arm that prevents seat from being used in most upright position.

Evenflo Travel Tandem child safety seats
When used with its base, the seat may not properly restrain a child in a crash.
Products: All Evenflo Travel Tandem infant seats made before 4/96. (Seats made after that date have a modified design.)
What to do: Call 800 233-5921 or 937 773-3971 to receive a free reinforcement kit, which includes a reinforcement plate that easily attaches to the buckle-assembly area that connects the seat to the base.

Evenflo Trooper car seats
With infant weighing less than 20 pounds, seat must be used only in rearward-facing position—not in forward-facing position as instructions imply.
Products: 10,423 seats with adjustable shield, models 219140, 219164, 219180, 219186, and 219188, made 11/95 through 1/96. Label bearing model number and manufacture date appears on seat.
What to do: Call 800 837-4002 for new instruction pamphlet.

Fisher-Price Safe Embrace safety seats
Shoulder-harness locking mechanism may malfunction, compromising protection in a crash.

Products: 55,000 "Safe Embrace" convertible child safety seats, made from 5/97 through 3/98. Model comes with a tether that secures the top of the seat to the car's rear shelf or cargo area.

What to do: Call Fisher-Price at 800 355-8882 for a free replacement harness-adjuster (consumers who registered the seat with Fisher-Price will automatically receive one). You can continue using the seat until the new adjuster arives, but inspect the seat each time that it's used to be sure the harness belts stay locked in place.

Kolcraft Secure-Fit and Performa infant safety seats

After crash, buckle may require too much pressure to release, making it hard to remove child. Also, shield pads on 1,000 Performa seats don't meet federal flammability standards and could catch fire.

Product: 159,400 safety seats made 1/96 to 7/97.

What to do: Call 800 453-7673 for free replacement buckle, tools, and installation instructions. Company will also provice new shield pad cover, if necessary.

Kolcraft car seat

Crotch-strap assembly can separate from car-seat shell.

Products: Travel About, Plus 4, Plus 5, and Infant Rider (model numbers 138xx and 368xx). Travel About, Plus 5, and Carter Travel model numbers 13833, 13842, and 13852. All seats were made from 3/96 through 9/96.

What to do: Call 800 453-7673 for written instructions on realigning crotch-strap retainer clip.

Built-in car seats
Chrysler Corp.

Shoulder-harness restraint webbing incorrectly installed.

Products: 1998 Plymouth Voyager and Grand Voyager, Dodge Caravan and Grand Caravan, and Chrysler Town & Country minivans equipped with integral car seats, all made 11/97 through 12/97.

What to do: Dealer will correct shoulder-restraint webbing.

Chrysler Corp.

Latch plate can remain in locked position when blocked by food or other items.

Products: 1996 and 1997 Plymouth Voyager and Grand Voyager, Dodge Caravan and Grand Caravan, and Chrysler Town & Country minivans equipped with integral child seats, made from 7/96 through 5/97.

What to do: Dealer will provide a videotape on proper use and maintenance of child seats, plus two new harness clips.

Chrysler Corp.

Bolts securing child-seat frame to automobile seat frame can break.

Products: 1996 Plymouth Voyager and Grand Voyager, Dodge Caravan and Grand Caravan, and Chrysler Town & Country minivans.

What to do: Dealer will replace bolts.

Strollers

Typical problems: Accidental collapsing; finger entrapment in unprotected tube holes; cuts on sharp hardware; failure of seat belts or buckles; seats that break or fall through; leg openings large enough to let a child slip through.

Safety standards: JPMA certifies specific strollers, but only a dozen manufacturers participate, with less than half their models. Sticker will refer to "compliance to ASTM F-833 safety standards for carriages/strollers." Tests cover sharp edges; locking devices to prevent accidental folding; stability; seat-belt systems; brakes; and leg openings.

Safety advice: Child should always be secured in the restraining system and never left unattended. Multiple-occupancy stroller labels should carry a sticker showing recommended sequence for placing and removing children. Enclosed literature should cover assembly, maintenance, cleaning, and operation.

Century TraveLite sport strollers

Restraint buckle could unlatch or stroller could fold suddenly and allow child to fall out.
Products: 166,000 strollers, model numbers 11-171, 11-181, and 11-191, made from 2/95 through 10/95 and sold for $60 to $80. Model number and date of manufacture are on stroller's side tubing.
What to do: Call 800 944-0039 for a free repair kit and installation instructions.

Cosco Geoby Two Ways tandem strollers

Plastic locks on folding mechanism could break, allowing stroller to collapse. Besides suffering injuries from fall, child could cut arm or hand on locking mechanism.
Products: 57,000 strollers, model numbers 01-644 and 01-645 (which includes car seat), made 2/97 to 2/98 and sold for about $110 and $170 at mass-merchandise and juvenile-product stores. Model number and manufacturing date (representing week and year product was made) are stamped on label on back of leg frame, just above wheel. Those made between 0697 and 0698 are subject to recall. Stroller is designed so two babies can sit one behind the other or face-to-face. Back seat reclines. Stroller has dual quilted canopies, market basket, and utility bag. "Cosco by Geoby" is written on plastic side-lock covers, and "Two Ways" is embroidered on front-seat crotch support.
What to do: Call 800 221-6736 for free repair kit.

Baby carriers

Typical problems: Leg openings allow small children to slip through; seats may be unstable; harnesses can entrap.

Safety standards: Baby carriers are covered by basic federal guidelines, such as having no small parts. There are no specific federal standards and no voluntary certification.

Safety advice: Read instructions carefully so you use carrier correctly. Never leave a child unattended in carrier. Do not use as a seat.

Baby Bjorn soft-fabric infant carrier
Baby could slip through leg opening and fall out.
Products: 240,000 infant front carriers sold 1/91 to 10/98 at juvenile specialty stores and by catalog for $75. Carrier came in navy blue, black, denim, green, and other colors. "Baby Bjorn" is printed on front and on strap. Straps fit over shoulders and around torso of adult; baby faces adult's chest.
What to do: Do not use carrier for children less than 2 months old. Call 877 242-5676 toll-free for kit to reduce size of leg openings. Carriers currently sold aren't being recalled.

Carter's infant carrier
Adjustable shoulder strap could come loose and allow infant to fall out.
Products: 5,400 infant carriers, style 89000, sold since 6/96 for about $30. Carrier is made of light blue quilted fabric with waist belt, padded shoulder strap, zippered leg openings with padding, and padded back and head supports. Padded fabric is light blue, white, green, and pink. Waist belt and shoulder strap are white nylon webbing with white stitching. "Carter's" brand label is sewn into seam. Carrier came in cardboard package labeled, in part, "Carter's Infant Carrier . . . 0–24 mos." Style number is on bottom of box. Infant carriers bearing style number 89200 (with black stitching at ends of shoulder straps, which are threaded through buckles) aren't being recalled.
What to do: Call 800 942-9442 for free replacement.

Evenflo Hike 'N Roll child carrier
Child could slip through leg openings and strangle.
Products: 22,000 child carriers, models 522101 and 522102, made 6/96 through 10/97 and sold 6/96 through 6/98 for about $65. Model number and date of manufacture are on white tag on bottom of carrier. Device, used as a backpack carrier or stroller, is green and blue, or blue and beige, with "Evenflo" on front and back.
What to do: Call 800 649-0071 for free seat insert to reduce size of leg openings.

L.L. Bean backpack child carrier
Child could become entangled in harness and strangle or wriggle out of harness and fall out.
Products: 10,000 child carriers, model number AC25, sold 1/97 to 10/98 for about $100 through catalog and web site and at company's retail stores in Del., Maine, N.H., and Ore. Carriers are forest green with gray harness; kickstand holds device upright. Model number AC25 is on tag on upper left side of rear storage compartment. L.L. Bean label is on back of carrier.
What to do: Call 800 555-9717 for instructions on returning carrier for refund.

Baby seats

Typical problems: Seats may lack a stable base; handle may have faulty locking mechanism; handle may break; kickstand may not hold seat stationary; toys or toy parts may break from toy bar.

Safety standards: Seats are covered by federal standards on small parts. There is no industry certification program.

Safety advice: Check for a wide base, sturdy seat belts, secure handle-locking mechanism.

Playskool Fold N' Travel infant carrier
Child could fall out and suffer serious injury.
Products: 38,000 lightweight plastic infant carriers, models 100, 101, 102, 103, sold 4/91 through 12/93 for $35. Carrier is blue or teal with fabric or vinyl pad. It measures 17 inches long folded, 26 inches fully extended. Carrier is adjustable in three positions—rocker, feeder, or sleeper—by pushing buttons on either side of handle where it attaches to shell. Device can be folded by squeezing levers underneath carrier.
What to do: Return carrier to store or to Playskool for refund. For prepaid shipping carton and return information, call 800 447-7707.

J. Mason infant carrier
Handle could break and allow carrier to fall.
Products: 18,200 white plastic carriers with fabric seat pad and matching removable canopy, sold 4/96 to 8/97 at Kmart, Rose, and State Enterprises stores for about $20. Fabric came in three designs: multicolored (pink, white, blue, and green) with geometric pattern; light blue with white squiggly lines; and light blue with pink and purple patterns. "J. MASON" is imprinted on handle. "MADE IN U.S.A" is imprinted on the bottom of the carrier, which also bears red sticker that reads, "Warning Do Not Use As A Car Seat."
What to do: Call 800 242-1922 for replacement carrier.

High chairs

Typical problems: Restraint bar may break or seat belt may malfunction, allowing baby to slip through leg holes; chair legs may lack secure folding mechanism, allowing for accidental collapse.

Safety standards: JPMA/ASTM has a certification program. Standards cover a locking device to prevent accidental folding; secure caps and plugs; sturdy, break-resistant trays; wide legs to increase stability; no springs or dangerous scissoring actions that could entrap a baby's fingers. Safety belts have to pass pressure tests. The sticker is on the tray or frame. New standards expected in 1999 call for a "crotch post" so babies cannot slip under a tray.

Safety advice: Check the folding mechanism on legs; rock chair to assess stability; examine all surfaces for sharp edges or entrapment hazards. Assess how securely small parts are attached.

Playskool 1-2-3 high chairs
Restraint bar could break off and allow unbelted child to fall out.
Product: 287,000 high chairs made 5/95 to 5/96 and bearing serial numbers TX51321 through TX61442. Number is on label on high chair's seat back. Chair sold for about $65. Restraint bar, which holds tray in place, is at center front of seat.
What to do: Call 800 555-0428 for replacement restraint bar.

Playskool 1-2-3 high chairs
Plastic joints could crack and make chair collapse.
Products: 300,000 high chairs sold 5/94 through 10/95 for $75.
What to do: Inspect chair, especially plastic pivot joints, and call 800 752-9755. Company will send repair kit—or, if chair has cracks, company will replace chair.

Infant swings

Typical problems: Swing frame is not stable; frame or seat may have sharp edges; child may become entangled in harness straps; seat can collapse.

Safety standards: Swings are covered by federal regulations involving small parts. There is no voluntary industry certification program.

Safety advice: Look for a sturdy, stable frame and a secure harness. Follow manufacturer's age and weight specifications.

Graco infant carriers and carrier/swings
Seat handle can unlock and let infant fall out.
Products: 564,000 products made 8/1/93 to 8/31/97, including model numbers: 1300, 1301, 1310, 1350, 1501, 1502, 1530, 1723, 2788, 5510, 8108, and 36264. Model number and date of manufacture are on label under seat or under top of swing. Carrier was sold separately for about $30, or as part of Graco Carrier/Swing set for about $100.
What to do: Call 800 281-3676 for repair kit and instructions.

Century Lil' Napper infant swings
Infants may become entrapped in harness straps, posing a strangulation hazard.
Products: 125,000 infant swings, including model numbers 12-344, 12-345, 12-347, 12-475, and 12-476 with shoulder harness straps. Model number is on a white sticker under bottom of swing's foot area. Swing has four white tubular metal legs, a plastic, two-position seat with removable plastic tray, and vinyl or fabric seat pad. Century brand name is on motor assembly at top.
What to do: Call 800 231-1448 for a free replacement seat pad and restraint system.

Cosco Quiet Time wind-up infant swings
Seat could fall off and injure child.
Products: 355,500 infant swings, models 08-975 and 08-977, made 2/1/93 to 9/30/95 and sold for $45 to $49. Label under seat lists model number and date-of-manufacture code. Recalled swings have date codes 0593 (fifth week of '93) through 4095. Swing consists of four tubular white metal legs supporting plastic swing seat, which has vinyl or fabric cover. Seat can be set in two positions. Fully wound, swing operates for about 30 minutes. "Cosco Quiet Time" is printed on label on top of swing.
What to do: Call 800 221-6736 for free repair kit and installation instructions.

Little Tykes Cozy Highback Swing
Could flip over and allow child to fall out.
Products: 245,000 swings, model no. 4637, designed for children nine months to three years and sold 1/96 to 4/96 for $15 to $18. Bright blue plastic swing is 13 inches wide, 12 inches long, and 14 inches high. "Little Tykes" logo is on stationary front crossbar. Swing hangs from four yellow ropes.
What to do: Phone 800 321-0183 for replacement swing or comparable Little Tykes product.

Playpens

Typical problems: Entrapment/suffocation pockets created by a lowered side and the playpen floor; rivets or other protrusions that catch clothing or pacifier strings, causing strangulation.

Safety standards: JPMA/ASTM certifies specific playpen models, testing for the following: Side mesh must be tightly woven to avoid finger or clothing entrapment; vinyl must be thick enough to preclude its being bitten or picked apart; pen should have no sharp edges, protrusions, or points, and a minimal potential for scissoring, shearing, or pinching; sides should measure at least 20 inches from floor, so babies cannot crawl out, and have a locking device; railings and floors should be sturdy, with no entrapment holes. Warning label should specify that dropside should not be left down; playpen should not be used when child reaches size limits of 30 pounds/34 inches; and child should not be left unattended.

Safety advice: The sides of some models lower only during the folding-away process, helping to prevent the suffocation-pocket hazard. Check pen for stability and for protrusions that could catch necklines and pacifier strings. Keep child away when folding the pen.

Various brands of foldable mesh-sided play yards/playpens
Child could strangle if clothing or loose strings catch on protruding rivets.

Products: More than 9.6 million play yards/playpens sold since 1960. Only models with protruding rivets are subject to recall; rivets stick out ¼-inch to ½-inch from the outside top rails. Rivets are similar to nut-and-bolt fasteners but can't be removed. Except for the Evenflo Houdini, all models are drop-sided mesh playpens that fold in half for storage. The Houdini is also mesh-sided but folds up compactly for storage or travel. The affected brands:
- 2 million Graco products made 1976 to 11/90 and sold for $35 to $55. Word "Graco" is written on floorboard or side rail. Company is offering $20 refund with proof of destruction.
- 409,000 Bilt-Rite products made through 1989 and sold for $35 to $55. "Bilt-Rite" is written on floorboard. Company is offering $20 refund with proof of destruction.
- 2.6 million Kolcraft and Playskool products made 1/86 to 5/98 and sold for $40 to $70. "Kolcraft" or "Playskool" appears on floorboard or side rail. Company is offering free repair kit.
- More than 4 million Pride-Trimble products made 1960 to 9/91 and sold for $35 to $55. "Pride-Trimble Corp." appears on floorboard. Company is out of business; discard play yard.
- 100,000 Pride-Trimble products—with words Pride-Trimble Inc. on floorboard—made 10/91 to 10/93 and sold for $35 to $55. Company is out of business; destroy and discard play yard.
- 205,000 Evenflo "Houdini" play yards made '94 to '96 and sold for $45. "Evenflo" is written on plastic hinge covers. Company is providing free repair kit. Note: Models are subject to recall even if they have plastic covers over rivets. Covers can crack, break, or come off.
- 100,000 Gerry products made '86 to '92 and sold for $35 to $45. "Gerry" appears on floorboard. Company is offering free repair kit.
- 200,000 Strolee products made through '83 and sold for $35 to $55. "Strolee" is on side rail. Company is out of business; destroy and discard play yard.

What to do: Call the Consumer Products Safety Commission at 800 794-4115 for the appropriate manufacturer's telephone number. If you own a suspect play yard from a company not mentioned above, call the CPSC's hotline at 800 638-2772 to report it.

All Our Kids portable playpens
Could collapse and strangle child in V formed by folding top rail.
Products: 13,000 playpens, models 741, 742, and 761, sold '92 through '95. Playpen comes in various colors, shapes (rectangular and square), and sizes. Some have detachable toy bag on one end. "All Our Kids" appears on two of four top rails.
What to do: Destroy playpen to prevent use. Since maker is out of business, refund is unavailable.

Graco playpens
Mesh netting could unravel at seam and strangle child.
Products: 133,000 playpens sold in juvenile-products and discount stores for $35 to $55. Drop-side playpen has vinyl-covered top rails and pad. Recalled units bear date-of-manufacture codes 11395 (Nov. 13, 1995) to 091296 (Sept. 12, 1996). Date-code is

first six digits of serial number, listed on floor label under pad (see arrow).
What to do: Call 800 423-9078 for free repair kit and instructions. Discontinue use if netting has started to unravel.

Portable play yards

Typical problems: Older model play yards collapse when hinges, centered on the top rail, are not in the locked position, or rotate open during use. Collapsed pens form a steep-sided V that entraps babies' necks. Since 1992, millions of travel play yards have been recalled by the CPSC for this and other problems, and 12 babies have suffocated.

Safety standards: Top rails on current-model play yards lock automatically when fully set up. Play yards carry a warning that play yard must be fully erected—side rails up, top rails locked upright—before use; and that child should not be left unattended.

Safety advice: Be sure your model meets current standards. Check sides for loose fabric; examine surfaces for sharp edges; and be sure locks function correctly.

Century Fold-N-Go Care Centers
Infant could become trapped in loose fabric in bassinet and suffocate.
Products: 50,000 devices, models 10-750 and 10-760, sold 3/98 to 8/98 for $100 to $130. Care center is multifunction portable device on wheels that serves as play yard, bassinet, and changing table with side storage compartment. Model 10-760 has canopy. Model number and manufacture date are on tube supporting underside of play yard. "Century" is imprinted on side of play yard. Only Fold-N-Go Care Centers with bassinet are being recalled. If bassinet has yellow inspection sticker on bottom tubing or was made 9/98 or later, it is not subject to recall.
What to do: Call 800 583-4092 for free repair kit.

Century Fold-N-Go Travel Playard
Could collapse and strangle child in V formed by folded top rail.
Products: 212,000 portable play yards, models 10-710 and 10-810. Model number appears on label on floor or on one of support tubes under floor. Model 10-710, measuring 26x38 inches, was sold at Toys 'R' Us from 6/94 for $50. Model 10-810, measuring 28x41 inches, was sold at juvenile-product and discount stores from 2/93 for $80. Both models fold compactly and fit into nylon carrying case. Other Fold-N-Go models have different top rails and are not subject to recall.
What to do: Call 800 541-0264 for repair kit and installation instructions.

Evenflo play yards
Hinges can collapse, trapping a child in the play yard.

Products: 1.2 million rectangular Happy Camper, Happy Cabana, Kiddie Camper play yards. Each play yard folds and comes with a carrying bag and mattress. Look for the words Evenflo and the model name on the top rail.
What to do: Call 800 447-9178 for a free hinge cover that prevents it from collapsing.

Evenflo Houdini portable play yards
Metal push caps (small metal washers) that connect components have small plastic covers that could break off and choke child. Also, exposed edges of push caps could cut child.
Products: 205,000 play yards sold '94 through '96 for $45. All Evenflo Houdini play yards whose model number begins with 332 are subject to recall; model number is on tag on bottom of play yard.
What to do: Inspect top rail. If plastic covers are loose, cracked, or missing, call 800 490-7549 and ask for free replacements and installation instructions. (Each play yard has 16 push caps and covers: three in each corner of top rails, and one in center of each top rail.) Even if plastic covers are intact, call for warning label to affix to the play yard.

Clothing

Typical problems: Decorative parts or fasteners can be chewed off, posing a choking hazard; strings on hoods or jackets create a strangulation risk.

Safety standards: The CPSC regulates flammability of sleepwear and relaxed its standards in 1996 to allow tight-fitting sleepwear in sizes under nine months to be made without added flame-retardants. In 1995, the CPSC issued guidelines to help prevent strangulation from strings on hoods, waists, mittens, or other children's clothing parts that become entangled on protrusions. Most major clothing manufacturers have agreed to remove or sew down and shorten strings on clothing.

Safety advice: Do not buy clothing with strings that could capture baby's neck or get caught on crib posts, doors, or other protrusions. Or cut strings on such clothing as hoods, necklines, and mittens. Do not buy clothing with small parts—buttons, bows, etc.—that might come off and pose a choking hazard.

Minnie Mouse nautical outfits for infant and toddler girls
Small cloth loop on bow around neckline could come off and choke child.
Products: 29,400 outfits sold 11/95 to 4/96 for $10 to $14. Outfits came in four styles: Knit dress with leggings (style 165000); infant dress (style 18500); toddler dress (style (19500); and short set (style 17214H). Short set features beach scene with Minnie Mouse on front. Other garments have embroidered appliqué of Minnie Mouse on

front. All outfits have long sailor tie at neckline, held together with small beige fabric loop that says "Minnie Mouse" in red letters. Label in short set says, in part: "Catton Brothers...60% Cotton/40% Polyester . . . Made in Hong Kong . . . " Labels in other garments say, in part: "MICKEY STUFF for kids . . . Catton Brothers . . . 70% Cotton/30% Polyester . . . Made in Thailand . . . "

What to do: Return garments to store for refund. For more information, call 800 357-6343.

'Little Me' baseball uniform for infants
Wooden buttons can come off and choke child.
Products: 5,000 one-piece, white-cotton jersey garments with thin blue stripes, sold during spring of '92 for $27. Red "24" is stitched onto left front of garment with blue thread. Outfit, which came with matching blue-and-white baseball cap, has three round wooden buttons, each measuring ¾-inch. Label on garment reads, in part: "Little Me . . . 100% Cotton . . . Made in USA . . . "
What to do: Send garment to Schwab Co., P.O. Box 1742, Upper Potomac Industrial Park, Cumberland, Md. 21501, for refund, including shipping cost.

Infant and toddler acrylic knit hats
One-piece chin strap could strangle child if it snags playground equipment or other catch point.
Products: 15,000 hats sold '85 to '98 at mass-merchandise and discount stores for $2 to $4. Hats, which aren't identified by brand, came in various colors and styles. Inside tag reads, in part "100 percent Acrylic . . . Made in U.S.A . . . . RN 36299" or "RN82864."
What to do: Cut one-piece chin strap in half. (The CPSC urges consumers not to put any type of cord around child's neck. The CPSC also recommends removing drawstring from hood and neck of any children's clothing and buying childrens' outerwear with other types of closures such as snaps, buttons, Velcro, or elastic.)

Pacifiers

Typical problems: Nipples separate from base; small pieces of nipples break off, posing a choking hazard.

Safety standards: Federal standards require two ventilation holes in shield to admit air if shield is caught in mouth or throat. Pacifiers must pass a "pull test" after boiling and cooling to ensure they will not come apart. Shield size is regulated to prevent choking. Package must carry warning label advising against hanging pacifier around child's neck due to strangulation risk.

Safety advice: Boil for five minutes before first use to remove chemical residues. Never hang from string around baby's neck or tie to crib bars due to strangulation risk. Discard when nipple becomes sticky and crumbly, or when baby starts chewing off pieces.

Atico International USA pacifiers
Nipples can separate from base, posing a choking hazard.
Products: 13,000 pacifiers, sold both as part of a diaper bag gift set and individually as a pacifier with a clip, at Bath & Body Works, from 6/98 to 9/98.
What to do: Stop using and return to Bath & Body Works for a refund and a $25 gift certificate.

Binky Newborn Orthodontic pacifiers
Nipple can detach from shield and choke child.
Products: 13,000 pacifiers sold 8/94 to 8/95 by Target Stores and other stores nationwide and 5/95 to 8/95 by University Hospitals of Oklahoma City, individually or in sets of two, for about a $1 each. Pacifier has red, mint-green, blue, or white butterfly mouth shield, with star and crescent vent holes on each side. Some white shields have crescent vent holes on each side. Some white shields have crescents, stars, and hearts stenciled on front. Knob on pacifier doesn't move if twisted, and well around knob is ¼ inch deep. Pacifier came in plastic shell with cardboard backing. Label on back of package reads, in part, "Made . . . in Malaysia . . . Griptight Malaysia Ltd." English-made pacifiers whose knob moves when twisted and whose well is ⅜ inch deep aren't recalled.
What to do: Return pacifier to store for replacement or mail it to Binky-Griptight, Inc., P.O. Box 3307, Wallington, N.J. 07057, for replacement and reimbursement of postage.

Gerber Clear and Soft pacifiers and nipples
Found to contain a chemical related to phthalate.
Products: One pacifier and two models of feeding-bottle nipples from the Clear and Soft line sold by Gerber through 1998. The company has stopped making these products and is removing phthalates from all future products. Stores have been directed to remove the phthalate-containing pacifiers and nipples from their shelves.
What to do: Do not buy these products and dispose of any you have.

Toys

Typical problems: Small parts break off or are bitten off, posing choking hazard; toys crack or break, creating sharp edges that can cut; toys can break, spilling out small parts that can choke; crib mobiles strung across crib pose strangulation hazard.

Safety standards: Voluntary industry standards stipulate that squeeze toys and teethers must be large enough to preclude a choking hazard; crib-toy strings must be short enough not to wrap around a child's neck; and crib gyms and mobiles must be labeled so parents know to remove them when the child can pull up on hands and knees (about age six months). Under the Federal Hazardous Substance Act, all toys sold in the U.S. must meet low lead levels for paint and have smooth surfaces rather than sharp points and edges. Rattles must be large enough not to lodge in a baby's throat, and cannot separate into small pieces. No small parts that could pose a choking hazard (this includes small balls and marbles) are allowed on toys intended for children under three.

Safety advice: Don't buy toys small enough to slip through the center tube of a toilet paper roll. Avoid any with small parts that can be broken or chewed off; strings or cords that can strangle; sharp edges; finger-pinching lids and hinges. Check regularly for loose parts, cracks, tears, sharp edges. Supervise your child's play.

Gerber Flip Fingers rattle
Small parts could spill out and choke child.
Products: 60,000 rattles with red U-shaped handle marked "Gerber," sold 5/96 to 10/96 for about $1.40. Rattle is 5¼ inches long, 2½ inches wide. Rattles with green handles are not being recalled.
What to do: Call 800 443-7237 for instructions on returning rattle to company for refund.

Fisher-Price crib mobiles
Part of mobile can detach and fall into crib, causing injury.
Products: 21,000 "Magic Motion Mobiles," model number 71153, sold for $24 at major toy and mass merchandisers nationwide beginning 6/97. The toy is a round, musical mobile, with a mirrored center and rotating beads and butterflies, suspended from the crib by a plastic arm. It can also be used as a floor toy.
What to do: Remove from crib and call 888 407-6479 for replacement parts.

Baby Buzz stretchable crib mobile
If strung across crib or playpen, could strangle small child. Lacks required warning label.
Products: More than 26,000 mobiles sold 12/95 to 12/96 at Dollar Value and other discount stores for about $1. Toy consists of four 1½-inch plastic balls and plastic animal figures strung on elastic, with white hook at either end for securing mobile to stroller, carriage, swing, or infant seat. Balls and figures come in various colors. Some plastic items are imprinted with word "China." Toy came in clear plastic bag with multicolored cardboard top labeled "Baby Buzz Baby Stretch Mobile." Picture of bee holding rattle appears on cardboard.
What to do: Return mobile to store for refund.

Activity Block Sets
Rods on one of blocks could break and release small hollow cylinders that could choke child.

Products: 4,000 block sets sold 5/97 to 6/98 for $7 or $8 in East and Midwest at Cook Brothers, Johnny's Toys, Meijer, and Ocean State Job Lot stores. Set consists of four colorful plastic blocks and plastic shape sorters. One block has beeper, one has clicker dial, another has mirror, and fourth has rollers—hollow plastic cylinders—on plastic rods. Toy came in multicolored window box labeled, in part, "QUALITY FunKids TOYS . . . Activity Blocks . . . ITEM NO. 38329 . . . T.S. TOYS . . . MADE IN CHINA."
What to do: Return toy to store for refund.

Brio wooden clown stacking toy
Clown's small hat could choke child.
Products: 79,000 toys sold '77 to 9/97 at specialty stores and by mail order for about $19. Clown is 9 inches high and consists of 12 brightly colored pieces, including base. When pieces are stacked, toy forms clown figure with yellow cone-shaped hat. "BRIO . . . MADE IN SWEDEN" is stamped on bottom of base. Toy came in red, white, and yellow cardboard package that includes pictures of toy, model number 30130, and words "BRIO . . . CLOWN." Latest version, which isn't being recalled, has redesigned hat and comes in box that says "CONTAINS NEW HAT DESIGN."
What to do: Mail hat to Brio Corp., N120 W18485 Freistadt Rd., Germantown, Wisc. 53022, for replacement toy and postage.

Summer Infant Products play yard and crib toys
Plastic flower stem can break when bent, posing cut and puncture-wound hazard.
Products: 5,000 Garden Play Yard Pals, which attach to cribs and play yard rails, in box with UPC number 0 12914 05802 2. Toy includes three figures on a plastic base: a gopher in a cup, a butterfly with a spinning-ball rattle, and a flowered mirror with red and purple clackers. "Summer" is written in white on the base front. The toy was sold for $12 at retail and specialty stores, including Babies 'R' Us, Ross, TJ Maxx, and Value City, from 2/98 through 11/98.
What to do: Call 800 426-8627 for a refund.

STK International baby rattles
Rattle handle can pose choking hazard if inserted in the throat.
Products: 15,800 baby rattles made of multi colored plastic. The handle, made of large colored beads with a whistle on the tip, is connected to a ring holding a rotating clear plastic ball. It was sold with a cardboard hangtag reading "Turning ball with whistle . . . No. BI-194 . . . Made in China," at discount stores nationwide for $1.
What to do: Return rattle to store for refund or call 800 536-7855.

Michael Friedman Corp. rattles
Small parts can break off, posing choking and aspiration hazards.
Products: 2,000 "Hobby Horse" rattles, shaped like a pink or purple "rose," with a green stem-like handle. "Hong Kong" is embossed on the lower part of the rose. Rattles were sold for $1 to $2 at small children's clothing and discount stores nationwide from 3/97 to 5/98.

What to do: Return rattle to store for refund. Call 800 431-3166 for more information. (In New York State, call 718 257-7800 collect.)

SnackTime Stroller Toy Bar
Rattle attached to bar could break apart and child could inhale small beads inside.
Products: 99,000 toys sold 7/95 to 6/96 for $13 to $15. Toy is 14 inches long and 3 inches wide and fits over front bar of stroller. It includes four plastic figures: green and pink flower, which doubles as cupholder; purple and pink caterpillar, with plastic rings that function as stacking teether; yellow bear, which holds rattle and jingle balloons and plays music; and frog whose head opens into removable, spill-resistant bowl. Toy came in cardboard box with see-through window labeled, in part: "SnackTime Stroller Toy Bar, Model Number 6679 . . . Combines Snacktime and Playtime for babies on the go! . . . Easily attaches to stroller crossbars . . . KIDS II . . . For Ages Up To 3 Years . . . " Toys sold after 8/1/96 and bearing model number 683 and date code are not subject to recall.
What to do: Return toy to Kids II, 1015 Windward Ridge Parkway, Alpharetta, GA 30202, for replacement bar.

Plush "Pajama" bears
Eyes could come off and choke child.
Products: 8,000 stuffed toy bears distributed 10/95 to 5/97 at amusement parks, including Busch Gardens in Tampa, Fla., Dutch Wonderland in Lancaster, Pa., and Play Day Amusements in Seaside Heights, N.J. Twelve-inch version is white with brown eyes and pink nose and mouth. It's dressed in one-piece floral-print pajamas (gray and mint green or yellow and peach) with ruffled collar and elastic cuffs; paws have same print pattern as pajama. Thirteen-inch version is also white, but with black nose and eyes. It's dressed in one-piece pajamas with multicolored fish or dinosaur designs and white collar with red bow; ears have same print pattern as pajamas. Sewn-in label says "Nadel & Sons Toy Corp . . . Made in China."
What to do: For a $5 refund plus postage, call 800 234-4697.

Stationary entertainers

Safety standards: Entertainers come under federal laws regulating such infant hazards as small parts. This product is not covered by voluntary industry safety standards.

Safety advice: Inspect entertainer regularly for loose parts. Limit time in entertainer to 15 minutes several times per day. Purchase a model with a stationary rather than rocking base or with a locking mechanism, and do not leave baby unattended.

Graco Stationary Entertainer children's activity toy
Screw securing clicker toy to tray can come out and choke or scratch child.
Products: 19,000 toys, model numbers 4118C, 4118RA, and 34429, made 4/24/98 to

8/6/98 and sold for $59 to $69. Device resembles baby walker without wheels and has plastic tray supported by three adjustable legs. Chair in center swivels so child can play with toys attached to tray. Model and serial number are on label under tray; first six digits of serial number are date of manufacture. Clicker toy, made of yellow plastic, has three knobs. Yellow "Graco" label is on front of tray.
What to do: Remove clicker toy and call 800 231-3676 for a free redesigned attachment screw and instructions.

Graco stationary entertainer
Sharp edges on seat rings can cut or scratch child's legs.
Products: 63,000 entertainers made prior to 3/96 with white plastic seat rings located under the padded seat cover. (Those with yellow plastic rings are not included in recall.) These were sold for $59 to $69 at juvenile product and discount stores nationwide beginning 11/95.
What to do: Call 800 423-9078 for a free replacement seat ring.

Safety 1st stationary play center
Snack-tray toys can be broken off, leaving a sharp plastic edge.
Products: 106,000 Bouncy Buggies with a cat "Stop" sign and dog "Go" sign attached signpost style to rods on the snack tray at rear. Look for "Safety 1st" between the car's headlights. "Product No. 45606" is in raised lettering on the bottom of the rocking base. The play center was sold for $50 in toy stores nationwide from 5/97 through 4/98. (If a white sticker reading "Product No. 45606A" appears on the base or the front of the box, toys are made of a more flexible plastic and not subject to this recall.)
What to do: Call 800 723-3065 for free replacement toys and instructions.

Baby monitors

Typical problems: Monitor wiring can pose a fire hazard.

Safety standards: There are no federal guidelines aimed specifically at nursery monitors, nor is there a voluntary industry safety standard.

Safety advice: Keep monitor (an electrical hazard) and cord (a strangulation hazard) out of child's reach. Do not prop on a soft surface, which can block air vents, causing overheating. Keep away from water to avoid shock hazard.

Gerry Deluxe Baby Monitor 602
Improperly wired monitor could cause a fire.
Products: 990,000 monitors sold between 6/88 and 5/90. The two-piece set resembles a pair of walkie-talkies. Embossed on the back of the affected transmitter are the words "GERRY DELUXE BABY MONITOR MODEL 602" and a date code that runs sequentially from 8806 to 9005. The date code may appear in the form of a clock with an arrow pointing to the month the monitor was made and the two digits of the year on either side of the arrow.

What to do: Call 800 672-6289 for how to return the monitor for a free replacement, or write to Gerry Baby Products Co., Attn: Building R-602 Recall, 1500 East 128th Ave., Thornton, Colo. 80241.

Gerry baby monitors
After an electrical short, the rechargeable battery causes parent's unit to smoke and flame.
Products: 86,000 Clear Choice model 618, consisting of baby unit, a parent unit, a recharging base and AC adapters, all white with light blue accents. The model number is on a silver plate on the front of the AC adapter. The monitor was sold for $40 at mass merchandise and baby stores nationwide from 4/96 to 3/98.
What to do: Discard blue battery pack from parent unit. Call 800 273-3521 for free replacement battery pack with safety fuse.

Safety 1st rechargeable monitor batteries
The dry cell battery can rupture and irritate skin.
Products: 25,000 batteries sold with Safety 1st Model 49226 nursery monitors, which consist of a gray and white plastic parent's receiver with recharging stand and baby transmitter (both labeled "Safety 1st"), AC adapter, and battery. The receiver holding the battery has a white date-code sticker on the back—recalled dates are between 00097 and 03097. The monitor sold for between $35 and $45 at retailers nationwide from 6/97 through 8/97.
What to do: Call 800 964-8489 for instructions on exchanging the recalled batteries for replacements.

Gates

Typical problems: Parts can break off, posing a choking risk; tops of old-style gates can form a V, a strangulation hazard.

Safety standards: JPMA certifies gates. The ASTM F1004 standard covers size of openings, gate height, strength of top rails and framing components (including vertical dislodgement test), bottom spacing, and configuration of uppermost edge. Certified gates provide permanent label warning consumers to install gate according to manufacturer's instructions, stating that gate is designed for children six months to two years and that it won't prevent all accidents.

Safety advice: Gate should not be used with child older than two. Pressure-mounted gates may easily come loose and should not be used to block stairways. Purchase a gate wide enough for door opening. Avoid gates with any protrusion that can catch clothing. Check all gates regularly for loose parts, stability, and holding power of hardware.

FirstAlert True Fit child safety gate
Plastic parts such as bumpers and hinges could break into small pieces and choke child or make gate insecure.
Products: 36,000 white plastic gates with gray handle, model CSSG1, sold since 10/96 for about $35. Label on gate lists brand and model. Expandable gate is pressure-mounted but can also be installed with screw-mounted hinges so it swings open like a door. One version fits 28-inch to 47-inch openings; other version, 29½-inch to 46-inch openings.
What to do: Call 888 777-5599 for refund. Note: In 9/97, company recalled same model, offering free replacement gate. This recall extends to all FirstAlert True Fit safety gates, including those replaced during previous recall. Company no longer makes safety gates.

RESOURCE GUIDE

Contents

- **Parent information web sites,** page 287
- **Health & safety agencies,** page 288
- **Web sites selling baby products,** page 290
- **Catalogs selling baby products,** page 291
- **Manufacturer and brand locator,** page 292

PARENT INFORMATION WEB SITES

Name	Web site
Baby Center Surveys of parents, polls on interests of parents, chatrooms and a store.	www.babycenter.com
Baby Talk and Shop Allows you to create your own registry and has a searchable database of articles from back issues of "Baby Talk" magazine.	www.babytalkandshop.com
Johns Hopkins University Department of Pediatrics A searchable baby and child medical information site with links to lots of other sites, too.	www.med.jhu.edu/peds/neonatology
Moms Online Moms writing columns and essays and posting recipes, messages and baby-care tips.	www.momsonline.com
Motherstuff Links to resources for breastfeeding and baby health and special section on preemies.	www.motherstuff.com
ParenthoodWeb Parent-to-parent advice, "ask the pros" section, and listings of baby product recalls.	www.parenthoodweb.com
Parents Place A huge site with experts, chat rooms, a library of baby information, breastfeeding help, the Internet Baby Store (iBaby).	www.parentsplace.com
ParentSoup Chat rooms, ongoing parent discussions, experts, and a library of parenting articles.	www.parentsoup.com
ParentTime Postings from "Baby Talk" and "Parenting," information from experts, and month-by-month guide to baby info.	www.ParentTime.com
SIDS Network Searchable information on SIDS and SIDS prevention, with links to other sources.	www.SIDS-network.org
The Baby Net Baby photo contest, baby-proofing tips, chat rooms, and mother-written poems and lullabies.	www.thebabynet.com

HEALTH & SAFETY AGENCIES

Name	Phone number/web site
Alliance to End Childhood Lead Poisoning Washington, D.C. 20002. Information on lead poisoning prevention.	202 543-1147 www.aeclp.org
American Academy of Pediatrics Send self-addressed stamped envelope to P.O. Box 927, Dept. C-Carseats, 141 Northwest Point Blvd., Elk Grove Village, Il 60009-0927, for free brochure on car seat safety.	847 228-5005 www.aap.org
Back to Sleep Campaign Bethesda, Md. 20892. SIDS prevention.	800 505-CRIB www.nih.gov/nichd
Centers for Disease Control and Prevention (CDC) Atlanta, Ga. 30333. Updates on immunization.	888 880-4232 www.cdc.gov
Danny Foundation Alamo, Calif. 94507. Newsletter posting major baby product dangers and recalls.	800 83-DANNY
Depression After Delivery Belle Meade, N.J. 08502 Postpartum depression clearinghouse.	800 944-4773
Federal Aviation Administration Washington, D.C. 20591. Child safety seats in aircraft.	800 FAA-Sure or 202 267-3484 www.faa.gov
International Association of Infant Massage Eugene, Ore. 97402.	800 248-5432
International Lactation Consultant Assoc. Raleigh, N.C. 27607. Referrals for professional breastfeeding support.	919 787-5181 www.ilca.org
Juvenile Products Manufacturers Association Moorestown, N.J. 08057.	609 231-8500 www.jpma.org
La Leche League International Schaumburg, Il. 60173 (Breastfeeding information and support).	800 LA-LECHE www.lalecheleague.org
March of Dimes Birth Defects Foundation White Plains, N.Y. 10605. Information on healthy pregnancy and birth defects.	888 663-4637 www.modimes.org
Mothers at Home Vienna, Va. 22182.	800 783-4666, www.mah.org
National Association of At-Home Mothers Fairfield, Ia 52556.	515 472-3202 www.at-home-mothers.com
National Easter Seal Society Chicago, Ill. 60606. KARS (Kids Are Riding Safely) program for children with special needs.	800 221-6827 www.seals.com
National Committee to Prevent Child Abuse Chicago, Ill. 60604.	312 663-3520
National Highway Traffic Safety Administration Washington, D.C. 20590. Child safety seats in vehicles.	888 327-4236 Fax: 202 366-3443, www.nhtsa.dot.gov
National Lead Information Center Silver Spring, Md. 20910. Reference materials on home lead reduction.	800 424-LEAD www.epa.gov/lead
National Organization of Mothers of Twins Clubs Albuquerque, N.M. 87192-1188. Referral to local support groups.	800 243-2276 www.nomotc.org

HEALTH & SAFETY AGENCIES, *continued*

National Safe Kids Campaign Washington, D.C. 20004. To reduce accidental injuries and safety-seat information.	202 662-0600 *www.safekids.org*
National Safety Council Itasca, Ill. 60143. Accident, fire, and lead-poisoning prevention.	800 621-7619 *www.nsc.org*
National Sudden Infant Death Resource Center Vienna, Va. 22182.	703 821-8955 *www.circsol.com/sids.*
Parents Anonymous Claremont, Calif. 91711. Support toward the prevention of child abuse.	909 621-6184 *www.parentsanonymous-natl.com*
Parents Without Partners Chicago, Il. 60611-4267. Single-parent support groups nationwide.	800 637-7974 *www.parentswithoutpartners.org*
Safety Belt Safe USA Safe Ride Help Line.	800 745 7233
Sudden Infant Death Syndrome Alliance Baltimore, Md. 21208.	800 221-SIDS (24-hour information and referral hotline) *www.sidsalliance.org*
U.S. Consumer Product Safety Commission Bethesda, Md. 20816. Baby product safety.	800 638-2772 (Consumer Safety Hotline) *www.cpsc.gov*
U.S. Department of Agriculture Washington, D.C. 20250. Meats in baby foods.	202 720-2791 *www.usda.gov*
U.S. Food and Drug Administration Rockville, Md. 20857. Baby food and skin-care product safety.	800 FDA-4010 (Hotline), 800 FDA-1088 (Consumer complaints), *www.fda.gov*

WEB SITES SELLING BABY PRODUCTS

Name	Web site
Baby Best Buy Claims to save parents 40 percent or more on its small selection of strollers and other items.	www.bestbuy.com
Baby Catalog of America Promises to save you 10 to 50 percent on pregnancy, baby, and toddler products. It has information on how to select products by categories and a closeout page, too, for baby bargains.	www.babycatalog.com
Baby Center A selection of strollers, car seats, backpacks, carriers, playpens, and other baby equipment.	store.babycenter.com
Baby Shop Created as a cooperative program to promote women in business on the Internet. Shops in the "mall" carry a selection of baby clothing and diapers.	mommy-mall.com
Baby Supermall Baby clothes, selected car seats, and other baby products, primarily mainstream brands.	www.babysupermall.com
BabyGap Lets you browse their pricey but wonderful baby clothing. Need some knitted cashmere baby pants for $75 each? Look in their top-of-the-line offerings.	www.gap.com
Babyzone Resource for expectant moms that includes features on pregnancy, books, and connections to maternity clothing and baby gear boutiques.	www.babyzone.com
Child Secure Catalog Offers a full range of baby products, including baby carriers, bouncers, breast pumps, etc., with an eye toward safety.	www.childsecure.com
Cybertykes High chairs, bedding, car seats, bassinets. Claims that it "guarantees to have the lowest prices."	www.cybertykes.com
Dad Gear Co Carriers dad-designed (mostly black) diaper backpacks, shoulder bags, and hip packs.	www.dadgear.com
eToys Source for baby toys (by age), along with music, games, and playthings for children, too.	www.etoys.com
Internet Baby Carries over 20,000 baby products from 200 brands at discount prices.	www.ibaby.com
Lands' End Baby items from flannel crib sheets to cozy baby clothes and mittens. Take a look at their outlet (overstock) section.	www.landsend.com
Rainbee Upscale bedding, soft carriers, infant seats, and gift sets.	www.rainbee.com
Toys 'R' Us Baby toys along with children's toys and software.	www.toysrus.com
White River Concepts Breast pumps and other breastfeeding equipment and advice.	www.whiteriver.com

CATALOGS SELLING BABY PRODUCTS

Name	Phone number/web site
Baby Club of America West Haven, Conn. 06516. Discounts for club members.	800 752-9736 *www.babycatalog.com*
Babyworks Portland, Ore. 97229. Carries diapering systems.	800 422-2910
Back to Basics Toys, Games and Hobbies Ridgely, Md. 21660.	800 356-5360 *www.backtobasicstoys.com*
Constructive Playthings Grandview, Mo. 64030.	800 832-0572, *www.constplay.com*
Discovery Toys Livermore, Calif. 94550. Toys for babies and children.	800 426-4777 *www.discoverytoysinc.com*
Genesis Direct/Biobottoms Secaucus, N.J. 07094. Reusable diapers.	800 766-1254
Gifts for Grandkids Secaucus, N.J. 07096.	888 472-6354
hand in hand Secaucus, N.J. 07096.	800 872-9745
Hanna Anderson Louisville, Ky. 40258. Apparel for babies, children and moms.	800 222-0544 *www.hannaanderson.com*
it's kids time Clearwater, Fla. 33765.	800 372-4244
JC Penney/Penneys from Heaven Milwaukee, Wis. 53201. Cribs and baby equipment.	800 709-5777 *www.jcpenney.com/shopping*
Lands' End Dodgeville, Wis. 53595. Crib supplies, baby clothes.	800 734-5437 *www.landsend.com*
Livonia Hendersonville, N.C. 28739.	800 543-8566 *www.ioa.babyshoe.com*
Natural Baby Catalog North Canton, Ohio 44720. Diapering systems.	800 388-Baby
Perfectly Safe North Canton, Ohio 44720.	800 837-KIDS
The Right Start Westlake Village, Calif. 91361.	800 548-8531, *www.rightstart.com*
Safe Beginnings Burlington, Mass. 01803.	800 598-8911, *www.safebeginnings.com*
Simple Alternatives Bellevue, Wash. 98004. Diapering systems.	800 735-2082 *www.simplealternatives.com*

MANUFACTURER AND BRAND LOCATOR

Name	Phone number	Web site
Ameda/Hollister Cary, Ill. 60013	800 323-4060	*www.hollister.com*
Aprica U.S.A. Compton, Calif. 90220	310 639-6387	—
Arm's Reach Concepts Agoura Hills, Calif. 91301-3358	800 954-9353	*www.armsreach.com*
Baby Faire Inc. Winchester, Mass. 01890	781 729-4500	*www.babyfaire.com*
Avent America Elk Grove Village, Ill. 60007	800 54-AVENT	*www.aventamerica.com*
Baby Bjorn/Regal & Lager Marietta, Ga. 30067	800 593-5522	*www.babybjorn.com*
Baby Jogger Company Yakima, Wash. 98907	800 241-1848	*www.babyjogger.com*
Baby Trend Ontario, Calif. 91761	800 328-7363	*www.babytrend.com*
Bailey Medical Engineering Los Osos, Calif. 93402	800 413-3216	*www.baileymed.com*
Bassett Furniture Industries Bassett, Va. 24055	540 629-6000	*www.bassettfurniture.com*
Beech-Nut Nutrition St. Louis, Mo. 63188	800 523-6633	*www.beech-nut.com*
Bravado! Designs Toronto, Ontario, CANADA M4M 3N9	800 590-7802	*www.bravado.org*
Burley Design Cooperative Eugene, Ore. 97402	800 311-5294	*www.burley.com*
Century Products Macedonia, Ohio 44056	800 837-4044	*www.centuryproducts.com*
Chicco USA Bound Brook, N.J. 08805	877 4-CHICCO	*www.chiccousa.com*
Child Craft Salem, Ind. 47167-0444	812 883-311	*www.childcraftind.com*
COMBI International Carol Stream, Ill. 60188	630 871-0404	*www.combi-intl.com*
Cosco Columbus, Ind. 47201	800 544-1108	*www.coscoinc.com*
CycleTote Ft. Collins, Colo. 80524	800 747-2407	*www.cycletote.com*
Dad Gear South Pasadena, Calif. 91031	888 847-7008	*www.dadgear.com*
Delta Enterprise Brooklyn, N.Y. 11212-8012	718 385-1000	*www.deltaenterprise.com*
Discovery Toys Livermore, Calif. 94550	800 426-4777	*www.discoverytoysinc.com*
Drypers Vancouver, Wash. 98661	360 693-6688	*www.drypers.com*
Early Development Co Charlotte, N.C. 28287	704 643-8400	—
Evenflo Co Vandalia, Ohio 45377	800 837-9201	*www.evenflo.com*
The First Years Avon, Mass. 02322	800 225-0382	—
Fisher-Price East Aurora, N.Y. 14052	800 432-5437	*www.fisher-price.com*
Gerber Products Freemont, Mich. 49413	800 443-7237	*www.gerber.com*
Graco Children's Products Elverson, Pa. 19520	800 345-4109	*www.gracobaby.com*
Homekeepers Publishing Richland, Pa. 17087	800 572-1826	*www.homekeepers.com*
Heinz (and Earth's Best) Pittsburgh, Penn. 15230	800 USA-BABY	*www.earthsbest.com*
Huggies Neenah, Wis. 54957	800 544-1847	*www.huggies.com*
Infantino San Diego, Calif. 92126	800 365-8182	—
International Playthings Riverdale, N.J. 07457	800 631-1272	—
Johnson & Johnson Skillman, N.J. 08558	800 526-3967	*www.johnsonandjohnson.com*
J. Mason Santa Clarita, Calif. 91355	800 242-1922	—
Kelty K.I.D.S. Boulder, Colo. 80301	800 423-2320	*www.kelty.com*
Kidco, Inc. Mundelein, Ill. 60060-3836	800 553-5529	*www.kidcoinc.com*
Kids II Alpharetta, Ga. 30005	770 751-0442	—
Kolcraft Enterprises Aberdeen, N.C. 28315	800 453-7673	—
Kool-Stop International La Habra, Calif. 90632	800 586-3332	*www.koolstop.com*
Lamby/Kapoochi Lynden, Wash. 98264	800 669-0527	*www.lamby.com*

292 ■ Guide to Baby Products

MANUFACTURER AND BRAND LOCATOR, *continued*

Name	Phone number	Web site
Learning Curve International Chicago, Ill. 60610	800 704-TOYS	www.learningtoys.com
LEGO Systems Enfield, Conn. 06083-1310	800 453-4652	www.lego.com/worlds.asp
Little Tikes Hudson, Ohio 44236	800 321-0183	www.littletikes.com
Manhattan Group Minneapolis, Minn. 55401	800 541-1345	www.manhattantoy.com
Maya Group. Huntington Beach, Calif. 92649	888 TINYLOVE	www.tinylove.com
McKenzie Kids Marietta, Ga. 30064	800 832-0969	www.mckenziekids.com
Medela McHenry, Ill. 60050	800 435-8316	www.medela.com
Mommy's Helper Wichita, Ks. 67208	800 371-3509	—
NoJo Rancho Santa Margarita, Calif. 92688	800 541-5711	www.nojo.com
North States Industries Minneapolis, Minn. 55427	612 541-9101	www.northstatesind.com
Pampers Cincinnati, Ohio 45201	800 285-6064	www.pampers.com
Playtex Products Westport, Conn. 06880	203 341-4000	www.playtexproductsinc.com
Nursery Needs Fitchburg, Mass. 01420	800 726-4869	—
One Step Ahead Lake Bluff, Ill. 60044	800 950-5120	www.onestepahead.com
Over the Shoulder Baby Holder San Clemente, Calif. 92674	800 637-9426	—
Peg Perego U.S.A., Fort Wayne, Ind. 46808	800 671-1701	www.perego.com
PlaySkool/Hasbro Pawtucket, R.I. 02862	401 431-TOYS	www.hasbro.com
Premiewear Auburn, Calif. 95602	800 992-8469	www.premiewear.com
Prenatal Cradle Hamburg, Mich. 48139	800 607-3572	www.prenatalcradle.com
PRIMO Irvington, N.J. 07111	973 926-5900	www.primobaby.com
Prince Lionheart Santa Maria, Calif. 93455	800 544-1132	www.princelionheart.com
PU Digital Mountain View, Calif. 94039	650 567-7585	www.flipnflush.com
Pugubop Hailey Idaho 83333	208 725-2057	www.pugubop.com
Safety 1st Chestnut Hill, Mass. 02167	800 723-3065	www.safety1st.com
Sassy Kentwood, Mich. 49508	616 243-0767	www.sassybaby.com
Seymour Housewares Seymour, Ind. 47274	800 457-9881	—
Simmons Juvenile Products New London, Wis. 54961	920 982-2140	—
Today's Kids Booneville, Ark. 75244	800 258-TOYS	www.todayskids.com
Tough Traveler Schenectady, N.Y. 12307	800 GO-TOUGH	www.toughtraveler.com
Tracers Furniture Mt. Vernon, N.Y. 10550	914 668-9372	—
Weebees Denver, Colo. 80227	888 342-7373	www.weebees.com

INDEX

Air bags
    and children, 70-71
    on/off switches, 71
Airlines, child restraint systems on, 71-73
American Academy of Pediatrics, 69
American Society for Testing and Materials (ASTM), 92, 133, 140, 230, 254, 260
Audio monitors, 248-252

Baby Faire Consumer Expo, 22
Baby fairs, 22, 34
Baby food, 206-214
    frozen, 207
    homemade, 32, 212-214
    labels, 209-210
    manufacturers of, 28, 206-208
    marketing, 207-208
    safety, 210, 212
    solids, introducing, 211-212
Baby powder, 33, 149
Baby-proofing your home, 237-247

Baby seats, 121-124
    models available, 123-124
    recalls, 272
    safety, 122
    seat belts, 122, 123
Baby showers, 22-24
Backpacks. *See* Carriers; Diaper bags
Backyard, baby-proofing, 245-246
Balloons, 219
Basements, baby-proofing, 243-245
Bassinets, 26, 55-56
Bath cushions, 147
Bathing, 19, 145-147
Bathroom, baby-proofing, 242-243
Bath seats, 148
Bathtubs, 25, 26, 147-148
    alternatives, 33, 146
    dangers of, 148, 242
    models available, 147-148
Beanbag chairs, 243
Bedding, 18, 57-58
    and Sudden Infant Death Syndrome, 39, 53

Bed proppers, 58
Bedrooms, baby-proofing, 243
Beds, adult, 243
Bedside sleepers, 54-55
Bed warmers, 58
Bicycle trailers, 108-110
    models available, 110
Blind cord protectors, 246-247
Booster seats (for chairs), 130-131
    models available, 130-131
    safety, 131
Booties, 181
Bottle feeding, 18, 194-202. *See also* Formula
    angle-neck bottles, 195-196
    disposable bottles, 196
    nipples, 196-199
    plastic bottles, 197
    safety, 197, 199
    sterilizing, 201-202
    temperature, 202
Botulism, 203
Bouncers, 26
Breastfeeding, 18, 31-32, 36-37, 183-187
    freezing milk, 194
    health benefits, 183-184
    storing milk, 193-194
Breast pumps, 188-193
    manual, 189-190
    models available, 190, 191-192
    types, 188-189
    vacuum problems, 189
Burns, 241, 243

Carriage/strollers, 102-103
Carriers, 25, 26, 111-120
    back carriers, framed, 118-120
    models available, 115, 117-118, 119-120
    recalls, 270-271
    safety, 116
    slings, 112-115
    soft carriers, 19, 115-118
    weight limits, 112
Car seats, 18, 26, 59-88
    on airplanes, 71-73
    booster seats, 60, 65, 72, 77, 78
    built-in, 60
    car-beds, 62
    convertible seats, 64-65, 76-77, 78
    discounts, 31
    harnesses, 61, 64
    in house use, dangers of, 64, 122
    infant seats, 63, 76, 77-78
    installation, 67-70
    Ratings, booster car seats, 82-83
    Ratings, convertible car seats, 79-81
    Ratings, travel systems: infant seats, 84-85
    Ratings, travel systems: strollers, 86-88
    recalls, 266-269
    safety precautions, 64
    special-needs babies, 66
    stroller combinations, 29, 62, 95
    testing, 75-78
    tethering, 65-66
    used, 62-63
Cereals, 208
Certification stickers, 92, 260-261
Changing tables. *See* Diaper-changing tables
Chemicals, storing, 244
Chests, 26, 34
Child safety seats. *See* Car seats
Choking, 139, 214, 240
Clothing, 19, 25, 173-182
    basics, 174
    footwear, 181-182
    outerwear, 179, 180
    recalls, 277-278
    safety, 176
    sizes, 31, 174-175

for toddlers, 179-180
underwear, 180-181
used, 177
Coffee tables, 239
Competition and product quality, 29-30
Consumer Product Safety Commission (CPSC), 39, 44, 47, 197, 216, 218, 229, 230, 243, 257, 259, 260
Cord holders, 239-240
Cradles, 26, 56-57
Crib alternatives, 54-57
Crib bumpers, 18, 57
Cribs, 18, 26, 39-50
assembly, 49-50
convertible, 49
drawers, 44
dropsides, 45-47
durability, 43
floor samples, 47
location, 36
mattress supports, 45
pricing, 41-43
railings, 44
recalls, 262-264
safety, 43, 44
standard, safety, 43
and toys, 219
used, 47-48
wheels, 45
where to buy, 40
Cribs, portable, 54

Decks, danger of, 245
Diaper bags, 18, 25, 161-163
backpacks, 162
models available, 162-163
Diaper-changing tables, 18, 26, 37, 157-159
alternatives, 34, 37, 157-158
models available, 158-159
safety, 157

Diaper pails, 18, 159-161, 242-243
Diaper rash, 150, 155-157
Diapers, 18, 25, 28, 32-33, 149-155
disposable, 18, 25, 28, 33, 150-154
environmental issues, 151
laundering, 154
overnight diapers, 167
Ratings, disposable, 169-170
superabsorbent, 154-155
testing, 166-167
Diaper service, 151, 155
Discount chains, 20, 34, 40
Dishwasher detergent, danger of, 237-238
Door-knob covers, 247
Dressing tips, 178
Drowning, 242, 244, 245

Electrical outlets, 240
Electrical shock, 243
Entertainers, stationary, 232-234
models available, 233-234
recalls, 282-283
safety, 234
Environmental Protection Agency (EPA), 204, 213
Exercisers. *See* Entertainers, stationary
Extension cords, 241

Falls, 157, 240, 243, 244, 245
Federal Aviation Administration (FAA), 72, 73
Feeding supplies, 18
Finger entrapment, 241
Fingernails, trimming, 19
Fire escape plans, 36
Fireplaces, 239
Food. *See* Baby food
Food and Drug Administration (FDA), 204, 210
Food Quality Protection Act, 213
Foreign companies, 28

Formula, 18, 28, 32, 200-202. *See also* Bottle feeding
    expiration date, 201
    preparation, 202
    storing, 201
    types, 200
Fruit juices, 202-203, 208-209
    storing, 203
Fruits, 209
Furniture recalls, 264-265
Furniture sets, 48

Garage doors, 244-245
Garages, baby-proofing, 243-245
Gates, 253-258
    alternatives, 258
    models available, 254-257
    pressure-mounted, 253-254
    recalls, 284-285
    safety, 256, 257-258
    standard, safety, 254
    types, 253-254
Gift certificates, 25
Gift registries, 22-24
Gifts, 23, 25

Heatstroke, 142
High chairs, 26, 124-130
    cleaning, 126-127
    models available, 128-130
    options, 125
    recalls, 272-273
    reclining, 128
    safety, 126, 129
    seat belts, 126
    stability, 125
    standard, safety, 129
    trays, 127
    wheels, 128
Homecoming, packing for, 33

Honey, 203
Hook-on chairs, 131-133
    models available, 133
    safety, 133

Imports, 28
Infant seats. *See* Baby seats

Juices, 202-203, 208-209
Jumpers, 235
    models available, 235
    safety, 235
Juvenile Products Manufacturers Association (JPMA), 92, 133, 140, 230, 254, 260-261

Kitchen, baby-proofing, 237-239

Lactation consultants, 187
La Leche League, 18, 185, 187
Lamps, 239
Lawn mowers, dangers of, 244
Licensed characters, 25, 34
Living room, baby-proofing, 239-242

Mail-order catalogs, 22
Mattresses, 18, 26, 50-54
    antibacterial claims, 51
    foam vs. innersprings, 52
    measurements, 52
    warranties, 51
Mattress pads, 57
Meat, 209
Medical supplies, 19
Medicine cabinets, 242
Milk. *See* Bottle feeding; Breastfeeding; Formula
Mobiles, 220
Monitors
    audio, 248-252
    batteries, 248
    models available, 250-252

recalls, 283-284
safety, 252
static, 249
video, 253

Nasal aspirator, 19
National Highway Traffic Safety Administration (NHTSA), 59, 63, 71, 259
National Safe Kids Campaign, 69
Night-lights, 19, 39
Nipples, 196-200
    flow, 199-200
    latex, 197-198
    orthodontic, 199
    silicone, 197-198
Nursery
    decorating, 37-39
    flooring, 39
    safety, 36
Nursing bras, 187
Nursing pads, 188

Pacifiers, 19, 198, 204-206
    recalls, 278-279
    safety, 205
    standard, safety, 205
Packaging, child-resistant, 247-248
Pain relievers, 19
Pediatricians, 32
Pesticides on produce, 212-213
Phthalates in plastic, 216, 218
Plastic bags, 239
Playpens, 137-141
    models available, 140-141
    recalls, 274-276
    safety, 139
Play stages, 219-222
Play yards, portable, 30, 141-144
    models available, 143-144

recalls, 276-277
safety, 139, 142-143
Potties, 164-165
    models available, 164-165
Power tools, dangers of, 244
Preparations (for new baby), 32-33
PVC, 216, 218

Railing guards, 247
Ratings
    car seats, booster seats, 82-83
    car seats, convertible, 79-81
    car seats, travel systems: infant seats, 84-85
    car seats, travel systems: strollers, 86-88
    diapers, disposable, 169-170
    training pants, 171
Recalls
    baby seats, 272
    carriers, 270-271
    car seats, 266-269
    clothing, 277-278
    cribs, 262-264
    entertainers, stationary, 282-283
    furniture, 264-265
    gates, 284-285
    high chairs, 272-273
    monitors, 283-284
    pacifiers, 278-279
    playpens, 274-276
    play yards, portable, 276-277
    strollers, 270
    swings, 273-274
    toys, 279-282
    warmers, 266
Receiving blankets, 25, 58
Refrigerators, hazard, 238
Return policies, 27
Rocking chairs, 26

Safety. *See also* Baby-proofing your home
   baby food, 210, 212
   baby seats, 122
   bassinets and cradles, 56
   bathtubs, 148, 242
   bedding, 39, 53
   booster seats (for chairs), 131
   bottle feeding, 197, 199
   carriers, 116
   car-seat precautions, 64
   clothing, 176
   cribs, 43, 44
   diaper-changing tables, 157
   entertainers, stationary, 234
   gates, 256, 257-258
   high chairs, 126, 129
   hook-on chairs, 133
   jumpers, 235
   mobiles, 220
   monitors, 252
   nursery, 36
   pacifiers, 205
   plastic baby bottles, 197
   playpens, 139
   play yards, 139, 142-143
   strollers, 92, 101
   swings, 136
   toys, 216, 218-219
   walkers, 228, 229-230
Seats. *See* Baby seats
Shampoo, 149
Sheets, 57-58
Shoes, 181-182
Skin-care products, 28, 33, 148-149
Sleeping, stomach vs. back, 53
Sleepwear, 176
Smoking (around baby), 53
Soap, 19, 149
Specialty shops, 20-21, 40

Standards, safety
   cribs, 43
   gates, 254
   high chairs, 129
   pacifiers, 205
   strollers, 92
   walkers, 230, 231
Storage units, 37
Stove guards, 238
Strangulation, 142, 240, 243, 257
Stroller/carriages, 102-103
Strollers, 18, 26, 89-108
   car-seat combinations, 29, 95
   guarantees, 94
   models available, 96-98, 100-101, 102-103, 105, 108
   recalls, 270
   safety, 92, 101
   sports strollers, 105-108
   standard, safety, 92
   tandem strollers, 104-105
   two-seaters, 103-105
   umbrella strollers, 96-97
   warranties, 94
   weight, 94-96
Sudden Infant Death Syndrome (SIDS), 39, 53
Suffocation, 56, 138, 142, 219, 241, 243
Swimming pools, 245-246
Swings, 26, 134-137
   bassinet attachment, 134
   models available, 135-136
   recalls, 273-274
   safety, 136
Swings, outdoor, 246

Talcum, 33, 149
Thermometers, 19
Toilet lid locks, 243
Toiletry kit, basic, 156

Toilet seat adapters, 164-165
    models available, 165
Toilet training, 163-165
Toys, 215-227
    age guidelines, 221-222
    recalls, 279-282
    ride-on, 219, 246
    safety, 216, 218-219
    size test, 218
    used, 217
Training pants, 180
    Ratings, 171
    testing, 168

U.S. Department of Agriculture (USDA), 210, 212

Vegetables, 209
Video monitors, 253

Walkers, 228-232
    models available, 231-232
    safety, 228, 229-230
    standard, safety, 230, 231
Walking skills, 228-229
Warmers, recall, 266
Warranties, 27
    mattresses, 51
    strollers, 94
Washcloths, 33, 149
Water, bottled, 203-204
Water beds, 243
Water heater thermostat, 244
Web sites, 21-22, 185
Window locks, 36
Windows, falls from, 243